The Borough Park Papers

SYMPOSIUM III

How Jewish Should the Messianic Jewish Community Be?

THE BOROUGH PARK PAPERS

SYMPOSIUM III
How Jewish Should the Messianic Jewish Community Be?

October 22 – 24, 2012

Borough Park Symposium
An imprint of
Messianic Jewish Publishers
Clarksville, MD 21029

15 14 13 12 5 4 3 2 1

Library of Congress Control Number: 2012951378
ISBN 978-1-936716-61-6
The Borough Park Papers, Symposium III
How Jewish Should the Messianic Jewish Community Be?

Printed in the United States of America

Published by
Borough Park Symposium
An imprint of
Messianic Jewish Publishers
6120 Day Long Lane
Clarksville, Maryland 21029
Distributed by
Messianic Jewish Resources Int'l.
www.messianicjewish.net
Individual and Trade Order line: 800-410-7367

Email: lederer@messianicjewish.net

******

COVER DESCRIPTION:
"Brooklyn Bridge with Manhattan buildings in background by night" (purchased from istockphotos.com)
The Brooklyn Bridge connects Brooklyn, New York with downtown Manhattan. Brooklyn is home to many Orthodox Jews who have not recognized Yeshua as their promised Messiah … yet.

******

TABLE OF CONTENTS

HOW THE BOROUGH PARK SYMPOSIUM CAME TO BE AND WHAT IT IS

The Borough Park Steering Committee

The time had come for leaders across the organizational spectrum of the Messianic Jewish/Jewish Missions world to unite as members of the Jewish community, leaders of a Remnant, with a responsibility to the God who called us his chosen people. On October 19-20, 2006, ten Messianic Jewish colleagues met in Brooklyn, New York. We agreed on a direction, a Steering Committee, and shared convictions that would determine who should actively participate:

> *We are Jews who believe in Yeshua and in God's covenant with Israel, and as members of the Jewish community, are committed to the welfare of our people.*
>
> *We feel compelled by the spirit of God to advance the good news of Yeshua among our people.*
>
> *We desire to preserve the unity and secure the future of the Messianic Jewish movement and our common mission through respectful dialogue, without acrimony, even in the face of critical disagreements.*
>
> *We believe in the authority of Scripture and the deity of Yeshua, and that eternal life is the gift of God in Messiah Yeshua our Lord.*

Since we held our planning meeting in an Orthodox Jewish hotel in the Borough Park neighborhood of Brooklyn, our setting provided a great name for this consultation—"the Borough Park Symposium." We scheduled it for a year later, October, 2007 and chose a topic that we knew would be controversial, but which seemed like a logical starting point for our dialogue: *The Gospel and the Jewish People.*

When the symposium arrived, we discussed the nature of the gospel itself, how it applies specifically to Jewish people, and what outreach should look like in light of all this. Participants were impassioned and not afraid of ideological clash or of expressing agreement when it was there. Leaders who had staked out opposite ends of the Messianic Jewish spectrum years earlier now sat down together and talked. Indeed, several leaders reconnected with colleagues with whom they hadn't spoken, for one reason or another, for twenty or thirty years.

When the Steering Committee evaluated the Symposium, we determined that it was a big success, not only in discussing the issues, but also in helping to "preserve the unity and secure the future of the Messianic Jewish movement and our common mission through respectful dialogue." Although we didn't want the Symposium to become institutionalized into an annual event, we started to think about a second one. The Steering Committee met in May 2008 and chose a topic that we imagined to be less controversial among us, *The Deity of Messiah and the Mystery of God.*

Paradoxically, this is the issue most controversial in the wider Jewish community, the boundary-marker that the Jewish community has set for centuries to define itself. No matter how Jewish in all other ways a person might be, a Jewish gatekeeper might say, belief in the deity of Yeshua, by itself, drives him or her out of Judaism into Christianity. And Messianic Jews are problematic (and even to be feared) because they refuse to accept that they've crossed this line.

From this perspective, all of us who gathered for BPS II, as diverse as we might have been, were on the same side of the divide, despite our differences, and even despite our lack of precise definition of the deity of Messiah. Our goal in meeting was not to produce a precise theological definition, but to discuss how we can embrace and share the truth of the deity of Messiah specifically as Jews. How do we respond to questions we often hear from non-Messianic Jewish friends? "Are you telling us to worship a man as God?" "Can it possibly be right for a Jew to acknowledge a Messiah who claims (or whose followers claim for him) to somehow be God?" "Why are you trying to bring such a non-Jewish idea into Judaism?" Much was accomplished by hearing the thoughts of others in our Community.

A clear benefit of the Symposium was the heightened sense of unity that came out of this event. Some of the panels included speakers who had been in robust debates with each other in recent years, who had widely different perspectives, and yet, at the Symposium, communicated with the greatest respect and deference. There were disagreements on many specific points, but an underlying sense prevailed that we are all in this together—marking out new territory as Jews who recognize the unique nature of the Messiah of Israel. It is our hope that this renewed awareness of our underlying unity will help the entire Messianic Jewish community to move forward. As one of the Steering Committee members remarked afterwards, "I guess this BPS Symposium was about more than our theology!"

No one expected that we'd ever have total agreement, but in the larger scope of things, we have more in common with each other than many other people in the world. We are Jews who all agree that Yeshua is the Messiah. We all believe that our people are the chosen people. We all hold that the Land of Israel was uniquely given and still belongs to the Jewish people. We all accept the Torah, and its obligations upon us as Jews, to one degree or another. Compared to the entire 6.6 billion people in the world, we have more in common with each other than many other groups in the world.

That's why these symposiums are so important. Our numbers are small, but great things can happen as we learn how to listen and work together. There's strength in unity. That's why we agreed that:

> The purpose of the Symposiums is to provide a forum for members of the broader Messianic Jewish community to articulate their beliefs with an expectation that they will receive a respectful hearing, but without the expectation that agreement concerning these beliefs will be achieved. The Symposium is designed to provide an internal platform for leaders to better understand each another and the various positions held within the Messianic movement.

So, as you read one or more of the papers in the Borough Park Symposiums, you may be challenged. You may read papers that present both sides of an argument, with few, if any, conclusions drawn. This is the way of the Jewish people.

In the Second Temple era, the time of Yeshua, there were quite a few sects of Judaism—Pharisees, Sadducees, Essenes, Zealots,

Herodians, and more—but they were all considered, and considered themselves, to be Jews. Judaism then was like Judaism today—pluralistic. Orthodox, Conservative, Reform, Reconstructionist, Hasidic, Zionistic branches may disagree today on many matters but all see themselves as part of the same people—the nation of Israel, the Jewish people.

That's the way we in the Borough Park Symposia see ourselves—Jews, albeit Messianic Jews. We are getting more comfortable talking about serious issues, in the hope of understanding God and his revelation better. You are invited to "read over our shoulders" as we have these discussions, much like when you read the New Testament, which also records discussions Jews had about critical issues. Please just remember that you are "listening in" and our discussions may not fit into your previously held pre-suppositions. You may need some paradigm shifting in your thinking.

There were response papers given to most of the papers in this volume. They can be read, as can the papers, on line at:

http://www.boroughparksymposium.com

or

http://www.boroparksymposium.com

We're pleased you are interested in the discussions we in the Messianic Jewish community are having. We believe that you will be challenged to think about these issues alongside us.

For more information, email: info@boroughparksymposium.com.

INTRODUCTION TO THE THEME OF BOROUGH PARK SYMPOSIM

Russ Resnik
Executive Director of the Union of Messianic Jewish Congregations,
Author of numerous books and articles on
Scripture and Messianic Judaism

The genius of the Borough Park Symposium is to bring together Messianic Jewish leaders and thinkers from a broad spectrum into "respectful dialogue, without acrimony even in the face of critical disagreements," and to focus this dialogue on issues that really matter to the Messianic Jewish community—the sort of issues that might actually stir up critical disagreements. The topics of the first two symposia reflected core doctrinal concerns—first, the nature of the gospel and, second, the deity of Messiah. The third symposium shifts the attention to the Messianic community itself, with the topic, "How Jewish Should the Messianic Jewish Community Be?"

This title is reminiscent of some books published nearly a decade ago, including *Messianic Judaism Isn't Jewish*, by Baruch Maoz;[1] *Messianic Judaism Isn't Christianity*, by Stan Telchin;[2] and *How Jewish is Christianity? Two views on the Messianic Movement*, edited by the late Louis Goldberg.[3] Telchin's title in particular was meant to frame a critique of Messianic Judaism as not being sufficiently "Christian," which Telchin attempted to soften with a gloss, *Some Messianic Jews say . . . Messianic Judaism isn't Christianity*, and the subtitle, *A Loving Call to Unity*. All three books, or at least their titles, reflect ambivalence about Messianic Judaism and Jewish identity.

Like these titles, the BPS III title, "How Jewish Should the Messianic Jewish Community be?" sounds ironic, but unlike them, it doesn't assume that Christianity is the benchmark for Messianic Jewish legitimacy. Numerous Messianic Jewish figures have advocated an unambiguous identification with Judaism and Jewish identity. For example, the Union of Messianic Jewish Congregations, an organization that I represent, defines Messianic Judaism as "a movement of Jewish congregations and groups committed to Yeshua the Messiah that embrace the covenantal responsibility of Jewish life and identity rooted in Torah, expressed in tradition, and renewed and applied in the context of the New Covenant."[4]

The Borough Park Symposium more broadly defines its active participants as "Jews who believe in Yeshua and in God's covenant with Israel, and as members of the Jewish community." Some participants affirm this self-definition and call themselves Christians at the same time; others would not apply the Christian label to themselves at all, arguing that belief in Yeshua does not diminish one's Jewish identity or connection to the Jewish people. But what is most striking, and unifying, is that all participants see themselves as members of the Jewish community, despite the wide divergence of views about the meaning of this membership. This combination of a shared commitment to the Jewish community and a wide range of differing applications of this commitment led inevitably to the emphasis of the third Borough Park Symposium, which is of the nature of the Messianic Jewish community.

The BPS III steering committee originally considered dividing this subject into three inter-related topics, Community, Torah, and Tradition, under the general theme of *What's distinctive about the Messianic Jewish Community relative to the Jewish Community and the Christian Church?* We wanted participants to consider what makes us a community, given our precarious position between two far more established communities. As with the first symposium, on the nature of the gospel, we knew we were on controversial ground, and after some discussion, we decided to re-frame the topics to reflect that controversy. The center of controversy isn't how the Messianic Jewish community is or should be distinctive, but how *Jewish* it should be.

In other words, even as the terms Messianic Judaism and Messianic Jew have gained increasingly wide currency, the issue of connection to Jewish tradition and community remains controversial; hence, "How Jewish Should the Messianic Jewish Community be?" Within this broad question, the steering committee identified four more specific questions that provide a framework for the entire symposium:

1. What is the role of Torah and Jewish tradition in the Messianic Jewish community?

2. What is our relationship with the wider Jewish community?

3. What is the role of Gentiles in the Messianic Jewish community?
4. How Jewish will the Messianic Jewish community of the future be?

Each of the papers presented at BPS III addresses one of these questions, and we can consider them in more detail by way of introduction.

1. What is the role of Torah and Jewish tradition in the Messianic Jewish community?

"Torah" in this context implies not just the Five Books of Moses, but the Jewish communal discussion and development of those texts within the rest of the Scriptures, within rabbinic literature, and within traditional Jewish practice. Nearly all Messianic Jews adhere to at least some aspects of Torah in this broader sense but would display a wide range of opinion concerning its authority and specific application. Furthermore, Messianic Jews hold diverse interpretations on the impact of the coming of Messiah on Torah and tradition and on how to adapt tradition specifically to the Messianic community.

2. What is our relationship with the wider Jewish community?

Not long after the three books mentioned above, *Postmissionary Messianic Judaism: Redefining Christian Engagement with the Jewish People* appeared.[5] As its subtitle indicates, the book is directed toward the Christian community, but it presents the Messianic Jewish community as an inherent part of the wider Jewish community, which provides the primary locus of identity for Messianic Jews. Messianic Jews are "postmissionary" because they do not relate to the Jewish community only, or primarily, in terms of witness, but in terms of participation. Such a stance is controversial, of course. This sub-topic doesn't reflect directly on Postmissionary Messianic Judaism, but it explores the witness-participation spectrum and the underlying issue of boundaries in relationship with the wider Jewish community.

3. What is the role of Gentiles in the Messianic Jewish community?

One of the striking and, some would say, troubling features of the contemporary Messianic Jewish community is the large numbers of Gentiles participating in it. It's not unusual for a Messianic Jewish congregation to have a majority of Gentile members, which raises questions about whether Gentiles should keep Jewish tradition and why, whether conversion of Gentiles is valid, and what, if any, are the different roles of Jews and Gentiles within the community.

4. How Jewish will the Messianic Jewish community of the future be?

One of the goals of the Borough Park Symposium is to "secure the future of the Messianic Jewish movement and our common mission through respectful dialogue," and this section considers that future in terms of its Jewish identity. It emphasizes the views of younger-generation Messianic Jews and how they may differ from older-generation views in response to questions such as these:

1. What role will Torah and tradition, marriage within the Jewish community, and the importance of Israel have in the years ahead?
2. What future do Messianic congregations have? What challenges do they face in forming Jewish identity for a new generation?
3. Where will future leaders of the Messianic Jewish community come from?

Loyalty to Yeshua as the Messiah of Israel and loyalty to the people of Israel have been seen throughout history as competing commitments. Messianic Judaism claims that they are compatible commitments, although with diverse views of how this compatibility is to be expressed. In all four sections of BPS III, presenters explore these diverse views in terms of how Jewish the Messianic Jewish community should be, and in the process, discover and deepen Messianic Judaism's biblical roots and enhance its relevance to Jewish people of every background.

ENDNOTES

1. Baruch Maoz, *Messianic Judaism Isn't Jewish: A Friendly Critique of the Messianic Movement,* (Fearn, Ross-shire, Great Britain: Mentor, 2003).
2. Stan Telchin, *Messianic Judaism isn't Christianity: A Loving Call to Unity*, (Grand Rapids: Chosen Books, 2004).
3. Louis Goldberg, ed., *How Jewish is Christianity?: Two views on the Messianic movement,* (Grand Rapids: Zondervan, 2003).
4. "UMJC," accessed Oct. 4, 2012, http://umjc.org/home-mainmenu-1/global-vision-mainmenu-42/13-vision/225-defining-messianic-judaism.
5. Mark Kinzer, *Postmissionary Messianic Judaism: Redefining Christian Engagement with the Jewish People*, (Grand Rapids: Brazos Press, 2005).

A RETROSPECTIVE LOOK AT OUR MOVEMENT

Chaim Urbach
M.A. in Biblical Studies from Denver Seminary,
A Leader of Congregation Yeshuat Tsion in Denver, Coloado,
Served as VP of the Fellowship of Messianic Congregations

I am honored to share a personal perspective on the Messianic Jewish Movement as I have experienced it. I'd like to illustrate this movement's development from its inception using my family's story because they had been part of the movement from those early days. Although our family story spans 3 countries—Israel, Canada, and the US—most of my comments will address the Messianic Jewish Movement in the US because that is where I have spent the bulk of my adult life.

OUR BEGINNINGS AS HEBREW CHRISTIANS—ROAD TO ASSIMILATION

History of Persecution in Israel

Our commitment to Yeshua in Israel of the 1950s-1960s came with a stiff price. When my *savta* (grandmother) discovered that my parents embraced a faith in Yeshua, she asked them: "Why didn't you wait till I died?" My Uncle Sh'muel, who had been a practicing attorney was interested in exploring ways to have my sister Nechama and I placed in a different home. Once the family found out that we were believers, we were personna non-grata in our uncle and aunt's seder. Now, 50 years later, our family has finally begun to connect with us. Our cousins invite my sister and my nephew to participate in family events such as weddings and seders.

In 1963, my father received a letter from Yad LeAchim, warning him to "cease and desist from his missionary activity," which amounted to the translation of sermons given by visiting expatriates in our congregation in Yaffo. Our family stayed away from Shabbat services until my father determined that it was more important to "obey God, rather than men" (Acts 4:19). That event illustrated the atmosphere of fear under which we lived, with the constant question on our mind: "What would happen if 'they' would find out that we were believers." That blanket of fear was especially noticeable during the Eichman Trial years (1961-1962). We were a despised, beleaguered, persecuted little community.

The Messianic Jewish community in Israel continues to pay a stiff price for their commitment to Yeshua but with a major difference: The Messianic Jews in Israel are no longer hidden. The Israeli public has become well aware of its existence. Israeli media (TV, newspapers, etc.) presented the Messianic Jewish community, sometimes with fairness and accuracy. They have become integrated into Israeli society.

Assimiliation in Israel and North America

In our time in Israel, the prevailing mindset for the believers was based on Hebrews 13:12-13:

> And so Yeshua also suffered outside the city gate to make the people holy through his own blood. Let us, then, go to him outside the camp, bearing the disgrace he bore.

It played itself out in our praxis: our worship services were essentially an Evangelical Christian service in Hebrew—we sang Christian hymns in Hebrew, and we were taught the Good News of Yeshua with a four-spiritual-laws approach on flannel board.

I did not become bar mitzvah because my father felt it would be inconsistent with our faith. On the 3rd floor of our apartment building, our neighbor Mr. Rivlin prepared boys for their bar mitzvahs. I heard the blessings for the Haftarah but the sounds could have been in Chinese for all their impact on me.

Our **identification as Jews was no different than the secular majority of Israelis** who defined their Jewish identity by the following statement: "I am Jewish because I am an Israeli." It was basically an **ethnic heritage**, with little connection to our God-given calling as Jews.

The picture was no different when we emigrated to Canada, and after 3 years, to the US. We were associated with Christian churches, faithfully attending services twice a week but had absolutely no connection to the Jewish community. Furthermore, there were no discernible differences in our spiritual lives between ourselves and fellow church members. We did not celebrate any of the holidays and we did not set foot in a synagogue until I was in my late twenties.

There were positive aspects to our upbringing; we became grounded in our faith and committed to the Word of God. We learned the meaning of persevering under fire.

In retrospect, it was difficult not to become insulated from the heart and soul of all that is good in rabbinic Judaism. We were taught to do so, both in Israel and in North America, and most Jewish believers followed suit. However, after thirty plus years of being part of the Messianic Jewish Movement, I realize that the instruction of the writer of Hebrews (as seen in Heb. 13:12-13) needs to be a last resort rather than one of the beginning steps in our relationship with fellow Jews.

THE TRANSFORMATION

The Beginning of the Change

The transformation in my father's appearance over 30 years provides a snap shot of what was happening among Jewish believers. When we were in NYC, while my father was training with Moishe Rosen, he was clean shaven, wore a white shirt and dark tie, and engaged in street preaching from a platform bearing the American flag. During the mid 1970s, he began to sport a short beard and wore a denim jacket with the emblem *Jews For Jesus* on it. By the 1980s, he could pass for one of the Chassidic rebbes.

In the summer of 1970, I attended a conference of the Fellowship of Christian Testimony to the Jews. Sid Lawrence, a rabbi from B'nei Brith was invited to address a gathering of the Fellowship of Christian Testimony to the Jews. Asked about his opinon on Hebrew Christianity, he responded with one word, *na'arishkeit*, child's play. The picture he was attempting to draw of us was analogous to little girls putting on lipstick and wearing their mother's high heels or boys seeking to get behind the wheel of their father's car and pretending to drive. Moishe Rosen, who was in attendance, found that answer unacceptable. This prodded him to take an aggressive approach in conveying the Good News of Yeshua. Over time, this resulted in the formulation of the Jews for Jesus' mission statement: "We exist to make the messiahship of Jesus an unavoidable issue to our Jewish people worldwide."[1]

I realize that there is a great deal of controversy surrounding that mission statement. However, for me, it represents the beginning of a decisive transformation for us, which until then was a small and marginalized community of Jewish believers. We began to exercise holy *chutzpah*. This was true in North America and as well became realized in Israel. Messianic Jews were engaging publicly in ways we could not have dreamed of when I was a child in Israel.

The Late 1960s and 1970s—The Heady Years

Books have been written about the "glory years" of the Messianic Jewish Movement and most of us in this room were part of it, in one form or another.[2] I will not seek to duplicate that material. Rather, I would like to approach it from a personal perspective. For me, the onset of the movement was a time of re-discovery—finally coming to terms with the dynamic tension involved in being part of two communities: a dedicated follower of Yeshua and a committed Jew. For the first time, my Jewish identity felt like a comfortable slipper.

This was a time of great ferment. In retrospect, I realize that like all new wines, much sediment accumulated. We have seen a great deal of confusion and heterodoxy typical of the aftermath of revival movements. God was doing amazing work in drawing Jewish young people into the Kingdom, but at the same time, there was much spiritual counterfeit, especially in the fringes of our movement. My father's stock description of our movement in the early years was, "The Messianic Jewish Movement is still in diapers."

I firmly believe that God has been at work, sifting out the sediment in our movement and bringing it through the process of maturation. It has been happening as the rush of the early years has slowed down.[3]

THE MATURATION OF THE MOVEMENT

God has been at Work through the Leaner Years

Indeed, God has been at work through the leaner years. Those of us who have been involved in ministry to our people have not always been able to see that, and consequently, the desire to recapture the glory years has been strong over the last 20 years. I have seen it take two radically different approaches: the strong emphasis on **the need for charismatic expression** in our congregations and the commitment to be more **firmly embedded within the Jewish community**.

Do we need to set these two emphases, the need for charismatic expression and the need for identification with our community, as polar opposites? I believe that it cannot be a case of "either/or," but rather, a more Jewish "both, and." We must place a high value on the need for the Ruach HaKodesh to be active in our congregations. The expression will differ from congregation to congregation but we humbly recognize the imperative for the power of God to be at work in our midst.

By the same token, our Jewish identification must be clearly visible and authentic. The early followers of Yeshua were clearly identified as Jews—for them that was not a window dressing but part and parcel of their life. We need to emulate their example.

REASONS FOR DISCOURAGEMENT AND FOR HOPE

Discouragement Comes from Time to Time

How we identify ourselves (e.g. more charismatically or more Jewishly) is a crucial question that does not yield to simple answers. However, I believe that underlying this question is a greater one—do we see our movement as a success or a failure? How do we thrive under the pervasive sense of discouragement that comes over us from time to time?

There are some discouraging factors. What follows is a limited list. After almost 40 years in existence, we comprise less that one percent of the Jewish community.[4] The believing community with which we identify is comprised of a large amount of those who adhere to Replacement Theology. The majority of Jewish followers of Yeshua choose to be part of the Church rather than identify with us. We recognize that each Jewish believer needs to be responsive to the Lord's personal call on his or her life. Yet, the fact that a large majority chooses to be part of the Church at large conveys a basic continuation of the assimilation of many of the Jewish believers of previous generations. It also conveys a lack of concern about the survival of Klal Israel and a lack of understanding of the preciousness of our election as a Jewish nation.

Why do so many of our fellow Jewish believers choose to distance themselves from us and from any semblance of Jewish life? There is a plethora of reasons and I will address some of those later on.

Our movement in the US is largely comprised of Gentile believers. Some of them have a Ruth-like call to join themselves to us. We value them as precious members of our movement who have been called to come alongside and present the message of one Messiah. However, many others connect with us because of a felt need to grasp the "Hebraic roots of the faith," but they remain in that frame of mind. There seems to be little interst regarding what our God-given vision is about—the restoration of Israel (Rom. 11:12,15).

Reasons for Hope

In a message given at Yeshuat Tsion several years ago, Mitch Glaser made an observation that was both profound and yet simple at the same time: **"We know how the book ends."** His point was that regardless of current appearances, we know that history is moving irrevocably towards God's plan to restore Israel and bring a world-wide revival. Yes, we are facing a period of trouble for Israel, as the sages called it *chevlei ha-mashiach* (birth pangs of Messiah), but what keeps us going is the bedrock conviction that God is at work to bring about his good, sovereign plans for our people.

There are visible reasons for hope. Profound interest has been developing among Jewish scholars during the past few years with three signficant works on topics relating to Messianic Judaism this past year alone.[5] Some of this scholarly development can be seen as a "Jewish Reclamation of Jesus"—i.e. that endeavor to strip away the layers of Hellenistic accretions that have obscured who the Jewish Yeshua is.[6] Even Rav Shaul, who had often been portrayed as the arch-villain, is being given a fresh coat of Jewish varnish.[7]

Over the past 10 years, a number of academic institutions have been established which grant graduate level degrees in Messianic Jewish studies. I represent one of those—Denver Seminary's M Div in Biblical Studies with emphasis on Messianic Judaism. There are others, including The King's University, which now grants D Min degees in Messianic Jewish studies. Accompanying that development has been the rise in the number of Messianic Jewish scholars with Ph. D. degrees in related fields. That gives us much hope for several reasons.

We are positioning ourselves to present a clearer voice to the larger Jewish community, which places a great deal of value on credentials and scholarship. This is also an effective statement to the rest of the Body of Messiah, especially to Christian institutions of higher learning because our movement is expressing a credible move of God. Our trained young people are able to go into positions of influence, countering the heterodoxy that is peddled by fringe elements of our movement. More importantly, they are able to present a Biblically-sound message to those under their influence.

SOME OF THE REMAINING CHALLENGES

How do we Connect with Fellow Jewish Believers

This is a formidable challenge. As stated previously, a majority of fellow Jewish believers are detached from any semblance of Jewish life. That does not only mean being disconnected from the Messianic Jewish Movement but being detached from the Jewish community at large.

There are many reasons. Some come to faith in Yeshua out of a sense of antipathy to all things Jewish. They find the "pearl of great price" and have no desire to go back to what they consider a dysfunctional community and a distastful familiar setting. Some were raised with a minimum of Jewish identification and they find it much more comfortable to be embedded in a church setting. The challenge of integrating their commitment to Yeshua and a weakened Jewish identity seems simplified—it is unipolar, with the Jewish heritage hidden in a corner.

For others, it is a matter of parental choices. They may wrestle with the question: "Where do I bring my children: to a smaller

Messianic Jewish congregation or to a mega church where there are lavish facilities and dedicated staff? Or, they may express the issues slightly differently: "I want my kids to play soccer, baseball, football, hockey, and lacrosse—and all the games are on Saturday mornings."

Fortunately, some of our fellow Jewish believers who are in churches have had their hearts sensitized by what it means to be "Jewish." Their hearts are touched at different points of the yearly cycle as they remember their childhood. Sometimes they ask for our assistance in processing grief Jewishly or in training their children for bar or bat mitzvahs. I have been privileged to interact with fellow Jewish believers on a number of these life cycle events. These provide us with opportunities to offer our assistance. Sometimes, the Lord draws them into a fuller understanding and appreciation of their heritage and brings them into a Messianic Jewish context.

This is an area of great need for us. We need our fellow Jewish believers to come alongside us and participate in the building of God's work among our people. We need to invest time in reaching out to them. We need to pray that God will bring about healing to those who feel antipathy towards our people, or perhaps, even total indiffierence to their God given heritage.

The Lord may call many individual Jews to be part of solid churches for a variety of reasons. However, nowhere in Scripture do I see that it is God's counsel for a majority of fellow Jewish believers to become assimilated. That clearly flies in the face of the prophetic passages that require a living, ethnic entity—known as Israel—in order for God's plans to unfold.

One example, although somewhat controversial, of a Jew who believed in Yeshua and insisted on a public Jewish identity was Cardinal Lustiger. Aaron Lustiger, a Polish Jew, converted to Catholicism as a 13-year-old boy and through it, escaped the Holocaust. He came into the priesthood, became the Archibishop of Paris, and eventually was elevated to the post of Cardinal. Although he was severely criticized by Jewish leaders in the US and in Israel, he was well accepted by the French Jewish community. Lustiger was a vocal supporter of Israel, despite the Vatican's officially neutral position towards Israel, for which he won Jewish support. He was also active in promoting Jewish-Catholic relationships, especially in regards to Sho'ah events. The Cardinal was instrumental in seeing to the Carmelitan convent in Auschwitz becoming inactive. On becoming Archbishop of Paris, Lustiger said:

> I was born Jewish and so I remain, even if that is unacceptable for many. For me, the vocation of Israel is bringing light to the goyim. That is my hope and I believe that Christianity is the means for achieving it.[8]

Our hearts grieve for our fellow Jewish believers in Yeshua. While they have become followers of the Jewish Messiah, they have done so with the **needless jettisoning of their calling as Jews**. Their assimiliation fulfills the long-term accusation of us by the larger Jewish community—"You believe in Jesus and you are lost to your people."

Urgency, Value, and Limits of Identification with our People

How do we put into practice the need to more strongly identify with our people? As we all know, Yeshua was part and parcel of the Jewish community of his day, as were the early disciples. I believe that we need to emulate their pattern, while recognizing that there are some potential pitfalls. I am eager to hear the *chochmah* the Lord has given our presenters during the conference on this subject but I would like to offer some reflections.

Our culture values honor intellectual prowess. God has been raising wise men and women in our movement who are equipped to engage our people on the highest intellectual levels. That is a dramatic move during the past 30 years. Our scholarly credentials have earned us the right to be heard by the Jewish scholarly community.

However, we must keep this dramatic intellectual progress in perspective. While our scholarship provides us the platform from which we can communicate our message, having sobriety and humility is absolutely essential. What brings individual Jews to know Messiah is not our intellectual prowess or even our superb connections within the Jewish community. ***We can be drawn away from a simple dependence on the supernatural power of God, at work in us who are the communicators and in the perception of the listeners***.

That is not a theoretical danger. All of us are aware of the siren call to return to the fullness of Jewish orthopraxis and turn away from Yeshua. All of us know indivdiduals who professed Yeshua, even engaged in serving him and at some point walked away from him, seduced by one siren call or another.

All of us experience rejection from our fellow Jews and that rejection can function as a low-grade fever. We may feel insecure about our identity as Jews and may feel the need to buttress that sense of identity. At some point, we must come to the bedrock conviction that our Jewish identity rests securely on our individual calling by God to be part of our people.

A deep engagement with our people is an absolute must but it carries with it additional risks, one of which is the temptation to make the Good News more palatable for our fellow Jews. That is a precipice that we want to avoid assiduously, knowing that the power of God comes through that rough-edged message of salvation. Consequently, we choose to anchor ourselves in a message that appears as gross foolishness to the twenty first century mind as it did to that of the first century.

Yeshua's message appears to be out of step with a pluralistic society, obssessed with moral authority of each individual to determine what is truth.[9] Yeshua called Nicodemus, a rabbi of rabbis, to come in repentance. He died an ignoble death and the means of his execution has been the symbol of our suffering for millennia. Yet, we remember his words to the first century disciples: "Yeshua said, 'If you hold to my teaching, you are really my disciples. Then you will know the truth, and the truth will set you free'" (John 8:31-32).

Unity: Chesed for Times when Bunions Get Stepped on

I am seeing significant movement towards unity despite a past often characterized by fractiousness. The LCJE conference this past March proved to me to be a wonderful example of that movement. One of the presenters there made the following statement: "Time is short; we are all on Yeshua's team. Let's work together!" That sentiment was echoed by others present. A number of representatives of Messianic Jewish academic programs gathered together to discuss the establishment of a Messianic Jewish academic consortium, through which students would be able to take advantage of the strengths of the various institutions. I also heard about the collaborative endeavor to reach young Israelis in India.

The attitude that was portrayed at the conference was a refreshing "kingdom mindset"—a desire to advance the Lord's cause rather than a provincial, territorial approach to sharing resources. **Much prayer has**

gone up before the throne for the unification of our movement. It is inspiring to see that beginning to come about.

Yet, like other aspects of our spiritual life, unity requires our on-going engagement. It is a cooperative venture, involving the work of the Spirit and our committed efforts. Rav Shaul defines that collaboration:

> As a prisoner for the Lord, then, I urge you to live a life worthy of the calling you have received. Be completely humble and gentle; be patient, bearing with one another in love (New International Version). Make every effort to preserve the unity the Spirit gives through the binding power of Shalom. (Jewish New Testament)[10]

We all have passionately held thought out positions on a number of hot button topics extant in our movement. We come from a culture that values plurality of opinion. We can't paper over the differences. Nor can we stiff arm each other to come to our respective points of view. We have often tried that in times past, unsuccessfully.

There have been times when our differences spilled over into the larger Jewish community and the Body of Messiah.

"Being completely humble" is based on our grasp that there is one Righteous Judge, who has all the facts. We often learn that reality through the school of hard knocks. Our unity is not at all costs—ignoring significant issues. However, over time, I believe that the number of issues for which we are willing to die shrinks as we recognize that we are fellow learners with our brothers and sisters. Part of the picture is our need to learn to **set aside our magnifying glass and no longer look to micro-analyze others's short comings.**

What does it mean to "bear with one another in love"? The NLT is helpful here: "making allowances for each other because of your love." Peter adds an additional insight: "Above all, love each other deeply, because love covers over a multitude of sins" (I Pet. 4:8).

For me it boils down to a simple, earthy metaphor—how do we respond when our bunions get stepped on because of comments that were delivered in an offhanded, but insensitive manner? Yes, it is only possible for us to be truly united as the Spirit draws us together. It is a miracle that comes about by the power of God in our lives, transcending our natural tendencies towards divisiveness. The Spirit brings it about through the bond of Shalom—somehow we find ourselves tied together by that power, sometimes despite ourselves.

Yet, we are called upon to play a major role in this ongoing, developing unity. "Make every effort" translates the Greek verb *spoudazontes,* which conveys the sense of **eagerness/readiness** and the **expenditure** of 'intense effort and motivation."[11] What does that look like? It implies that we learn to be people of *chesed*: covenant, committed loyal love, as well as mercy, kindness, and despite inclination to do otherwise.

It is so easy to accentuate the negatives and observe the specks in our brother or sister's eyes. If we do that, we typically miss the larger picture of what God is doing in our midst. Perhaps a wiser approach is to observe and affirm positive developments that are taking place with others in our movement. God is at work with the collection of clay pots known as the Messianic Jewish Movement.

How do we relate to each other on those points of divergence? We learn to sit and learn from each other, even from those with whom we disagree vociferously. I have observed over the years how God has taken us, when we were full of ourselves, and brought us into humbling situations. For that we can say, *Todah, Adon.* Ultimately, we remind ourselves that our movement has been spawned and nurtured by the Almighty. We know that He operates out of the divine counsel of his will. We make our highest priority to depend on Him to establish HIS counsel, and that He will fashion what that looks like for each of us.

For us as a movement, an increasing commitment to unity is perhaps the strongest indicator of growing maturity. Scripture is very emphatic that disunity is indicative of spiritual immaturity.[12]

Most of all, a commitment to unity suggests that we are serious about lining up with the Lord's priorities. **Our Messiah prayed and continues to pray for unity**:

> Holy Father, protect them by the power of your name—the name you gave me—so **that they may be one** as we are one. (John 17:11)
>
> My prayer is not for them alone. I pray also for those who will believe in me through their message, **that all of them may be one**, Father, just as you are in me and I am in you. May they also be in us so that the world may believe that you have sent me. I have given them

> the glory that you gave me, **that they may be one** as we are one: I in them and you in me. **May they be brought to complete unity** to let the world know that you sent me and have loved them even as you have loved me. (John 17:20-23)

The phrase "that they may be one" appears 3 times in his prayer. That conveys the supreme priority that the Lord gives the need for unity. The additional expanded phrase, "may they be brought to complete unity" expresses the reality that this is an on-going process.[13] It will be completed when we see the Lord. In the meantime, we need to emulate Yeshua in this prayer and urgently seek Him for increased unity in our movement.

The Primacy of Our Messiah: Yeshua + Nothing

Is it possible to place Yeshua backstage instead of center stage? I believe that all of us can relate seasons in our life when that was the case. It does not take much for us to see ourselves drifting from a wholehearted devotion to the Lord. The Torah reminds us that because the Lord is the source of our life, we do not want to drift from him:

> Love the LORD your God, listen to his voice, and hold fast to him [i.e. cleave to him like glue]. For the LORD is your life. (Deut. 30:20)

Why do we drift and lose our focus on Messiah? We all face the temptation to help God when He seems to be slow in delivering. We become ***impatient with the Lord and seek to find quick fixes***. We worship him in his temple and then, to cover our bases, we come home and worship the teraphim (the household gods). It is easy to look for solutions in which God is absent.

The Ruach may guide us into new ways of doing things. However, the bottom line for us must be the basic concern: Where is the Lord in all our new endeavors? Do we sense His presence as we engage in doing His work? Are we interested in our ventures being Peniel, the place where we encounter God, or is that a distraction that keeps us from doing what we desire?

It is so easy to ignore the fact that Messianic Judaism is first and foremost about Messiah. Rav Shaul, a Torah observant Jew, made a radical statement about what was the ultimate priority in his life: "I consider everything a loss compared to the surpassing greatness of knowing Messiah my Lord. . . . I consider them rubbish, that I may gain Messiah" (Phil. 3:8).

That needs to be the plumbob in our lives: where are we today in our relationship with the Lord as contrasted to 5 years ago? There is a basic programmatic statement given to us about our priorities:

> Therefore God exalted him to the highest place and gave him the name that is above every name, that at the name of Yeshua every knee should bow, in heaven and on earth and under the earth, and **every tongue confess** that Messiah Yeshua is Lord, to the glory of God the Father. (Phil. 2:9)

We all long to see the power of God displayed in our movement in a greater measure.

We want to see a strengthened movement, to see more Jewish people come into the Kingdom of God, to see these new talmidim properly established and brought to maturity, and to see these same people embrace their God-given calling as Jews. We want to see the **power of God displayed through the moving of his Ruach**. It behooves us to remember that the major **goal of the Spirit is to bring glory to Yeshua**. The recipe is simple but it operates on God's time.

> Let us acknowledge the LORD; let us press on to acknowledge him. As surely as the sun rises, he will appear; he will come to us like the winter rains, like the spring rains that water the earth. (Hos. 6:3)

ENDNOTES

1. "Jews for Jesus," accessed on Oct. 1, 2012, http://www.jewsforjesus.org/about.
2. What follows is a limited listing of some of the books which address this history: David A. Rausch, *Messianic Judaism: Its History, Theology and Polity*, (NY: Edwin Mellen Press, 1982). Michael Schiffman, *Return from Exile: The Re-Emergence of the Messianic Congregational Movement,* (Columbus: OH, Teshuvah Publication Co, 1990). Carol Harris-Shapiro, *Messianic Judaism: A Rabbi's Journey through Religious Change in America*, (Boston: Beacon Press, 1999). Dan Cohn-Sherbok, *Messianic Judaism*, (NY: Cassell, 2000).
3. This was true with some notable exceptions, such as the ministry among the Jews of the FSU.
4. The numbers are difficult if not impossible to nail down. According to the 1990 Council of Jewish Federation cenus [http://www.ajcarchives.org/AJC_DATA/Files/1992_14_WJP.pdf], there are two million Jews who identify themselves as believing in Jesus. I believe that those include Jews who are minimally committed as believers. More conservative estimates put the number of Jewish believers in the US at 50,000 and in Israel at 15,000.
5. Amy-Jill Levine and Mark Z. Brettler, *The Jewish Annotated New Testament*, (New York: Oxford University Press, 2012). Shmuley Boteach, *Kosher Jesus*, (NY: Gefen Publishing House, 2012). Needless to say, Boteach's book stirred tremendous controversy in the Jewish community. The most severe critic has been respected rabbinic scholar [Chabad], and counter-missionary Dr. J. Immanuel Schochet has labeled the book heretical and has issued the following ban: "I have never read a book, let alone one authored by a purported frum Jew, that does more to enhance the evangelical missionary message and agenda than the aforementioned book." (http://jewishisrael.ning.com/profiles/blogs/kosher-jesus-judging-a-book-by-its-cover, accessed October 7, 2012). Daniel Boyarin, *The Jewish Gospels: the Story of the Jewish Christ*,(NY: The New Press, 2012). Also by Boyarin: *A Radical Jew: Paul and the Politics of Identity; Border Lines: the Partition of Judaeo-Christianity.*
6. Donald A. Hagner, *The Jewish Reclamation of Jesus: An analysis & a critique of the modern Jewish study of Jesus*, (Eugene, OR: Wipf & Stock, 1997).
7. Pamela Eisenbaum, *Paul was not a Christian: The original message of a misunderstood apostle,* (New York:Harper one, 2009).
8. Quoted in *The Economist* obituary, August 18th 2007, p.76.
9. A vivid example of that pluralism is a synagogue in Denver is named "Judaism as you like it."
10. Eph. 4:1-3.
11. *Spoudazontes* is the present participle of *spoudazo* . The present tense conveys on-going activity, Louw & Nida, *Greek-English Lexicon of the New Testament: Based on Semantic Domains*, 2nd ed., New York: United Bible Societies, 1999, accessed through http://www.accordancebible.com/, October, 14, 2012.

12. "Brothers, I could not address you as spiritual but as worldly [carnal/fleshly] — mere infants in Messiah. . . . You are still worldly. For since there is jealousy and quarreling among you, are you not worldly?" (1 Cor. 3:1,3).
13. The Greek verb for "brought to completion," is a paraphrastic form of the verb *teleioo* (teleiow), with the verb itself expressed as a perfect participle. The perfect tense implies past action with on-going consequences. Also, the preposition eis (ei˙ß) associated with the accusative conveys a sense of purpose and direction, Louw & Nida, *Greek-English Lexicon of the New Testament: Based on Semantic Domains*, 2nd ed., New York: United Bible Societies, 1999, accessed through http://www.accordancebible.com/, October, 14, 2012.

GUIDELINES FOR THEOLOGICAL DIALOGUE

Akiva Cohen, Ph.D.
Former Dean of the Israel College of the Bible

Before we begin to hear our first presentations, I have been asked to offer some guidelines for theological dialogue.[1] It may be helpful to listen together to the purpose statement of BPS as it appears on the Symposium web site, after which, I will attempt to parse some of its salient points:

> The purpose of the symposium is to provide a forum for members of the broader Messianic Jewish community to articulate their beliefs with an expectation that they will receive a respectful hearing, but without the expectation that agreement concerning these beliefs will be achieved.

The first point I would like to bring to our attention is that in order for our Symposium to succeed, we need to be engaged in authentic listening. The "articulation of some of our leaders' beliefs" is the expressive component (of our Symposium), however, the "respectful hearing" is what determines whether or not 'communication,' takes place. Without such communication, we are not engaging in a symposium, but rather a monologue with hardened a priori prejudices against the speaker or her or his views, before they have even spoken their first word. Note, also, that a 'respectful' hearing is one in which the hearer honors the presence of the speaker. The speaker is received as someone who is an integral part of our community leadership and a brother or sister who comes to us in Messiah's name, seeking to be understood by her or his audience.

Based upon this value of BPS, it is entirely in order for the speaker to expect such a respectful hearing, however, note the following qualification which relates to the *limits* of the speakers' expectations: "but without the expectation that agreement concerning these beliefs will be achieved." In other words, the speaker also needs to have a disposition of tolerance and humility to represent their view in a way that, while granted a respectful hearing, will realistically not result in changing the beliefs of her/his hearers. This does not mean, however, that the important aspect of 'persuasion' should not be adopted in a speaker's presentation. On the contrary, we expect each other to have clear positions on the issues under discussion; however, we also realistically do not expect a fifteen-minute speech to fundamentally change our views on the key issues under discussion.

The purpose statement then goes on to say: "The Symposium is designed to provide an internal platform for leaders to better understand each another and the various positions held within the Messianic movement." This statement notes the *internal* nature of our Symposium and the goal of enhancing our mutual understanding of one another and our doctrinal positions. The language in this section of the BPS purpose statement speaks to the creation of a 'safe' place for us to hold such a discussion. By stating that the discussion is 'internal,' we are declaring that what is spoken within the walls of this hotel today and tomorrow will have the sacred trust of an inner-community dialogue that will not see publication in electronic or print media outside of the agreement of the BPS participants. Such agreement is properly expressed in the dissemination of BPS papers for wider consumption. To this may be added a further affirmation of BPS:

> We desire to preserve the unity and secure the future of the Messianic Jewish movement and our common mission through respectful dialogue, without acrimony even in the face of critical disagreements.

This statement emphasizes our responsibility to contribute towards the unity of our movement that will impact future generations and the trust of our common mission by coming here to engage in respectful dialogue. We know that the Ruach HaKodesh is truly working in our midst when a room full of approximately one hundred Jews are able to listen to one another with an open mind and a soft-heart, dialogue concerning the issues, and enjoy table fellowship, all, "without acrimony even in the face of critical disagreements."

Remember that by coming to BPS, that is your commitment if and when you hear a view that you strongly disagree with. The BPS model is an inclusive one that commits to agree or disagree *as a family*. Even if some tough love (i.e. brotherly doctrinal correction) is expressed, we have seen some mature modeling of what that should look like in our former Symposia where we can transition from the lecture hall to the dining room and still enjoy fellowship with those brothers or sisters with whom we have significant doctrinal differences but share the same core faith and community commitments.

In my remaining few minutes, I would like us to consider some important aspects of theological reflection:

> 1) Theological reflection takes place in the context of a community.
>
> 2) Because theology is communal, it is also collaborative and dialogical.

Even though we all end up with our own 'operational theology,' we need to refine and test our theology by sharing it with others within our community and beyond it and be grateful for their feedback. Richard Harvey has put us all in his debt by mapping MJ Theology so we can now more clearly see that we have a common basis within our emerging diversity based upon two basic epistemic priorities, namely, "the Messiahship of Yeshua (Jesus) and the continuing election of Israel (the Jewish people)."[2] Our movement's leaders will easily agree with those two claims, and all of us present at this Symposium—representing a broad and diverse spectrum of theological views that flow from those two basic convictions—are indicating by our presence here, that we are *also* in agreement with BPS's four basic convictions that undergird our participation in this movement-wide theological symposium:

> 1) We are Jews who believe in Yeshua and in God's covenant with Israel, and as members of the Jewish community, are committed to the welfare of our people.
>
> 2) We believe in the authority of Scripture and the deity of Yeshua, and that eternal life is the gift of God in Messiah Yeshua our Lord.
>
> 3) We feel compelled by the Spirit of God to advance the good news of Yeshua among our people.

> 4) [As I noted already above]: We desire to preserve the unity and secure the future of the Messianic Jewish movement and our common mission through respectful dialogue, without acrimony even in the face of critical disagreements.

We will shortly begin to hear papers presented on this year's Symposium theme of "How Jewish Should the Messianic Jewish Community be?" Clearly, one of our most basic tasks will be to make sure we understand what each of us means by the descriptor 'Jewish,' and only then will be able to attempt to argue to what degree that defined essence should characterize our movement. Of course each presenter's view on this topic reflects a number of underlying presuppositions.

My hope is that we can demonstrate the kind of empathetic listening to one another that will help us to identify first *what* someone is saying about our topic, and then discuss the more important level of discourse that challenges underlying foundational convictions that need to be hammered out on the anvil of community scrutiny, reflection, and respectful debate. Let's remember our commitment to maintain a safe place of trust in dialogue, our commitment to protect the unity of our movement and guard the stewardship of our common mission for the next generation. The challenge for all of us is to remain humble and be good listeners, (on that note a re-reading of David Rudolph's previous BPS paper on "Guidelines for Theological Dialogue" is always a good refresher exercise).[3] All of us need to realize that there are aspects of our own theology that we hold onto with a noticeable defensiveness that is not necessarily commensurate with a deep and critical reflection upon the premises that underlie our convictions. I have noticed (in my own life, and the lives of other leaders) that the gap between what we *claim* to believe and what we actually *demonstrate* we believe, is sometimes a very glaring one.

My prayer is that the Ruach HaKodesh will help each of us here at this Symposium to drop our defensiveness and be open to reflect on our beliefs with a true humility before God and one another that reflects the prayer of the Psalmist, (I am reading it in the plural person): "Teach us thy way, O LORD; and we will walk in thy truth: unite our hearts to fear thy name."[4] Only if we embody the spirit of

Messiah in true humility, love, and faithfulness, will we be able to fulfill our generational call also outlined by the Psalmist:

> For he established a testimony in Jacob, and appointed a law in Israel, which he commanded our fathers, that they should make them known to their children: 6 That the generation to come might know them, even the children which should be born; who should arise and declare them to their children: 7 That they might set their hope in God, and not forget the works of God, but keep his commandments."[5]

ENDNOTES

1. My presentation is dedicated to the memory of our sorely missed friend and gifted leader, Jhan Moskowitz, who lived a life that modeled what intelligent and gracious theological dialogue should look like.
2. Richard Harvey, "Toward a Messianic Jewish Theology of Reconciliation in the Light of the Arab–Israeli Conflict: Neither Dispensationalist Nor Supersessionist?" in *The Land Cries Out: Theology of the Land in the Israeli-Palestinian Context*, ed. Salim J. Munayer and Lisa Loden (Eugene: Wipf & Stock, 2011), 83; cf. also, Richard Harvey, *Mapping Messianic Jewish Theology: A Constructive Approach* (Milton Keynes: Paternoster, 2009).
3. *Borough Park Papers: Symposium II* (Clarksville, MD: Borough Park Symposium, 2012).
4. Psalm 86:11.
5. Psalm 78:5-7.

THE ROLE OF TORAH AND OF JEWISH TRADITION IN THE MESSIANIC JEWISH COMMUNITY

Baruch Maoz
Translated and edited over 50 books in Hebrew,
Served as founder and chairman of the International Jewish Evangelical Fellowship,
Founded the Messianic Action Committee

I never enjoy flying: there is but sparse wriggle-room. By the end of the flight, I feel cramped, barely able to walk. My assigned title is "The Role of Torah and Jewish Tradition in the Messianic Jewish Community." Such a title provides necessary room to stretch comfortably.

The title serves well as a map for our discussion. My purpose in this short paper is to present the right—no the necessity—of a distinct Messianic identity within the nation of Israel, and therefore of maintaining the Jewish identity for those of us who are Jewish and who belong to the body of Christ. At the same time, I shall seek to present a case against maintaining our Jewish identity as an element of our relations with God or with others in the body of Messiah.

COMMUNITY—ECCLESIA VERSUS KOINONIA

There are at least two ways we might use the term "community." One is synonymous with the New Testament Greek term *ecclesia*, which, in brief, serves in the NT primarily to denote a fellowship of saints gathered for the worship of God according to his word. The second way we might use the term denotes a society of individuals who share a complex of substance, which may be made up of common histories, goals, concerns, interests, cultures, languages, and preferences. Thus, the Ephesian gathering described in Acts 19:39-41 is likewise referred to in terms of an ecclesia.

Ecclesia Koinonia

In an ecclesia of believers in Messiah, God's word is authoritatively preached. He is worshipped according to his word, the sacraments and discipline are administered, all conduct is organized according to scripture, and the body's officers are appointed and function by the same standard, to which nothing may be added and from which nothing may be subtracted. In the context of ecclesia, members are united by the finished work of Messiah and his presence through the Holy Spirit. Ecclesia has the glory of God as its primary goal.

Community—*koinonia* in Greek—is an important aspect of the life of an ecclesia. One cannot be a faithful member of the ecclesia without sharing koinonia. Membership in the koinonia of an ecclesia is by grace and through faith. We relate to one another on the grounds of grace, not on those of ethnic or cultural identity, of personal achievement, or of shared interests and purposes; nothing more than a living faith in God through Messiah, the product of the grace of God and regeneration by the Holy Spirit is necessary. God as he is known in Messiah is all in all. He is the ground, goal, and focus of all that is done in ecclesia. He is the one and only legitimate distinctive, and he shares this central role with no one and with no other issue.

In the ecclesia, we meet other brethren to whom we have been united into one new man: Jews and Gentiles, males and females, bond and free. The ecclesia does not consist of Jews and converts to Judaism, but of Jewish and Gentile sinners converted to God, between whom there was no difference in sin and there is no difference in grace.

Nor may we establish any difference. All sinned and came short of the glory of God. All are justified freely by his grace through the redemption that came by Messiah Yeshua. The same God is rich toward all who call upon him. The middle wall of partition has been broken down.

This lack of difference constitutes an important aspect of the Gospel, and is the logic behind Paul's repeated and sacrificial insistence that Jews and Gentiles should live, worship, and serve together on the same grounds on which they were justified and within the same congregational context.

Any erosion of that unity is an erosion of the Gospel because it is tantamount to attributing spiritual standing to something other than God's amazing grace. We are not, therefore, entitled to insist on national, gender, or social distinctions with regard to our communal worship, our walk with God, our obedience to him, our spiritual advancement, or fellowship/shared service in the body of Messiah. The same kind of obedience is required of all. The goals and duties of all are identical; no spiritual advantages or disadvantages are attached to culture or to ethnic identity. In Messiah, we are all one, one in the ecclesia, which is his body.

Our oneness does not consist merely in that we are spiritually equal but also in that we are spiritually identical. In Messiah, that is to say, in the context of ecclesia, there is neither Jew nor Gentile, male nor female, freeman nor slave. Wherever else differences may legitimately exist, in Messiah they have been done away with and a single identity is shared by all: we are followers of Yeshua.

In the ecclesia, Messiah—not our distinctions—has pride of place. His primacy outshines the differences between us. He is the Alpha and Omega of salvation, history, and of all we do in the context of ecclesia. His saving work is sufficient for every aspect of our salvation: in him we are circumcised with a circumcision not executed by human hands, sanctified by grace, forgiven, secure, and complete. Nothing is obtained in Messiah but by his virtues and his accomplishments. However as much we may differ in gifts of function and ability, no spiritual advantages or spiritual privileges are accorded to one individual in Messiah over another.

This is in accordance with the hope inculcated by scripture. We would do well to remember that our Hebrew Bible does not begin at Genesis chapter twelve but at chapter one; not with Abraham but with creation as a whole and, more specifically, with Adam and Eve. They, not Abraham, were the beginning of humanity, created in the image of God. God did not begin history by creating Jews but by creating humanity, and his purpose of blessing and salvation neither began nor ends with the Jewish people. Scripture goes on to speak of the nations, indicating Israel's essential relationship to them, demonstrating that Israel's calling had the blessing of the nations in view.

Of course, this is not to deny that Israel differs from the nations. But it does so in a manner that was ultimately intended to characterize all nations so that Isaiah could speak of the day when "all nations will stream" to the worship of God, saying one to another, "Come, let us go up to the mountain of the Lord, to the house of the God of Jacob. He will teach us his ways, so that we may walk in his paths." After all, is

God the God of Israel only? Is he not also the God of the Gentiles? Indeed, he is the God of the Gentiles as well.

Abraham's call entailed Gentiles as well as Jews. God's promise through Isaiah goes so far as to put Egypt and Assyria—Israel's traditional enemies—on a par with Israel when the prophet says that the Lord will speak of Egypt as "my people" and of Assyria as the product of his creative activity in history, just like Israel. Even when God performs his terrible work through and on Gog and Magog, he describes his purpose in universal terms: "I will bring you against my land that the nations might know me."

There is no room within the ecclesia for ethnic or cultural boundary markers, and we must not nullify the grace of God by asserting distinctions that formerly played a role in our thinking. Whatever we formerly viewed as gain, we now consider loss for the sake of Messiah. Everything is a loss compared to the surpassing worth of knowing Messiah Yeshua, our Lord, for whose sake we have willingly lost all things. The one aspiration that now drives us is to know him whom to know is life eternal, to experience the power of his resurrection, and to participate in his sufferings, becoming like him in his death so as to attain to the resurrection from the dead.

We recognize that the attribution of any spiritual gifting to anything but the work of Messiah is to imply that he died in vain, an implication from which we shrink in horror. In the past, we related to people in terms of a spiritual walk according to their national identity, gender, and social standing, but we do so no longer.

The primacy and sufficiency of Messiah's finished work are the grounds of our unity. We have turned our eyes upon Yeshua, looked full on his wonderful face, and the things of the earth have grown strangely dim in the light of his glory and grace. Any weakening of the unity he has created threatens the clarity with which we testify to Messiah's place in our lives. We must, therefore, maintain the biblical tension between the Bible's particularity and its universalism. For that reason, any role our ethnic and cultural identity—or the Torah or tradition—may be allowed to play in our private and communal lives must be overtly visibly and very clearly subordinate to Messiah.

We are one in Messiah with those of all nations despite how much we may differ from them due to our Jewishness. That oneness must find practical expression in the context of local ecclesia life; there should be neither Jewish nor Gentile ecclesiae. Our congregations should reflect the essence of the Gospel. Ethnic and cultural differences do not distinguish us in the context of local congregations. We relate to one another on the grounds of the grace that purchased our salvation, and on no other grounds.

We would do well to remember that most of the conflicts Yeshua had with the synagogue had to do with what has become fashionable to describe today as "boundary markers," such as the Sabbath and dietary laws, that distinguished Jews from Gentiles and faithful Jews from others. Most of Paul's conflicts had to do with those markers in the context of ecclesia, with the addition of circumcision. The reason for the addition lies in that fact that Yeshua's audience was comprised primarily of circumcised Jews, while many of Paul's converts were uncircumcised Gentiles.

Contrary to much of modern practice, there is no biblical legitimacy for ethnically-based, culturally-orientated, or linguistically focused congregations, any more than it is legitimate to separate into white and black churches, blue or white collar churches, churches for the young and for the elderly, etc.

Of course, each of these groups differs from the other. But that is the beauty of the Body of Messiah: it is a coat of many colors, in which each culture, each set of national interests, clashes with others, challenges them, and thus promotes a process of sanctification in which all are made to be more like him who saved them. Human differences are put into their proper place by being made secondary to God in Messiah, secondary to spiritual and moral concerns, and secondary to the unity of the body of Messiah. We should not seek meaning in self-fulfillment—individual or communal—but in God, as he is known through Messiah.

It never occurred to the apostles to form separate congregations for Jews and for Gentiles—although tensions between the two were the main source of difficulties within the body of Messiah for decades. The obvious solution would have been to divide into separate but fraternal entities, respecting each other from a distance and assisting each other where agreement was found. But such an option would have constituted a denial of the grace on which all—Jews and Gentiles—stood. It would have laid the grounds for elitism in the church: "You're OK, but not like us," thereby eroding the primacy of Messiah and the completeness of his work by allowing distinctions to divide in spite of all that unites.

Nor is there room in the ecclesia for the introduction of human traditions, however much we might cherish them. God's worship is to be pure, as he has commanded it to be, with neither adulteration nor dilution. Our forefathers were forbidden to introduce into God's worship anything but what he had commanded. Aaron's sons were punished for offering strange fire, defined as fire the Lord had not commanded. Our worship is not to be taught to us by precept of man, not even by rabbis, but by the commandment of God.

Community in a Broader Sense

At the bare minimum, community means shared concerns, interests, and goals; common duties and privileges; and a common language—and culture is a language. Charles Sherlock describes language as "perhaps the most fundamental aspect of human culture."

Community, in the broader sense, is of extreme importance. Human camaraderie, moral, and intellectual and emotional encouragement is essential to mankind's health and happiness. God is an eternal community of Father, Son, and Holy Spirit. Human society was designed to be a reflection of the godhead. Community is, therefore, essential to the image of God in man. Surely, this is an important implication of the divine "let us make man in our image."

In the Garden of Eden, man lacked nothing material or spiritual. He was in a perfect world, in intimate fellowship with his Maker. The world was his domain and mandate. Still, God described man as alone and evaluated this situation as not good.

Worship and spiritual obedience do not exhaust man's humanity; he was created with a need for human community in a broader sense, as well as in the narrow. Man not only needs the company of peers for worship—the special domain of ecclesia—but he needs their company for the cultivation and maintenance of his humanity in the many God-given areas of life other than worship.

Prior to sin, at the time of man's innocence, man needed help to be and to do what he was made to be and do. So God created for him an ezer kenegdo, one to assist him, ezer, by complementing him, kenegdo. Without community, both in a spiritual and in a broader sense, no individual is all he can be, all he is meant to be, or all he needs to be. However valuable ecclesia is, broader community is also needed. Such a community meets legitimate needs and opens legitimate vistas for which ecclesia was not designed. All the more is this so since sin invaded the world. Community is now needed in areas that would not have otherwise existed.

In contrast with ecclesia, distinctions are valid in the context of community. People commune with some and not with others over shared interests, concerns, and identities that distinguish them from others and form the rationale of each community's existence. People who meet to play chess do not meet to play basketball, Democrats are not Republicans (some might wish they were), and Jews are not Gentiles. Ecclesia does not exhaust our humanity. We were made for community in a sense broader than that afforded by ecclesia.

The broader the sense is, the narrower the community. Many who belong to the ecclesia do not and ought not belong to one or another kind of community. No kind of superiority is involved but differences are acknowledged. We were made to differ one from another and thus contribute to the amazing variety involved in being human.

Community is for mutual enabling in areas designated by each community for an ongoing contribution to specific aspects of life in exclusion of others and for the creation of a distinct sphere in which important aspects of our God-given humanity come to expression. Our God-given potential is realized in other than spiritual realms. In the ecclesia, we are neither Jews nor Gentiles, but in community we may be—and, I suggest, we Jewish followers of Yeshua very much should be—what God has made us to be: Jews.

In community, individuals are Jews or Gentiles, male or female, freemen or slaves. As such, they have differing duties and privileges. This is the primary sphere in which, if we are circumcised, we should not seek to undo our circumcision, nor seek circumcision if we are uncircumcised. Jews should remain Jews and Gentiles, Gentiles. We should each continue within the context of the social and national callings that we found when we responded to the gospel of grace.

In this paper, I shall not use the term "community" to denote the ecclesia, nor that aspect of ecclesia life characterized by koinonia. I enlist the term here to describe a body of individuals—in our case, a body of Jewish believers—united by common interests and concerns that are not the domain of ecclesia, for the promotion and enjoyment of those interests and concerns.

Such interests and concerns may well be compatible with scripture, but they do not fit the description of ecclesia koinonia in important areas. Messianic community membership, for example, is contingent on ethnic and cultural distinctive characteristics—the focus is on the ethnic and cultural identity that unites the Messianic community's members and distinguishes them from others; the goals which direct and the duties incumbent on members are implied by the shared identity of the community's members. Here too, of course, members are obliged by the word of God because no area of human life is exempt from his reign. But their obligations and privileges differ greatly from those in an ecclesia, and are not necessarily derived directly from scripture.

THE NEED FOR A VISIBLE MESSIANIC JEWISH ENTITY

God has not forsaken his people, for this is his covenant with them: A redeemer will come out of Zion and turn ungodliness away from Jacob. Their restoration will be such a blessing to the world that Scripture compares it to nothing less than a resurrection. Is it not yet just a little while before Lebanon will be turned into a fertile field, and the fertile field will be considered as a forest? On that day the deaf will hear words of a book, and out of gloom and darkness the eyes of the blind will see. The afflicted also will increase their gladness in the LORD, and the needy of mankind will rejoice in the Holy One of Israel. For the ruthless will come to an end and the scorner will be finished, indeed all who are intent on doing evil will be cut off.

Like Paul, Isaiah tells us that this happy event is related to another: Thus says the LORD, who redeemed Abraham, concerning the house of Jacob: "Jacob shall not now be ashamed, nor shall his face now turn pale; but when he sees his children, the work of my hands, in his midst, they will sanctify my name; indeed, they will sanctify the Holy One of Jacob and will stand in awe of the God of Israel, those who err in mind will know the truth, and those who criticize will accept instruction."

God has declared his intention to bring Israel back to himself and to do so by means of a Jewish believing community—obviously composed of Israel's children but no less obviously the work of his hands—bearing the imprint of the spiritual and moral transformation that the divine work of regeneration implies. The result of such a visible believing community within the nation of Israel will be that the people will stand in awe of the God of Israel, those who err in mind will know the truth they rejected, and those who criticize will accept the very instruction they refused.

Paul never spoke of his Jewishness as a thing of the past. Judaism was no longer his religion, but he continued to speak of his Jewishness in the present tense many years after he turned his back on Judaism. In Gal. 1:13-14, he speaks of his Judaism as a thing of the past and in 2:14, describes Peter as one who lived like a Gentile. Judaism was no longer Paul's religion, but he continued to speak of his Jewishness in the present tense. He remained Jewish to the day of his death, although he knew himself to be bound no longer by the dictates of the rabbis he formerly obeyed or by the covenant God made with his forefathers at Sinai. He exulted in the hope of God's faithfulness to his covenant with Abraham.

The distinction Paul drew between Judaism and Jewishness needs to be maintained. Judaism is a religion rooted in Phariseeism and framed in the course of many years by the rabbis. It affirms a theology that includes the denial of Yeshua's Messiahship and divinity. It teaches salvation by human effort, regardless of modern claims to the contrary and asserts the authority of the rabbis as authoritative interpreters of the Law of God. Jewishness, on the other hand, is an ethnic identity with cultural implications impacted by rabbinic tradition but not bound by them.

Jewishness is an intensely communal affair. It is also a calling to which we should not turn our backs. Jewishness is a wonderful thing. I am grateful to have been created Jewish, I love being Jewish, and I call upon all Jews in Messiah not to submerge their Jewishness in the context of the ecclesia in such a way that they de facto erase it. In the ecclesia, we are neither Jewish nor Gentile, but our national and cultural identity has not been obliterated by faith in Yeshua, nor should we obliterate it. Men and women do not lose their gender following conversion. Slaves are not transformed into freemen, or freemen into slaves, when their sins are forgiven for Yeshua's sake. Jews do not cease to be Jews or Gentiles, Gentiles by virtue of their faith in Messiah.

An ongoing Jewish identity is not merely a secular matter; it has deeply-rooted theological implications. Our faith in Messiah does not conflict with our Jewish identity. It is, rather, a fulfillment thereof: the faith of Yeshua is the true faith of our fathers. Yeshua is the hope of Abraham, the son of David, the fulfillment of our national hopes of the covenant God made with our fathers. In him are and will be accomplished all the promises God made to the fathers. The ongoing reality of a visible remnant that believes in Messiah and conducts itself within the context of Israel's national life is a testimony to God's faithfulness and a call to the nation to turn to God in Yeshua. It is also an expression of the confidence we have that he, who is still in covenant with our people, will yet graft them in again and render their salvation a blessing to the world.

Our continued national existence is a testimony to the gracious faithfulness of God in spite of our people's sin and a potential instrument for the salvation of our people whom God foreknew and chose, in whom he will yet be glorified. We are obliged by the biblical tension between the Bible's particularity on the one hand and its universalism on the other and must maintain that tension.

If following Yeshua entailed the obliteration of our national identity, such following would constitute a denial of the biblical covenants, promises, and history that are inextricably associated with it. If one cannot be Jewish and believe in Yeshua, then Yeshua is not the promised Messiah of Israel and, if that is the case, he is no Messiah at all. That is precisely why rabbinical Judaism insists that Jews ought not believe in Yeshua and why the rabbis equate such unbelief with Jewish identity. Concerning Yeshua, they wish to deny exactly what we wish to affirm. There are few things a Jew may believe or disbelieve without being accused of denying his Jewish identity; the rabbis deem believing in Yeshua to be a demarcation line between "us"—the Jewish people—and "them."

There is need, therefore, for a distinct, vocal, well-organized, and lively Messianic Jewish community within the nation of Israel that will prove the lie involved in such assertions. It is by way of such a community that we Jewish followers of Yeshua can and should strengthen each other, reach out to our people, respond to their needs, and contribute to their welfare. It is by way of such a community that we can come to the defense of our people in times of distress and assert our national and cultural identity vis-à-vis the ecclesia on the one hand and our nation on the other. It is by way of such a community that we can address our nation as a nation, from within, and call it to Messiah, while the church (to which we also belong) addresses our people from the outside.

Such a community can provide a context where needs that have not been addressed by the ecclesia may be recognized and met. A Messianic Jewish community is called for and should be assiduously cultivated by those of us who are Jews and who love and honor Yeshua. Here I rest my case in defense of a Messianic Jewish community.

TORAH

Before we discuss the role of Torah in a Messianic Jewish community, it would be helpful to define what is meant by the term in the context of this paper. I offer the following working definition: Torah is that conglomerate of commandments God gave our forefathers at Sinai as the outline of their national covenantal duties. In some circles it has been customary to divide the Torah into three distinct laws: moral, ceremonial, and civil—as if one could stand without the other. The moral law is considered as having to do with issues of spiritual and moral conduct, the civil law with administrative conduct in the secular affairs of life, and the ceremonial with the conduct of divine worship. There is a measure of truth in such a division. There is, I suggest, also a large measure of untruth.

The law of the covenant was given as a unit. Israel's transgression of any facet of the law was to be punished (we've already had occasion to reference the death of Aaron's two sons when they transgressed a purely ceremonial restriction). The so-called civil requirement to leave the fringes of one's field for the poor had obvious moral implications. More examples could be given.

Yeshua fulfilled the whole Torah on our behalf. His sacrifice was in fulfillment of ceremonial facets of the law and, at the same time, of its moral and civil facets, for we transgressed all three, are guilty, and are atoned for the three.

However, one facet of the law had prominence over the others: the moral requirements enshrined in the Ten Commandments were given pride of place in the Ark of the Covenant. The prophetic message had to do primarily with transgression of the moral facets of the Torah. The prophets repeatedly insisted in God's name that observance of ceremonial duties, however strict when moral duties were neglected and moral boundaries transgressed, negated the value of ceremonial observance. Israel's prophets did not hesitate to call even the Gentile nations to account for their transgression of God's moral demands.

These demands are not discovered by human enterprise but are generally recognized, particularly by man's conscience. They are discovered through a reading of God's word as a whole, both Old and New Testaments, preeminently the Ten Commandments.

The New Testament recognizes this distinction within the one Torah. It repeatedly measures man's moral actions by the moral demands of the Torah and calls upon the faithful to exercise themselves in holiness in terms that sit well with Torah morality. There is not an inkling of a call to celebrate the feasts, practice circumcision, or maintain the dietary laws. Quite to the contrary: by way of example, and in the vein with Israel's prophets, Matthew informs us that Yeshua repeatedly castigated those who observed ceremony while neglecting what he described as the weightier things of the Torah.

Yeshua said, Woe to you, scribes and Pharisees, hypocrites! For you tithe mint and dill and cumin, and have neglected the weightier provisions of the law: justice and mercy and faithfulness; but these are the things you should have done without neglecting the others. You blind guides, who strain out a gnat and swallow a camel.

That is the Law which, Paul insists, is inscribed on every human heart and by which all will be judged, which—obviously—had nothing to do with fringes on one's garment or dietary restrictions.

So much so that, In I Cor. 7:19, Paul juxtaposes circumcision with God's commandments when he says, "Circumcision is nothing, and uncircumcision is nothing, but the keeping of the commandments of God." James, whose dedication to the Torah is well known, speaking of the law in terms meant to bind a believing conscience, makes reference only to moral issues, never to civil or ceremonial.

Such a distinction within the Torah was known even to rabbinic Judaism, which affirmed that with the coming of Messiah (The commandments terminate). They did not mean that men would be free to lie, covet, and murder. The moral facet of the Torah was not in view, but was what some Christian theologians term civil and ceremonial. Moral duties remained and will remain forever.

Let it not be thought that we can better impact our people if we put on a show of keeping the law and the traditions. Remember Josephus' testimony that James, the brother of our Lord, was put to death "as an offender of the law" in spite of his strict observance of the Torah simply because he believed in Yeshua.

Our protagonists understand clearly what we are sometimes loath to recognize, namely that reliance on Yeshua for justification and for sanctification is exactly contrary to what Judaism teaches on the role of the Torah. So long as we affirm a biblical view of Yeshua, Judaism will reject us. We must, therefore, chose between Judaism and Jewishness, as well as between Judaism and Israel's Messiah.

Tendencies among us to erode a clear vision of the biblical view of the savior are the product of our back staging him because our focus is not on him, where it should be, but on finding acceptance by affirming our Jewishness. God, having spoken long ago to the fathers by way of the prophets in many partial revelations, has spoken to us in these last days by way of his Son, whom he appointed heir of everything that exists and through whom he also made all that exists. That Son is the radiance of God's own glory and the most exact representation of his divine nature. He upholds all that exists by his powerful word. It is He who offered the sacrifice that purifies sin, and having accomplished that, he is now seated at the right hand of the Majesty on High. He should fill the whole of our vision.

We conclude, then, that one facet of the Torah remains man's eternal duty, being a reflection of the image of God in which we were created. That facet is moral. However, our relation to it has been fundamentally transformed by the coming of Messiah. We love God's Torah and not because it is the grounds of our standing with God or a means to spiritual advancement. Our love of the Torah is the product of the sanctifying work of the Spirit in our hearts and is an expression of our devoted gratitude and our loving obedience. In the moral facets of the Torah, we discover glorious reflections of the image of God and long to shape our lives in accordance with that glory.

Such is the power of the Gospel. We do not invite the righteous to this feast of grace and glory, even as our Master did not come for the righteous; we invite poor, failing, fumbling sinners, with the promise that God will create in their hearts a longing for holiness that, in the last day, will find complete satisfaction. They will be conformed to the image of his Son. Meanwhile, they will be empowered to struggle in confident hope of the glory of God and with the constant support of his grace. Jaroslav Pelikan put it well: "The church was not a moral all-star team for which one could qualify by being an athlete of holiness; it was a moral hospital in which . . . one could be gradually healed."

JEWISH TRADITION

We need not spend time on defining tradition beyond stating that it is the means by which any human community identifies itself. Jewish tradition is that living body of consensual mores by which Jews define themselves as Jews, celebrate the present, preserve the memory of their past, and express their hopes and aspirations for the future. As Saadya Gaon put it, "Our people the children of Israel, are a people only by virtue of our laws."

We should pause, however, to reflect on two words in my proposed definition of Jewish tradition: consensual and living. In the interest of clarity, we view them in the reverse order. The term living serves to indicate what is true of any national tradition: it changes over the years, accruing new features and discarding others. Although Jewish culture is religiously orientated, it is not fossilized. The ways Jews, even Orthodox Jews, express their Jewishness today is as dissimilar as it is similar to the way Jews did so a mere 200 years ago. Many features continue through the centuries; many change. Modern rabbis determine *halacha* precisely because they realize that Jewishness needs to meet the challenges of the day.

The term consensual serves here to indicate that not every rabbinic dictum, not every feature handed down through the centuries, is adopted for all times by the majority of the people. There are features of Jewish tradition that are not embraced by the majority of the Jewish people, and therefore do not serve as consensual boundary markers of Jewishness. Fasting on the Day on Atonement, eating *matzah* during Passover, celebrating the biblical and traditional feasts in one way or another are part of the consensus; avoiding the use of electricity on the Sabbath (or lighting a fire) and eating kosher are not. The consensus is that part of Jewish tradition that the majority of Jews observe by virtue of which they consider themselves—and are recognized to be—Jewish.

A large part of Jewish tradition has its roots in the Bible. Some are directly biblical. The biblical feasts are a prominent example, while many of the dietary restrictions are not. Jewish tradition is not wholly biblical. Hanukkah is not a biblical feast, nor do most features of the Passover seder have biblical authority. The *arba minim* used during sukkot is the product of rabbinic creative thinking, incorrect but part of a hoary tradition. The custom of men covering their heads has no biblical roots. The use of a *goy shel Shabbat* is contrary to the divine commandment. Hillel's famous prosbul is a convoluted attempt to resolve a difficulty that was the product of a biblical command and unbiblical selfishness. The Mishnah informs us that Hillel introduced the prosbul "seeing that the law which prescribed the release of debts every seventh year . . . brought about the harmful consequence that people refused to loan one another and thus violated what was written in the law, namely, that a money loan should not be withheld because of the approach of the sabbatical year" (Deut. 15:1-3, 9-11). As is true of any national tradition, the roots and ground of Jewish tradition are primarily religious, both biblical and rabbinic. The extent to which this determines the ongoing authority of Jewish tradition, in whole or in part, is to be considered next.

THE ROLE OF TORAH AND JEWISH TRADITION

For obvious reasons, we begin with a consideration of the role of Torah. However valid we may deem other aspects of Jewish tradition to be, the Torah is God's word. As such, it has priority.

We noted above the three facets of the Torah and affirmed that Messiah fulfilled all three on our behalf. We also noted that Yeshua and Paul applied the moral facets of the Torah to all mankind, not by virtue of the covenant at Sinai but because it is expressive of the image of God in man and, therefore, of God's eternal will. All three facets remain, to a varying extent, part of our national tradition. The moral facet is far more than that. All human communities are bound by the will and authority of God and must, therefore, adhere to his moral demands.

Community—any community—should be concerned with the promotion and maintenance of moral law. It should pursue its common interests, promote its common concerns, and forward its common goals in accord with divinely imposed moral duties. Whether playing chess or engaging in politics, human communities should manage their affairs in light of mankind's obligation to accommodate itself to God's will. There is little need for discussion of this issue and, therefore, we will soon proceed to the next. Before doing so, there is an important point to be made.

Learning from the prophets and from our Lord Messiah, we recognize the priority, or God's moral demands, over all other considerations. We therefore further recognize that a community of Messianic Jews must not allow its national interests, concerns, and aspirations to override the moral obligations imposed by God's law. We must not succumb to selfishness, national or personal. We are not free to ignore the interests, concerns, and aspirations of others, even if they conflict with our own. We must courageously exemplify the morality of our Maker and the Messiah he sent for our people—his kindness, his sacrificial generosity and his surprising grace—even as we identify with our own people. Eschatology ought not be used to secure us from God's call to a boldly humble kindness as we relate to the Israeli-Palestinian conflict, for example. That is the burden of the prophetic message, and its accomplishment is a major feature of the prophetic view of the future.

We may not turn a blind eye to the moral failings of our people in the conduct of this conflict. Holiness, truth, and righteousness are as much part of our duty as is any other aspect of our calling under God. As a community, we should exercise a truly prophetic ministry to our nation, putting the emphasis where the prophets put it: not in a predicted future but in promoting righteous conduct in the present.

So much for the moral facet of the Torah. Some aspects of the civil and many of the ceremonial facets of the Torah continue to be part of our national tradition. But we no longer stone adulterers; we no longer maintain cities of refuge; we no longer hand murderers over to be slain by the families of their victims; nor are we obliged in terms of our duties to avoid pork, attend temple worship in Jerusalem thrice a year, or offer sacrifice. However, belonging to a people entails certain obligations, including cultural obligations. Tradition is a way by which families, communities, and nations identify themselves—to themselves and to others.

Of course, there are aspects of our national tradition to which we cannot adhere and, at the same time, be faithful to God in Messiah. We cannot thank God for commanding us to light Sabbath or Hanukkah candles because he never issued such a command. We cannot and do not share the Orthodox view of Gentiles. We also recognize that most of the extra-biblical traditions our people have embraced did not exist in New Testament times, that some of them are reactionary, vis-à-vis the Gospel, and some are contra-biblical.

But where our traditions are compatible with the scriptures and form part of the national Jewish consensus, we adhere to them because they are part of our identity, part of who we are. We celebrate the arrival of the Sabbath with a festive Sabbath meal, bless God for the bread and wine, and light candles. We masquerade on Purim and have a Passover seder, preserving most of the elements of that tradition. We're Jews, and we love being Jewish. Maintaining our traditions in the context of our community is not a gimmick. Nor is it a means of evangelism, a way to find acceptance, a means to a greater spirituality, or an authoritative grid through which we understand the scriptures. We maintain our Jewish culture because of what we are, sincerely, naturally, honestly, whole-heartedly.

At the same time, we must maintain a clear distinction between what has become national Jewish tradition and our walk with God. We recognize that Jewish tradition, including those parts that issue directly from the Covenant of Sinai, provide no spiritual advantage and should play no role in our walk with God. They are now part of national custom and, to the extent that we practice them, we do so on a cultural basis, for cultural purposes, not as an act of religion.

Some of us might choose to maintain a kosher kitchen and prefer to wear a *yarmulke*, but we recognize that we're free to eat whatever we wish and do not pray with our heads covered so as not to dishonor Him who is our head. Nor do we separate into ethnic or cultural-based congregations. Our Jewishness is for community, not for ecclesia.

We insist on remaining Jews for yet another reason: we believe. Our affirmed, overt, and communal Jewishness is an expression of our confidence that God has not forsaken his people, that he will yet labor a work of grace among them. It is the fruit of our faith in God and an expression of the expectation his word has created in us.

A brief and final point: Jewish national tradition is not only communal. It is first and foremost familial. One belongs to the community by way of practicing Jewish tradition in the context of one's home—as much would also be expected of those who belong to a Jewish Messianic community. Too much of traditionally Jewish customs have been moved by the Messianic Movement out of the family and into the congregation or the community, thereby transforming its essence and eroding its Jewish character. We are also engaged in too much nonsense that goes by the name of Jewishness, and that is not truly such any more than pork—or bagels—can be.

I am a Jew. I continue to be Jewish. In every area of my life—except the spiritual—I view and identify myself as Jewish. But I practice my Jewishness at home and do not impose or recommend it to those who are not of my people. At the church I attend, provisions are made for those who wish to celebrate Christmas. None are required, nor is any spiritual advantage attached to such a celebration. The same holds true for Jewish customs. Those of us who are Jewish offer no apologies, while Gentiles are not encouraged to consider themselves disadvantaged. They do not need to dig into their distant past to discover some purported inkling of Jewish blood to be accepted as equals. They do not need to embrace our cultural distinctive characteristics; they maintain their own. Here we strongly disagree with our people's traditional religion expressed, for example, by Rabbi

Yehuah HaLevi's in *The Khazari*: "Any Gentile who joins us sincerely shares our good fortune, but he is not equal to us . . . we are the pick of mankind."

We studiously avoid obscuring what God, in fulfillment of promises given to the fathers, has done for us in Messiah. Our lives, thinking, hoping, praying, worshipping, and celebrating are focused on Messiah, not on Torah or tradition. He is our tree of life, teaching us holiness and enabling us thereunto. What Torah could not do, God has done for us in Messiah. In Messiah we have a better covenant, a better sacrifice, better promises, and ultimate fulfillment. Yeshua accomplished what the Torah could not do. The temple and its ritual have been replaced by the Son of God, who came to seek and to save that which was lost, and who offered one final sacrifice by which he forever perfected those who turn to God through him. The Law of Moses no longer holds the primary place in our lives: Messiah has come, and he is our all in all. We ought not nullify the grace of God by reestablishing Torah. Nothing need be added to Messiah's finished work, and any attempt to do so is to diminish it. Through him we have access within the veil and discover God in Messiah to be a very present help in times of need. The Torah no longer serves as the focus of our obedience; Yeshua is.

We are disciples of Messiah, dedicated to keeping his commandments and living our lives in unrestrained devotion to him. To reestablish the law as a central feature of our walk with God is in Paul's stark words—already quoted above—to set aside the grace of God. We, through the law, are dead to the law that we might live for God. We have been crucified with Messiah and no longer live: Messiah lives in us. We live by faith in the Son of God, who loved us and gave himself for us. This, as C. K. Barrett reminds us, "is not mysticism but eschatology."

It is the future lived out in the present, for Messiah has come, and he has made all the difference. In him all the promises of God are 'yes' and 'amen!' "The significance of Torah as Law and Commandment is the most characteristic feature of Judaism."

But Yeshua is our distinctive. He is also the ground of our victory, for the lamb slain before the foundation of the world is the lion of Judah, conquering and still to conquer. What overcame the Roman Empire was nothing less than "adherence to the person of Jesus Christ and to the church he was believed to have established."

Our faith is the power that overcomes the world. As Jocz succinctly points out, "What the Jew owes to the Torah, the Christian owes to Jesus Christ." Our message to our people is that they, too, owe him what they believe they owe the Torah.

We must teach our people to distinguish between Jewishness and Judaism. Jewishness is our national identity; Judaism is that false religion created by the rabbis.

THE MESSIANIC JEWISH COMMUNITY

What, then, is the purpose of a Messianic Jewish community? If we agree on what I have proposed above, the answer is clear; it is also clear whom the Messianic Jewish community is for. The Messianic Jewish community is for Jewish followers of Yeshua, not for Gentile wannabes, however sincerely motivated. Why on earth would chess players want to be members of a football club, or Democrats members of the Republican Party (a note of apology to Republicans)? There are no spiritual advantages to being Jewish. It therefore goes without saying that there are none for those who act as if they are Jewish.

The Messianic Jewish community is the context in which Jewish believers encourage one another as Jews in Messiah, where they share their concerns, promote their common interests, and enlist their resources for the good of their nation and the good of others. It is the context in which they can exercise an important aspect of their being, without dilution, without constituting a threat to anyone, and without their identity being inappropriately impinged upon or threatened by external forces.

One of the main purposes of the Torah was to distinguish the people of the covenant from other peoples.

Torah now informs Jewish traditional culture to a meaningful extent with the same purpose in view. After all, one of the functions of a culture is to distinguish those it unites from those it does not. Culture not only provides a means of mutual identification; it also serves as a means of disassociation, which is precisely why, on the one hand, there is no room for it in ecclesia and why, on the other, it is so necessary to community. It is an expression of our recognition that, even in an ecclesiological Garden of Eden, we would need the kind of give-and-take for which human community was intended.

Such a community does not supplant the ecclesia; it supplements it in areas for which the ecclesia was not designed. Our confusion of

Ecclesian and of koinonia has led us to unbiblical thoughts as to how to reduce the number of Gentiles among us. I agree with Rich: "the very nature of Messianic Judaism demands distinctions between Jews and Gentiles." Brethren, that needs to be amended.

CONCLUSION

Ecclesia is the context in which all Messiah's followers gather for the worship of God and mutual edification in the things of God. In the ecclesia, there is no room for national or cultural distinctions. Community, on the other hand, is the context in which Messianic Jews meet to promote interests and defend concerns that distinguish them from others, be the followers of Yeshua or otherwise. Here, distinctions between believers are eminently valid.

There is both great need and clear justification for a Messianic Jewish community. Such a community is not and should not become an ecclesia. In the context of such a community, the consensus of Jewish national tradition would be practiced, barring those aspects of the consensus that contradict the word of God. Together, we would work for the salvation of our people, and for any other national need that may arise. This is the course that is most likely to appeal to the majority of us Jewish Christians, who have rightly chosen to worship God in churches rather than in Messianic synagogues.

I sincerely believe that we have mistakenly conflated the two—ecclesia and community—and that this does not serve the glory of God, does not meet the requirements of the word of God, and does not serve our truest interests.

It is time for us to rethink our positions, and draw closer to the standards God has laid out in his word. Surely, it is not without reason that we have been so ineffective in our calling with regard to our nation. Most of those who have been impacted by our movement are Gentiles, and most of our influence is on churches, while Israel remains in darkness and in desperate need of the Gospel of Messiah. That is where our focus should be, not in affirming our Jewishness, but in affirming our Messiah's legitimate claim on the allegiance of our people, for the Gospel is God's power to save, Jews first.

BIBLIOGRAPHY

Babylonian Talmud.

Flavius, Josephus. *The Antiquities of the Jews.* Lawrence: Digireads.com Publishing, 2010.

Gaon, Saadiya. *Book of Beliefs and Opinions.* New Haven: Yale University Press, 1989.

Hagner, Donald A., ed. *Conflicts and Challenges in Early Christianity.* Harrisburg: Trinity Press International, 1999.

Harvey, Richard. *Shaping Messianic Jewish Theology.* Colorado Springs: Paternoster, 2009.

Jocz, Jakob. *The Jewish People and Jesus Christ.* London: SPCK Publishing, 1962.

Lewy, Hans. *Three Jewish Philosophers.* Edited by Isaak Heinemann and Alexander Altmann. New Milford: The Toby Press, 2006.

The Mishna.

Midrash Rabbah

Sherlock, Charles. *The Doctrine of Humanity, Contours of Christian Theology.* Downers Grove: InterVarsity Press, 1996.

Schreiner, Thomas R. *Romans (Baker Exegetical Commentary on the New Testament).* Grand Rapids: Baker Academic, 1988.

Schreiner, Thomas R. *The Law and Its Fulfillment: A Pauline Theology of Law.* Ada: Baker Publishing Group, 1993.

Yalkut Shimoni.

THE ROLE OF TORAH AND JEWISH TRADITION IN THE MESSIANIC JEWISH COMMUNITY

Joshua Brumbach
Spiritual leader of Ahavat Zion Messianic
Synagogue in Beverly Hills, California,
Worked with the Union of Messianic Jewish Congregations (UMJC)
and the Messianic Jewish Theological Institute (MJTI),
Degrees in Anthropology and Biblical Studies,
MJS candidate in Rabbinic Writings

The Torah and the Jewish people are interwoven together and cannot be separated. The Torah, and the way it has been uniquely interpreted and applied over time, defines us as a people. In a play on the famous quote from Ahad Ha'Am,[1] one could say: *More than the Jews have kept Torah, Torah has kept the Jews.*

For us as Jews, the Torah is more than the stipulations of the covenant between God and ourselves. It is more than just 613 different ways to connect with our Creator. The Torah speaks into the deepest places of our souls and tells us where we came from, who we truly are, and where we are going. It defines our behavior and shapes our interaction with the world around us.

Throughout the millennia, we Jews have guarded, preserved, and held tightly to the Torah. Whether through expulsions, pogroms, or even the Holocaust, we have risked our lives for the sake of the Torah. For as it is promised:

> *It is a tree of life for those who take hold of it,*
> *all who support it are to be praised.*
> *All its ways are pleasantness,*
> *and all its paths are peace.*

Without the Torah, we would not know what it means to be holy and what God expects of us. Furthermore, without the Torah, there would be no "Prophet greater than Moses"[2] or the renewal[3] and greater realization and internalization of that covenant in and through our Messiah, Yeshua.

In fact, if we are to take the Gospel of John seriously, then for us as Messianic Jews, the Torah is our ultimate symbol of faith because if Yeshua is the Living Torah (i.e. the Word made flesh which dwells among us),[4] than the Torah service is not only a sacred re-enactment of the events of Sinai but also a dramatic re-enactment of the Gospel message.

The "New Covenant" is not the replacement, but rather the renewal, of a greater intensification and internalization of the Torah through the Living Torah, Yeshua the Messiah (see Jeremiah 31 and John 1). Additionally, the outpouring of the Spirit is not only to spiritually empower and comfort us, but according to Ezekiel 36:27-28 and 37:24-28, it is to enable us to observe the *mitzvot* as well.

Although there may be emendations to the Sinai covenant as a result of this renewal through Yeshua, those emendations do not do away with the entirety of the Torah. In fact, obligatory observance of the Torah is assumed throughout the New Testament for Jewish followers of Yeshua (as well as the decision of non-obligatory observance for Gentile followers of Yeshua).[5]

The role of Torah and Jewish tradition within the Messianic Jewish community is a discussion that is far more nuanced and complicated than most people are willing to acknowledge. Such a discussion requires a thorough grasp of the biblical text, history, theology, recent scholarship, as well as Jewish tradition itself. Therefore, as we delve headfirst into this discussion, rather than try to assume all the answers, I'd rather we establish some important points to consider that will help guide and inform the rest of our conversation.

JEWS AND JUDAISM

The Jewish people remain God's covenant-elect people and have an ongoing role in redemptive history.[6] And as Jewish believers, we are the remnant within our people, prophetically calling them back to HaShem.[7]

Furthermore, the faith of the Jewish people (particularly post-Sinai) has always been Judaism. This was also true for the Jewish followers of Yeshua in the early centuries[8] (and for a handful of individuals and pockets of communities throughout history).[9]

Additionally, you cannot separate "Jewishness" from "Judaism." Attempts throughout history to do so have primarily resulted in failure. At Borough Park Symposium I, some argued that "an ethnic Judaism of bagels and lox cannot maintain Jewish identity over time, or over the span of multiple generations."[10] This has been further confirmed by recent Jewish population surveys and studies.[11]

CENTRALITY OF YESHUA

The existence of Messianic Judaism is a realization of a Yeshua-centered Judaism. There is no "Messianic" without the Messiah. Therefore, Yeshua must exist at the center of our Judaism, informing and infusing it with greater meaning and richness. After all, if Yeshua really is the Jewish Messiah, then faith in that Messiah should lead us to become better Jews (in all the different ways that it can and should mean).

We also recognize that not only is it possible, but it is preferable (even obligatory) to be both faithful Jews *and* faithful followers of Messiah. As David Stern once wrote, "We are both 100% Messianic and 100% Jewish." We don't have to choose between the two. Yet, as Dr. Stern also cautions, "If we call ourselves Messianic Jews we must intend to back up our words with actions demonstrating that our Jewishness has substance."[12]

Having a substantive Yeshua-centered Jewish spirituality is also supported by Mark Kinzer, who in discussing the term Messianic Judaism, writes, "It is significant that the term we selected was one which is primarily descriptive in nature, while also containing a strong claim to a unique position within the world of Judaism. Ours is a Judaism that believes that the Messiah has come, and that his name is Yeshua of Nazareth."[13]

Kinzer goes on to write, "As Messianic Jews, we affirm two truths as central to our faith and identity: (1) God's irrevocable covenant with the Jewish people, embodied in and guarded by the Torah, and (2) God's reconciling and revealing work for Israel and the nations in Messiah Yeshua."[14]

The remainder of our discussion hinges on whether or not we accept these above truths to be self-evident, as they are foundational principles not only for a Jewish spirituality, but especially for a Yeshua-believing movement within and among our people.

With these assumptions in place, we can now delve even further into the discussion of tradition and its role within the Messianic Jewish community.

THE PROBLEM WITH "BIBLICAL JUDAISM"

If the Jewish people continue to have an ongoing role in redemptive history and the Torah continues to be obligatory for Jews (in whatever that means), then our next question is: How are we supposed to embody those realities as Messianic Jews?

Whenever we interpret what the Bible says, we are doing "theology." And when we try to actually live out those principles outlined in the text, we end up forced to consult and establish tradition. Why? Because the Bible is a complicated text, and the differences in time, context, geography, and sometimes limited information, force us to recognize that following our canon is impossible without some form of interpretation and tradition.

I am, of course, in no way arguing against the canon of Scripture being our ultimate authority. Rather, I am simply acknowledging that when we seek to interpret and apply what the Bible says, it does not take long before we realize things get complicated.

Furthermore, we have to ask what we even mean by the term "biblical." Are we implying other forms of Judaism are not biblical? Do we mean that we are the Judaism of the Bible? If so, then which Judaism of the Bible—Pharisaic, Essene, Sadducean, Zealot . . . ?[15] And is it even possible to be a re-emergence of a form of Judaism that has not existed since biblical times?

CHALLENGE OF TRADITION

It may be helpful to think of the Torah as a set of statutes needing regulatory interpretation. Statutes lay out broad-brush policies and establish legal norms, but they still need to be interpreted and applied to a variety of contexts. Hence the body of case law, whereby legal authorities consult not only the original set of statutes, but all their interpretations and applications as well.

If we think of the Torah as the Constitution, then the body of interpretative case law would be the *halachic* codes and responsa. Just as a body of courts was established to interpret and apply the Constitution, so too Jewish courts and *halachic* authorities were established to interpret and apply Torah. As such, just as the United States cannot operate in accordance with the Constitution without the interpretative guidance of the judiciary, so too we as a movement cannot operate in accordance with the Torah without the interpretive guidance of our tradition.

Therefore, you cannot escape tradition. Such an attempt is impossible. Furthermore, there is not a single observance that can be defined as "Jewish" that is not "untainted" by tradition, whether it is wearing a *Tallis*, blowing a *shofar*, praying liturgy, or saying a *bracha* over wine. Although some of these practices may have origins in the biblical text or date back to biblical times, how they are observed is entirely tradition.

I already mentioned a *Tallis*. Although people are quick to argue that this is a purely biblical command, Numbers 15:37-41 tells us is to put *tzitzit* on the corners of our garments and attach a thread of blue. *What does THAT mean?* What are *tzitizit*? What defines a 'garment'? What should it look like? Who should create it? All of this is defined by tradition—what *tzitzyot* (plural of tzitzit) are, how they should be tied, the stripes, neckband, etc. It's all tradition.

Another example people are quick to highlight as purely biblical is the shofar. *Really?* This too is all tradition—how it should be made, the sounds (*tekiah, shevarim, teruah* . . .) and the protocol for sounding the *shofar*. It is all tradition.

This leaves us with a further question—is it even possible, then, to have a Judaism that is truly *Jewish* (in accord with the sensibilities of the Jewish people) without drawing upon, for example, the *Siddur*, the *Machzor*, or the *Haggadah*?[16] The answer is no.

No matter how hard we try, we cannot escape tradition. In reality, Jewish history and practice did not freeze in time with the resurrection of Yeshua or the destruction of the second Temple. And this should not be seen as a terrible thing either. Rather, Judaism and the Jewish people have evolved over the past two millennia. Furthermore, the few attempts throughout Jewish history to deny the role of tradition have not succeeded over time (a truth eventually realized even by the *Karaites*, for example).[17] For whatever reason, just as God chose the historic Church as the vehicle to preserve Yeshua-faith and believers throughout the past two thousand years, so too God chose Rabbinic Judaism as the vehicle to preserve the Jewish people and our way of life.

However, acknowledgment still leaves room to lovingly correct those elements where we may disagree. One can embrace the tradition and yet engage it in lively debate. This is especially true within Jewish history. There are plenty of examples of renewal movements who have sought to revive and reconstruct the Jewish experience—from the Essenes to the Chassidim—and yet have done so while simultaneously embracing and being a part of that tradition.

CHOOSE YOUR OWN ADVENTURE

When I was in elementary school, the most popular books at the time were the Choose Your Own Adventure series. These books enabled you to choose how you thought the story should go, giving options for actions, characters, and even the choice of which ending you thought best.

But this is not reality. If we continue trying to ignore tradition and avoid establishing certain normative practices and theology, we encounter a problem. We leave it to the individual to decide. When we leave it to each person to "choose their own adventure," the result is that everyone has their own interpretation and tradition without any cohesion.

Only in our modern, Western culture do we find this lone-ranger mentality when it comes to spirituality and how to interpret and apply Scripture. Although we want to praise individual discernment and maturity, we must also balance it with collective intellect and historic continuity. Leaving it up to each individual to decide what the Bible means and how it should be applied results in, for example, congregations around the country with few, if any, Jewish members who blow shofars-at-will, use *Tallits* as tablecloths and banners, and often suffer from identity crises. The reason for all the confusion within our movement is largely because there have been no parameters.

We should also consider how arrogant it is to assume that after a few thousand years, only now have we come along with all the correct answers. This is a little ridiculous. To outright reject tradition (whether Jewish or Christian) makes an assumption that all those previous generations of people were idiots and have nothing valuable to contribute to our current understanding and practice.

It would be much more honest to consider that many generations of individuals and communities have wrestled with the Biblical text, its meaning, and how to apply it to their own circumstances. Therefore, it would be much wiser to learn from them and use their collective wisdom as models for how to apply the Bible to our own lives and circumstances. Otherwise, it becomes a "choose your own adventure" with each person "doing what seems right in their own eyes."

CONTINUITY

Leaving these decisions up to each individual also undermines Jewish continuity. What we consider "Jewish" has always been defined by the community itself. So when we decide we are going to make up our own rules, we should not be surprised when our wider Jewish community does not recognize it as being Jewish.[18]

Just recently I was asked to give a eulogy for the father of one of our members at a very large and prestigious synagogue in Beverly Hills. The fact that I was able to participate and then speak from a perspective defined by our tradition elicited a very positive and respected response. People were moved by what I had to say but also because it clearly established my identity as still being part of our people—both in word and deed.

Although there are exceptions, by remaining Jews familiar with our tradition and living a lifestyle consistent with that message, my wife and I have repeatedly experienced positive results with family and friends. After all, the biggest fear within our Jewish community towards faith in Yeshua is that one who makes such a decision stops being Jewish. This emotional response is first and foremost on most people's minds. Consider the usual arguments why you cannot believe in Yeshua as a Jew—because of the Holocaust, pogroms, anti-Semitism, etc.[19] They are often emotional responses rather than theological. So when we practice a lifestyle consistent with, and recognizably Jewish, it breaks down the stereotypes that faith in Yeshua equals the abandonment of Jewish life. Furthermore, it establishes us as being within the boundaries of our people and faith. But this only happens when we embrace and find value within our tradition.

ROLE OF TRADITION FOR YESHUA AND PAUL

So the real issue is not whether we can escape tradition, because that is a given. Rather, the real question becomes how are we to engage with our tradition in light of Yeshua and the New Testament?

The best examples for how to navigate our tradition come from the New Testament itself. Judaism teaches that when the Messiah comes, one of his roles will be to clarify ambiguities within *halachic* matters. Interestingly, this is exactly what Yeshua does in the Sermon on the Mount—which serves as a parallel to, and a sort of "re-giving" of the Torah on Mt. Sinai. Through halachic formulas known from the Second Temple period, Yeshua sets out to clarify and set straight popular misconceptions of specific *mitzvot*.

Before dealing with each specific issue, Yeshua usually begins with the phrase, *"You have heard that our fathers were told."* This was a halachic formula whereby a Sage would state a particular halachic understanding, and then clarify its proper interpretation. This phrase is actually paralleled in a similar way within the Dead Sea Scrolls, in a text known as 4QMMT—*"Miksat Ma'aseh Torah" (Some rulings pertaining to the Torah)*. The text introduces disagreements between the Qumran community and their opponents (namely the Sadducees) with the phrase: *"You say . . . but we think/say."*

Yeshua uses this same traditional formula, known from the Second Temple period, to clarify and give the proper understanding to certain interpretations of Torah commands, which is also a fulfillment of one of the expectations Messiah would do within Jewish tradition. This is a clear example of Yeshua not only affirming, but adhering to, standard traditional practice.

Additionally, in Matthew 23:23, Yeshua addresses a specific group of Pharisees, and reprimands them for violating certain ethical considerations in halachic matters:

> *You pay your tithes of mint, dill, and cumin; but you have neglected the weightier matters of the Torah—justice, mercy, and trust. These are the things you should have attended to without neglecting the others! Blind guides!—straining out a gnat, meanwhile swallowing a camel.*

Yeshua does not criticize them for adherence to halachic minutiae, but for their hypocrisy. For in their striving to be oh-so-extra-pious, they missed the mark. What is particularly important for our discussion is that these additional tithes of "mint, dill, and cumin" are not actually required by *mitzvah de-oraita* (commanded directly in the Torah), but are rather supplemental/additional tithes known later from the Talmud (i.e. from tradition). Yeshua does not berate this practice. In fact he says, "*You should have done these things without neglecting the others.*" Yeshua's reprimand was an issue of weightier matters within Torah. He was establishing ethical considerations and priorities within the halachic process, which takes precedence over other matters of halachah, especially when those details are matters of tradition and not found within the Torah itself. This is something we should also be careful to consider.

Yeshua did not criticize the traditions of the fathers except when necessary and only where they conflict with the Tanakh. For example, in Matthew 23:1-2, Yeshua instructs the crowds "to be careful to do" all that the Torah teachers and that the Pharisees "sit in the seat of Moses." But he also teaches us "not to do as they do!"—for our righteousness must *exceed* theirs in order to enter the Kingdom of Heaven (Mathew 5:20).

In his paper, Baruch Maoz claims that although "Paul never spoke of Jewishness as a thing of the past," he does say that "Judaism was no longer his religion."[20] This is an incorrect interpretation of Pauline literature. Furthermore, the New Testament and recent scholarship[21] all paint a completely different picture. Paul himself claims not only Jewish cultural identity but always refers to himself in the present tense as a Pharisee[22] who continues to observe Torah,[23] attend synagogue regularly "as was his custom,"[24] and encourages circumcision for those who are Jewish[25]—all of which are matters of religious observance. Paul remained a devout Jew. Where he is challenged, and where there is often confusion, is in regard to his expectations of non-Jewish followers of Yeshua.[26]

Therefore, Paul shares a similar view of tradition as Yeshua. He not only upholds it when necessary, but he even subjects himself to its enforcement. In Acts 23:1-5, Paul is brought before the *Sanhedrin*. During the interrogation, a command is issued for Paul to be physically struck, after which, Paul responds with a strong rebuke. When it is made known to Paul that it was the High Priest himself who commanded him to be struck, and the one whom Paul is insulting, Paul quickly apologizes and states: "I didn't know, brothers, that he was the High Priest; for it says in the Torah, 'you are not to speak disparagingly of a ruler of your people.'"[27]

Lastly, in Acts 28, Paul convenes a meeting with the local Jewish leaders. In his address to them, he clearly argues, "I have done nothing against either our people or the traditions of our fathers."[28] This would also support his statement in Philippians 3:6 where he states that even in regards to the strictest observance of the Torah, he was "blameless."[29]

THOUGHTS ABOUT HALACHAH

If Messianic Judaism claims to be a Judaism, than it behooves us to consider the place of *halachah* in our midst. We have already established that Messianic Judaism is more than simply "Biblical Judaism." To make such a claim denies the history of the Jewish people over the last two thousand years and the fact that other forms of Judaism are also "biblical."[30] Such a perspective also fails to acknowledge the role Rabbinic Judaism has played in determining Jewish life, teaching and practice, as well as the preservation of us as a people throughout history.

As we proceed with discussing the role of tradition in the Messianic Jewish community, we must first understand *halachah* for what it is and what it is not. What has been lost in the strictest forms of Orthodox Judaism in recent years is the fluidity of the *halachic* structure and the innovation out of which it was birthed. Gordon Tucker, of the Jewish Theological Seminary, points out:

> The body of Jewish law is not uniform in texture, but is rather composed of materials which fall into two main categories, usually referred to as *de-oraita* (biblically ordained) and *de-rabbanan* (rabbinically developed). That which is *de-oraita* can be considered to be the very core of the system, which holds it in place and provides a frame of reference. It therefore must be treated as inviolable. Tampering with that which is *de-oraita* is tantamount to destroying the core of the Jewish pattern of life as it has existed for millennia . . . The much greater (that is, in terms of volume) overlay which is *de-rabbanan*, on the other hand, comes with procedures for change and development. What is *de-rabbanan* can develop, is in fact meant to develop, as the conditions of the Jewish community change. That is what ensures the vibrancy and the continuity of the *halakha* as the coordinate system which roots all Jewish communities.[31]

The myth that rabbinic tradition trumps the Bible is false. In fact, halachic development recognizes, as Tucker puts it, the "inviolability" of the Torah and places precedence on biblical commands over rabbinic ones, and even acknowledges the difference in the blessings that we recite over them.[32]

Furthermore, Jewish law was never meant to be static but rather to be reinterpreted in every generation. Rabbi Wayne Dosick describes *halachah* as "ever-developing" and "ever-evolving."[33]

Halachah is derived out of evolving case law, which is based upon prior precedent (much like our own American legal system).[34] As such, it is developed by wrestling with texts, the practicalities of daily life, and the teachings of previous generations in order to decide *halachic* matters. It is a process. A process that is not set in stone and not without inerrancy.[35] However, while engaging with rabbinic texts and deciding *halachah*, Tucker guides, "Development in the domain of *de-rabbanan* must not be abrupt or discontinuous, [but] must be rooted in traditional exegetical methodologies, and above all, must be ratified by the community of the committed and informed.[36]

This must also be true for us. We as Messianic Jews are obligated to engage in knowledgeable discussion with Jewish law and contribute our own unique voice. At times we may interpret it differently, especially in light of New Testament understanding. Yet that does not mean we can just "do as we see fit." We have a responsibility to ourselves and the larger Jewish world to engage our tradition through a knowledgeable and informed process.

CONCLUSION

According to *Pirkei Avot* (2:21), "Rabbi Tarfon would say, 'You are not obligated to complete the work, but neither are you free to desist from it.'" If the Messianic Jewish community is to evolve and mature, we must take seriously the role of Torah and tradition in our midst. As Jews, we are interconnected to the Torah in a deep and powerful way. And as Jews who have put our trust in Yeshua, this is an even greater reality, as Yeshua is the Living Torah, the Word made flesh that dwells in our midst; and the Gospel message is the greater renewal and internalization of the promise of Jeremiah 31.

It is impossible to take Torah seriously without considering the role of tradition, which plays a bigger part then we realize. The answer is to be engaged. The point is not to always agree on everything but to see our tradition as a collection of complex conversations between individuals and generations. There are things you will agree with, things you will not, and others that will challenge you. But the only way to understand and be involved is to participate in the conversation. We must add our own voice to the ongoing dialog.

Furthermore, as Messianic Jews, we have our own unique voice to add to the collection of voices of our people over the generations. But to do so, we must develop a love and admiration for our tradition and its accompanying body of literature. As mentioned earlier, it is not always about being "right," or agreeing with every single thing. The answer is to engage rather than disengage. We must dig deeper and swim in the conversation.

The question of the role of Torah and Jewish tradition within the Messianic Jewish community is a question that should be seriously wrestled with. There are no simple answers. But we need to also recognize that what we Jews are seeking today is really the same thing we have always sought—to simultaneously connect with God and to find our place within thirty centuries of Jewish history. And that simply cannot be done without Torah and wrestling with our tradition.

ENDNOTES

1. Asher Zvi Ginsberg (1856-1927) was a famous Zionist thinker and ideologue who wrote under the pen name, Ahad Ha'Am, and is attributed with the famous quote, "More than the Jews have kept Shabbat, Shabbat has kept the Jews."
2. Deuteronomy 18:15.
3. Jeremiah 31:30-33.
4. John 1:1-5, 14.
5. A great example for both positions is found in Acts 15. But also refer to Mt. 5:17-20, Acts 21:20, Acts 24:14, etc.
6. Ex. 31:17, Deut. 4:32-40, Deut. 5:3, Deut. 7:6-8, Jer. 31:34-36, Rom. 3:1-4, Rom. 11, etc.
7. Romans 11:1-5.
8. Acts 2:46-47, Acts 21:20, Acts 24:14, etc.
9. In the earliest centuries were groups like the Ebionites and Nazarenes. And in more recent history, consider Joseph Rabinowitz and his congregation, Beth Israel-Judea, in Moldova during the 19th century, and figures like Rabbi Daniel Zion, Rabbi Ignác Lichtenstein, Theophilus Lucky, Rabbi Yechiel Zvi Lichtenstein, etc.
10. Joshua Brumbach, "The Nature of God and the New American Jew: A Response to Akiva Cohen and Jhan Moskowitz." in *The Borough Park Papers: Symposium II* (Clarksville: Borough Park Symposium, 2012).
11. 2000 National Jewish Population Survey (NJPS), 2002 Report of the Union of Jewish Communities (UJC), etc. This has been a widely published and studied issue.
12. David H. Stern, *Messianic Jewish Manifesto* (Clarksville: Jewish New Testament Publications, 1991), 26.
13. Mark Kinzer, *The Nature of Messianic Judaism* (West Hartford: Hashivenu Archives, 2000), 7.
14. Kinzer, 21.
15. For more on this discussion, see: Kinzer, 7-13.
16. Kinzer, 9.
17. The *Karaites* were a group of Jews in the 7th-9th centuries who also advocated a Judaism based solely on the *Tanakh* and opposed the authority of rabbinic tradition. However, they eventually all but disappeared for the same reasons we wrestle with today. For more on this, see: Jacob Neusner, *An Introduction to Judaism* (Louisville: Westminster/John Knox, 1991), 284.
18. The most obvious exception to this would be historic consensus against faith in Yeshua. However, even here, there is a better way to live out and express our faiths that maintain Jewish continuity.
19. Sadly, for much of history this has actually been the reality. In ages past, faith in Yeshua *did* mean the abandonment of Jewish life and identity.

20. Baruch Maoz, "The Role of Torah and Jewish Tradition in the Messianic Jewish Community." in *The Borough Park Papers: Symposium 3* (Clarksville: Borough Park Symposium, 2012).
21. In fact, there is a whole new arena within Pauline studies called the New Perspective on Paul (NPP), which advocates understanding Paul within his Jewish context.
22. Acts 23:6, Acts 26:5, Philippians 3:5-6, etc.
23. Acts 21:20-26, Acts 25:8, Philippians 3:5-6, etc.
24. Acts 13:1, 13:14, 13:42-44, 14:1,17:2, 17:10, 17:17, 19:8, etc.
25. Acts 16:1-5.
26. Who are not obligated to the same religious obligations of Jewish observance, but share in the blessings.
27. Acts 23:5
28. Acts 28:17
29. Also see: Acts 25:8.
30. For a much deeper discussion on this point, see: Kinzer, specifically pages 6-10.
31. Gordon Tucker, "Final Report of the Commission for the Study of the Ordination of Women as Rabbis." in *The Ordination of Women as Rabbis,* ed. Simon Greenberg. (New York: JTS Press, 1988), 13-14.
32. For commands directly from the Torah, we use the longer formula, *"asher kidshanu b'mitzvotav vetzivanu . . ."* verses the shorter blessing, which is used for rabbinically derived mitzvoth—like *Kiddush* or *HaMotzi.*
33. Wayne Dosick, *Living Judaism* (New York: Harper Collins, 1995), 95.
34. Ibid., 104.
35. Ibid., 93-94.
36. Tucker, 14.

REFLECTIONS ON THE ROLE OF TORAH AND JEWISH TRADITION AT CONGREGATION SHA'AREI SHALOM

Seth N. Klayman, Ph.D.
Graduate diploma in Jewish Studies from Oxford University,
M.A. and Ph.D. in Religion (Judaic Studies) from Duke University,
Rabbi of Congregation Sha'arei Shalom in the
Research Triangle area of North Carolina

I would rank the question, "What is the role of Torah and Jewish tradition in the Messianic Jewish community?" in the top three most controversial questions among Jewish Yeshua-believers today. We may find ourselves engaged in lively debate over what the other two highly controversial questions in that hypothetical list might be. But, I think we would generally agree that the question posed in this session would be on that list.

I endeavor to approach the question not as a theologian or biblical scholar, but as a practitioner. I lead a Messianic Jewish community in Raleigh-Durham, North Carolina, USA, called Sha'arei Shalom. Our congregation is currently comprised of almost 70 family units, with a nearly equal percentage of Jewish and non-Jewish families. As a congregation of devoted Jews, devoted to Yeshua, together with Yeshua-believers from diverse backgrounds with Ruth-like callings, the question of the role of Torah and Jewish tradition in our local community is continually relevant. I think about the question primarily in practical terms and in a pastoral capacity. This paper is written from that perspective. In this paper, I seek to relate some practical reflections on the role of Torah and Jewish tradition in our congregation.

I will address the question in two parts. In Part 1, I will offer our guiding approach to the role of Torah in our local Messianic Jewish community. Part 1 is more-or-less a summary of the material presented in the course we require of everyone interested in becoming a "Vision Bearer" (member) of Sha'arei Shalom. In Part 2, I provide a practical example of the role of Jewish tradition in one area of our local community: our congregational kitchen. Part 2 provides reflection on why and how Jewish tradition informs our practice with respect to our kitchen.

By separating the discussion of "Torah" and "Jewish Tradition" into two parts, I do not intend to communicate that they should—or necessarily even can—be divorced from one another. I also by no means set out to give a comprehensive treatment of the question. My overarching goal is modest. I hope to promote constructive reflection on the topic in general, both here and in our respective home contexts. I also hope that these reflections might offer some help and encouragement, especially to those charged with leading local Messianic Jewish communities.

TORAH AND SHA'AREI SHALOM

I have developed an acronym describing our approach to Torah at Sha'arei Shalom. The acronym is: SHA'AREI. Each letter stands for a principle that guides our relationship to Torah. Here I present each principle, and then provide some general comments on it. Please note that the sequence in which I present these principles is driven only by the acronym; other than that, there is no special significance to the order in which I present the principles.

S—Salvation is by grace through faith

We approach the question of the role of Torah in our individual lives, and in the life of our community as a whole, in light of this teaching that we consider a foundational presupposition to the discussion at hand. Trust in the God of Israel, and in the God of Israel alone, is the essential element necessary for right standing with God and entry into his eternal promises. The Torah itself reflects this truth. Abraham "*believed* the Lord, and he counted it to him as righteousness."[1] Although faith results in obedient action (though not perfection of course), God's acceptance of us, and eternal favor toward us, hinges on our faith in him. Without faith, it is impossible to please God.[2] If faith is absent from our lives, then fastidiousness in Torah observance and the proliferation of benevolent deeds in general cannot gain us acceptance by God.[3] When we put our trust in God on God's terms, God extends mercy and grace.[4]

There is a strong current in Judaism that affirms our dependence on God's extension of mercy for salvation rather than on our earning salvation through good works. The climactic High Holiday prayer *Avinu Malkeinu* illuminates this current. "Our Father, our King, we have erred and we have sinned. For, we have in ourselves no [good] deeds. Deal with us charitably and mercifully and save us." *Avinu Malkeinu* acknowledges that our own goodness is not adequate for our salvation and encourages total reliance on God's righteousness and mercy for salvation.

In these last days, God has spoken to us through his Son,[5] whom he has provided as the way of salvation for Jews and Gentiles alike. Whoever *believes* in him receives salvation, an inheritance of life eternal.[6] There is no difference between Jews and Gentiles with respect to how we come to God.[7] That is to say, as I understand the scriptures, all people must come to God in the same way: through Yeshua. This reality does not answer the question of the role of Torah in the life of the Messianic Jew (or the Gentile Yeshua-believer). However, in our context, it is an important and foundational presupposition for approaching the question.

H—Humbly approach the question of the role of Torah in Messianic Jewish life

It is especially important to approach the topic at hand in a spirit of utmost humility. Let's not be so narrow-minded as to think that this is not a very difficult issue. There are some good reasons to exercise humility as we consider this topic. First, we should exercise humility because we do not address the question apart from our own respective theological and experiential influences, both positive and negative. Of course we all seek to believe what the Bible teaches about the role of Torah in the life of the Jewish believer. But, a mature and humble view is proffered in the knowledge that we have deeply ingrained ways of thinking about the question that well may be imperfect. A mature and humble view acknowledges that it is possible that experiences in Jewish life, or lack thereof, can sometimes color our perspective on the question. Even if we currently find ourselves a long way away from where we were once positioned on the question (we were so wrong back then and so much more enlightened now), our migration to a different viewpoint may not be solely a result of what we would like to believe is a deeper understanding of the Scriptures; it might be a reaction, for one reason or another, to something else.

By raising awareness of our respective influences and biases, I am not saying that we cannot get to a right understanding. I am also not discounting the impartation of the wisdom of the *Ruach* and the power of the *Ruach* to eliminate obstacles to a right understanding of the teaching of the Scriptures on the subject. I am simply reminding us that we are all coming to the question from different places, with different training, different life-experiences, and different biases. All of this is sufficient ground for humility when we state our position and evaluate the merits of other positions.

A second reason for exercising humility is because we are highly susceptible to misunderstanding one another on this issue. Sadly, misunderstandings have led to incorrect characterizations of people or groups, and resulted in unnecessary and unfortunate *lashon ha-ra* and even division. Humility means being careful with our words and not being quick to jump to assumptions about what another person means. For example, phrases like "observe the Torah," "keeping Torah" and "being free from the law" mean different things to different people. We should sincerely hear one another out and never resort to labels.

Third, we should exercise humility because we may well have some inconsistencies in our own views and practice. For example, some in our communities who are generally Torah observant cannot clearly articulate why they may not observe a particular mitzvah (*Niddah*, *Shatnez*, *Pe'ot*). Some mitzvot may be overlooked. Some people who are not so positive on Torah "observance" in general certainly believe that there is much in the Torah that we must keep. Sometimes there is inconsistency in the way those distinctions are made. Though we may have our own reasoning and understanding, it may be faulty, and it may not be satisfactory in the mind of another. Let's be humble.

A—Ask first, "How does the Torah point me to Messiah?" and, "What does it say to my heart?" before addressing questions of observance

Sometimes there is a tendency among people in our communities to launch immediately from a passage in the Torah to the question, "What do I do?" I do believe that is a question worth asking. However, we must first remember that the Torah points us to Messiah Yeshua. This is one vital role of the Torah: it focuses us on Messiah. Yeshua said, "Do not think that I have come to abolish the Law or the Prophets; I have not come to abolish them, but to fulfill them."[8] Shaul taught,

"For, Messiah is the end of the law for righteousness to everyone who believes."[9] Since Yeshua fulfills (fills full, is the end-goal of, brings to completion) the Torah, then as we read it, we should certainly be asking the question of how he does so. "What is it," we should ask, "about Yeshua's life, teaching, ministry, death, and resurrection that brings this passage in the Torah to its fullest meaning?"

After Yeshua rose from the dead, he explained to his disciples that he fulfilled everything written about him in the Torah (as well as the Prophets and Writings). He opened their minds to understand the fact that the Scriptures (that is, the Tanakh) say that "the Messiah should suffer and on the third day rise from the dead, and that repentance and forgiveness of sins should be proclaimed in his name to all nations, beginning from Jerusalem."[10] As followers of Yeshua, we should read the Torah in the light of God's revelation of his Son. We should prioritize the quest to understand how a given passage in the Torah points to Messiah Yeshua. Explicit messianic prophecies and typologies of biblical figures such as Joseph and Moses are examples of places in the Torah that most clearly point us to Yeshua. But Messiah is by no means limited to those passages alone. Of course, in this quest, we must simultaneously resist imposing a connection to Yeshua that is contrived or forced.

Not only is Yeshua the one to whom the Torah points, he is also our great teacher and interpreter of the Torah. His "You have heard" teachings in the Sermon on the Mount[11] provide an excellent example of Yeshua's exposition of some passages in the Torah. Yeshua corrects misunderstandings, misconceptions, and erroneous teachings about various mitzvot held by some of his contemporaries. In the course of Yeshua's discourse, we learn that the intended teaching of the Torah is to call us to obedience deeper than the level of what we do, on the level of the source of our actions in the heart. This is another vital role that the Torah fulfills in our lives. Thus, according to Yeshua, it is not enough to refrain from engaging in the physical act of adultery. Scrupulous observance of the command, "You shall not commit adultery,"[12] means not succumbing to lust in the deeper level of the heart. By focusing attention on the level of the will and intent from which the action flows, Yeshua is certainly not replacing or "spiritualizing" the literal command. Rather, he is correcting a solely superficial understanding of the mitzvah. He is calling us to continually look introspectively into our own hearts as we seek to understand and apply the Torah in our lives.

A—Acts 15 Paradigm

Like the vast majority of Messianic congregations, ours is comprised of Jewish people as well as individuals from diverse backgrounds with a recognized calling to be a part of our congregation. Because so-called "One Law" groups have contributed to some confusion with respect to the orientation of the Gentile believer to the Torah, it is important in our context to point to Acts 15 as a paradigmatic passage for the non-Jewish believer. By stating this view, we have seen many Gentile believers who do not understand Messianic Judaism rightly decide not to become a part of our congregation.

According to Acts 15,[13] after some debate, the Jerusalem Council decided that the Gentile Yeshua-believer is not required to "be circumcised and keep the Law of Moses," but is required to abstain from things polluted by idols, sexual immorality, strangled meat, and blood.[14]

For our purposes, I find three things noteworthy about the account and decision of the Council. First, the stipulations seek to eliminate unnecessary offense to observant Jews (whether Yeshua-believers or not), especially in the context of sharing table fellowship together. Second, it is clear that the Gentile believer is not bound to circumcision and observance of the Torah. I find this aspect of the decision of the Jerusalem Council interesting in light of our question about the role of Torah in the Messianic Jewish community. It seems to me that underlying this decision is the assumption that a Jewish follower of Yeshua *would* live a lifestyle of general Torah observance. We cannot come to a strong conclusion from this admitted argument from silence, but I find it conspicuous that the question of whether a Jewish follower of Yeshua should observe Torah does not come up directly here or in any other passage as the question does for Gentiles. Third, neither Acts 15 nor any other passage seems to limit the freedom of the non-Jewish believer to cast his or her lot among the Jewish people and observe the Torah. Of course, it is the great exception that a non-Jewish Yeshua-believer would be called to cast her lot among the Jewish people. Sadly, all too often Torah observance among Gentile believers is born not out of a calling, but rather out of misplaced focus, or confusion over theology or identity. In the congregational context, we must be sensitive to these challenges.

R—Right and Wrong

The Torah teaches us right and wrong. Shaul writes: "Yet if it had not been for the law, I would not have known sin. For I would not have known what it is to covet if the law had not said, 'You shall not covet.' But sin, seizing an opportunity through the commandment, produced in me all kinds of covetousness. For apart from the law, sin lies dead."[15] The Torah, in all of its holiness, righteousness, and goodness, provides a means by which we can identify the sin in our own lives. Once there is an understanding of the presence of sin, the ground of the heart can be prepared for conviction, leading to repentance and restoration of our relationship with God.

Elsewhere, Shaul says it this way: "So then, the law was our guardian until Messiah came, in order that we might be justified by faith."[16] The guardian, or "attendant, custodian" in Greco-Roman society, had the role of accompanying, training, and disciplining a child. As such, the Torah functions as a trainer in right and wrong to lead us to Messiah. Sometimes this passage is understood to mean that after trusting Messiah, we should stop observing the Torah or Torah observance has no value. My son is in third grade. In math class, he is already learning to write a check. One day he will no longer be under regular instruction in how to do this. But, he will continue doing it his entire life just the way he was taught. Once we encounter the grace of Messiah, are we to somehow forget or disavow the very means God has set in place for us to show us we need him?

E—Example of the Apostles

There is no extended discourse in the Apostolic Writings that has as its primary goal a direct and comprehensive explication of the issue at hand. Tragically, there is no historically continuous Jewish Yeshua-believing community to help us answer the question. Hence, the fertile ground for our differing views. In order to answer the question, we need to "peer behind the scenes," so to speak, of various passages in the Apostolic Writings in order to discern the example of the apostles and early Jewish Yeshua-followers. Among contemporary Jewish and Christian scholars of Judaism in the Greco-Roman period, the view of Yeshua as a first-century Torah observant rabbi is by and large accepted as axiomatic. The glimpses we receive into the lives of the apostles, especially the life of Shaul, indicate that, like their rabbi, Messiah, and Lord, the apostolic example is that of a Torah observant lifestyle.

I would like to mention a highlight from the life of Shaul. When Shaul arrived in Jerusalem and was received by Ya'akov, Ya'akov informed him of the rumor that Shaul was teaching Diaspora Jews to "forsake Moses."[17] Ya'akov seems to have known that this was a false rumor and asks Shaul to prove that "there is nothing in what they have been told about you, but that you yourself also live in observance of the law."[18] Shaul then consents to the direction of Ya'akov in order to demonstrate to the thriving Torah observant Jewish Yeshua-believing community in Jerusalem that Shaul lives in observance of the Torah.[19]

I have chosen to highlight this one example (and could refer to others as well), but I realize that there are other passages in Shaul's writings that do not seem *prima facie* to be consistent with the example I have cited.[20] I do not believe there is a problem, though, because in those contexts, Shaul is usually speaking to non-Jews and/or correcting a misunderstanding about the purpose of the Torah, not lambasting observance performed in the right understanding and spirit. Unless we believe Shaul to be duplicitous on the matter (a view I have actually heard before), we must come to the conclusion that passages in Shaul's writings that have historically been construed as antinomian must be read in light of his actions in Jerusalem in submission to Ya'akov's leadership.

From a young age, it has baffled me that as Jewish followers of Yeshua, we often need to defend a lifestyle lived in the spirit of Yeshua and the apostles to some of our well-meaning Christian brothers and sisters, and even sometimes to our fellow Jewish believers. I have wondered if the reason we do not have a lot of direct treatment of this topic in the New Covenant is because for those authors, in that time, in that place, it was a given—it was assumed—that generally speaking a Jewish person who seeks to follow God and trusts Yeshua would generally live a lifestyle that honors the Torah. For Jewish people today, removed as we are in time, and as a result of various historical forces, this is no longer a given.

For me, the apostles are the greatest examples of who we are called to be and how we are called to live as Jewish followers of Yeshua. They were Jewish. So are we. They were born from above through Yeshua. So are we. They sought to communicate the good news that the Messiah has come to their Jewish brothers and sisters and to peoples among the nations. So do we. They expected the fulfillment of the hope of their ancestors: the establishment of the kingdom of Messiah here on earth, which they knew would come in fullness at Yeshua's return. So do we. I believe that in the legacy of the apostles, a Torah-honoring lifestyle—and we will of course continue to discuss what that means in all of its specifics and complexities—is an important part of who we are as the unique remnant of Israel on this earth.

Too often we approach the question of the role of Torah in our lives and communities by asking something like this: "What sort of an orientation to the Torah is most effective for reaching our Jewish people for Messiah?" To be more blunt, we ask, "What is evangelistically expedient? What works?" I am inclined to ask different questions: "Who are we? Who are we called to be as the remnant of Israel on this earth? How do we most effectively shine the light of Messiah as the remnant? What does that look like in our lifestyle?" When I ask these questions, I cannot escape a vision that includes the Torah, just as we have in the example of the apostles—though we must update it in a new day and time. I believe that the more we gain common understanding of the answers to these questions, the more fruit we will see in our people turning in repentance to Messiah Yeshua.

I—Informed Practice: Messianic and Jewish

Our faith in Yeshua informs our Torah observance. For example, our Passover seder culminates in relating what we do to the death and resurrection of Messiah Yeshua. We make this explicit through readings from the Besorot, songs, and exposition of how the story of our redemption from Egypt points us to the story of our Messiah Yeshua. Thus, when we ask the question of the redemption from Egypt, "How does this point me to Messiah?" our answer does not just relate to theology or even spiritual application, but it is also reflected in our practice. We view this as vital, particularly in the identity formation and shaping of our children as Messianic Jews. I do long for more sharing among our respective communities of how our faith in Yeshua informs our Torah observance. I hope that my children have more commonality in their Messianic Jewish observance with children in other Messianic congregations than I did when I was growing up in this community.

Jewish tradition also informs our Torah observance. There are many mitzvot for which the Torah does not give specific detailed "how to" guidance. Let's take, for example, the four species during Sukkot. "And you shall take on the first day the fruit of splendid trees, branches of palm trees and boughs of leafy trees and willows of the brook, and you shall rejoice before the Lord your God seven days."[21] Conceivably, we could take up the fruit of what we consider to be a "splendid tree" and what we consider to be a "leafy tree," put them together with a branch of palm and some willows of the brook, and observe the mitzvah. However, such an application would only serve to disconnect us from the broader Jewish community and other Messianic Jewish communities who apply this mitzvah by defining the unnamed species as an etrog and myrtle. Our application is therefore informed by Jewish tradition. I am certain that if those of us in Messianic Jewish communities were to describe the way we observe any mitzvah, from holidays to lifestyle practices and lifecycle events, we would find—whether we realize it or not—that our customs are generally informed by Jewish tradition.

By saying that Jewish tradition informs our practice, I certainly do not mean that we never deviate from a strict *halakhic* application of Torah observance. Returning to our example, in our congregation, we have decided to wave the lulav and etrog on Shabbat. Traditionally, the lulav and etrog are not waved on Shabbat because bringing them to the synagogue would violate the traditional proscription of carrying on Shabbat. We, however, consider the following: (1) after commanding the taking of four species, the Torah says, "You shall rejoice before the Lord your God seven days;"[22] (2) Shabbat is our largest gathering of the week and it is a great blessing and encouragement to rejoice together with the lulav and etrog in such a gathering; (3) some in our community do not have a lulav and etrog and passing them around affords everyone who desires the opportunity to take them up. You may agree or you may disagree with our practice.[23] But, we can talk about it. For us, it is important that we seek to think through why we deviate when we deviate from the traditional application of a mitzvah. Thoughtful reasoning places us in the wider conversation, gives us increased integrity as the remnant of Israel, and strengthens our stand for Messiah Yeshua among our people.

AN EXAMPLE OF JEWISH TRADITION APPLIED AT SHA'AREI SHALOM: OUR KITCHEN

Summary of Our Kitchen Guidelines[24]

We have a non-meat congregational kitchen and facility. Only dairy and pareve foods may be prepared in our kitchen and served within our building. When people prepare food in their homes to bring to a community oneg, we ask that the food contain only kosher ingredients. Among our members, we seek to raise awareness of common pitfalls to be avoided, such as the presence of animal rennet in some cheeses. We ask that if people bring packaged food to the congregation for a community oneg, the packaged food be marked with a *hechsher*. We do not ask that people in our congregation keep the same *kashrut* standard in their homes as we do as a community in our building. We invite anyone to bring food to community onegs, regardless of the kashrut practice of the home/kitchen in which the dish was prepared. When someone brings food, the food stays on the private platter on which it came, and then is taken home after the oneg. We *kasher* the kitchen at least twice per year—once prior to the High Holidays and once prior to Passover—through a traditional *kashering* process with modifications based on the circumstances we have to work within our kitchen. For our larger celebrations and events, we have served full meals to well over 200 people, so maintaining these *kashrut* standards is no small endeavor!

The Question

This has been our practice for the four years that we have owned our own facility. I think that relatively speaking within our Messianic Jewish congregational community, our practice falls on the more traditional side. Why have we chosen these kashrut standards for our congregational facility? We have not set out to model ourselves off of an Orthodox or Conservative Jewish congregation. Every non-Messianic Jewish visitor we have had in our gates, except for a handful, is generally non-observant. We do not have a particular calling to reach out to our observant Orthodox or Conservative Jewish brothers and sisters any more than we do any other Jew. In fact, the percentage of strictly kosher families within the Jewish community in our city is very low. We do not feel that the kashrut standards we have adopted are the kashrut standards that we, and everyone else, are somehow obligated to adopt. Our practice necessitates a lot of forethought, a lot of communication, a lot of repeated vision casting, and a lot of organization. So, why have we chosen these standards for our congregational facility?

Our Process

When we acquired our own facility, we immediately faced the question of how we would handle our kitchen and our onegs. We began to answer this question by first looking into the Torah to find the general definitions of which foods are kosher (meaning "fit" or "appropriate for consumption") and which foods are not kosher. In summary and simplified terms, we found that the Torah teaches the following:

- Land animals must have split hooves and chew the cud (Lev 11:1-8)
- Poultry must fly and not be a bird of prey (Lev 11:13-19)
- Fish must have fins and scales (Lev 11:9-12)
- The blood of a kosher animal must be drained out before the animal is eaten (Lev 17:13-14)
- Animals that die on their own are not kosher (Deut 14:21)
- It is not permissible to boil a young goat in its mother's milk (Deut 14:21)

After looking into the Torah, we turned to the teaching and practice of Yeshua and the apostles. In summary and simplified terms, we highlighted the following:

- Yeshua kept the laws of kashrut
- Yeshua taught his disciples not to forsake the Torah (Matt 5:17-20)
- There are a number of passages sometimes adduced to argue that what the Torah teaches about kashrut has been radically altered or nullified by the teachings of Yeshua and the New Covenant. Some examples of such passages are: Mark 7:1-23; Acts 10; Gal 2:11-14. We did not find any of these passages to radically alter or nullify what the Torah teaches. But, even if we are incorrect in our understanding, we determined that there is certainly no prohibition against observing the plain meaning of the Torah.

- Shaul claims to have kept the Torah (Acts 21:15-26; 25:8) and to "have done nothing against the customs of our fathers" (Acts 28:17)

Equipped with this understanding, we considered how the Torah has been applied historically within Jewish communities worldwide. In summary and in simplified terms, three applications stood out to us:

Proper Slaughter of Animals: Because Leviticus 17:13-14 says the blood of a slaughtered animal must be drained out completely, only meat that has been slaughtered by a *shochet* (someone trained in the ritual slaughter of an animal according to the laws of kashrut), is considered kosher. If meat is not certified as kosher, then there is no way of knowing whether the blood was properly drained out and eliminated from the animal after it was slaughtered.

No Mixing of Milk and Meat: In traditional rabbinic interpretation, the command in Deuteronomy 14:21 not to boil a young goat in its mother's milk is understood to mean that milk and meat should never be eaten together at the same time. This constructs a fence around the commandment so as to ensure that it will never be transgressed.

Separate Dishes: In order to ensure milk and meat are never eaten together, the laws of kashrut require that separate dishes be kept for meat products, dairy products, etc.

Finally, we reflected on the way we had experienced kashrut observance within Messianic Jewish communities over the last few decades. We noted that the most common practice is refraining from pork and shellfish.

We were very familiar with the common description of Messianic Jewish kashrut practice as keeping "biblically kosher." While we understood that the phrase is intended to mean keeping the commands of the Torah, not rabbinic law, we found some problems with the phrase "biblically kosher." For example, those who use this phrase generally do not restrict themselves to eating only certified kosher meat. This means there is no way of knowing if the blood of the slaughtered animal has been properly eliminated as the Torah requires. There is, therefore, a question as to whether the person really is keeping kosher according to the Scriptures. In addition, the phrase "biblically kosher" does not formally exist in the wider Jewish community. Therefore, use of the phrase does not provide an occasion of commonality and connection when relating to non-Messianic Jews. We found that it actually creates more of a distance. For these reasons, we decided to discourage the use of the phrase "biblically kosher" in our congregation. Instead, we prefer to speak of our practice in terms of "our kashrut standards."

Our Vision

After going through this process, we were in a position to formulate our vision. The first point of the vision for our kitchen is to be faithful to Scripture. As a Messianic Jewish congregation, it was a "no brainer" that we would honor the plain meaning of what the Torah teaches on the subject. We would certainly not have any unclean meat (pork, shellfish, etc.) within our facility. Even if there is "freedom" for us to eat unclean meat, we did not see how such a practice within our congregation would honor the Torah and the role it has played in the life of our people historically, support our identity as Jews, and illuminate Messiah Yeshua's true identity among our Jewish visitors. We also faced the question of having meat in general in our facility. In our area, there are only a very few places within a very large radius where one can buy kosher meat. Therefore, we decided that having only kosher meat in our facility was not feasible. Thus, we next faced the question of whether to accept meat that is not certified kosher within our facility. In the end, we decided that the foolproof way to support this point of our vision—faithfulness to Scripture—was to eliminate meat from the equation altogether.

The second point of our vision is that our kashrut practice enrich our relationship with the Lord through Messiah Yeshua. We determined that in the course of our practice, we would continually ask how it points us to Messiah, and what it speaks to our heart. We decided that a kashrut standard such as the one we chose would continually remind us that preparing and eating food is a holy enterprise. This is truly the physical sustenance for us provided by the Lord. When we make a distinction between what we eat and don't eat, it reminds us of God's holiness. We are reminded that it is through Yeshua that God counts us as holy. We also decided that keeping a clear and common standard would bind us together more deeply as a community. It would entail more learning together, more communication and organization, more discussion, and more thought. It would provide opportunities to show deference to one another, to lovingly and kindly work through any misunderstandings that may arise, and therefore promote unity among us. We envisioned our practice as providing an opportunity for us to grow in Messiah-likeness in a general sense.

The third point of our vision for our kitchen is to engage and foster respect for Jewish tradition. We seek to serve God from the heart in a way that draws upon and is conversant with historic Jewish practice in the area of kashrut. We concluded that a positive orientation toward traditional practice in this area would establish a point of commonality between our community, non-Messianic Jewish congregations, family members, friends, and visitors. We believed this would increase the integrity of our claim to be a Messianic Jewish community. We did not see it as something we felt we needed to "prove" to ourselves or to anyone else. We simply viewed it as an opportunity to be a Jewish expression of faith in Yeshua in the day and time in which we live and in a substantive manner.

Outcome

We have always sought to communicate the vision of and the "heart behind" the kashrut standards we have chosen for our kitchen. At the same time, I do not think we have ever placed undue focus on our kitchen. As a result, over the past four years, I have never received one complaint from anyone related to our congregation, even though the vast majority of people in our congregation do not hold to the same kashrut standards in their own homes. Once in four years I recall a visitor bringing a meat dish to the congregation and this was handled in such a way that there was immediate understanding and no offense on either side. We have found that our kashrut standards have sparked important conversations with non-Jewish Yeshua-believing visitors concerning the Jewish roots of faith in Yeshua and have given us opportunity to promote understanding of kashrut and Judaism in general.

Out of the hundreds of non-Messianic Jewish visitors who have come through our doors, I have never encountered one of them being surprised or put-off by our practice. In fact, I have found that our Jewish visitors, no matter what their level of observance, generally expect that we would have outlined kashrut standards. Our standards seem to engender in our visitors a deep level of connection, even a feeling of coming home. Perhaps one of the reasons that our kashrut standards seem odd or especially stringent among some of our own is because we Messianic Jews are so entrenched in defining kashrut in our own "Messianic" way.

Every time we *kasher* our kitchen, it is a deeply impactful spiritual experience for those who participate. Some may find it ironic that my wife Rachael generally opens the process by reading Mark 7:14-23. After that, prayer and discussion ensue based on Yeshua's teaching there: What is going into our heart? What is coming out? After that, the *kashering* process then serves as a reminder to those involved of the defilement that can so easily seep into our lives over time, the necessity and often difficult work of walking in repentance, and the assurance of forgiveness through Yeshua.

CONCLUSION

Through these reflections, I have sought to provide a window into the way I think about the question at hand practically and pastorally, and how we approach the question of the role of Torah and Jewish tradition at Congregation Sha'arei Shalom. I envision these reflections as more of a beginning of a discussion than an end. I hope something here has sparked some inspiring thoughts and ideas in our own respective contexts so that we might continue to learn and mature as a Messianic Jewish community.

APPENDIX

Our Kitchen Guidelines[25]

A. A Non-Meat Kitchen

Our kitchen is a non-meat kitchen. Only dairy and pareve items are permitted in our kitchen. This includes individuals' meals brought to the building (such as by staff or volunteers). The kitchen may not be used by anyone, including a caterer, for meat or poultry products. The refrigerator may be used to store perishable dairy or pareve items only.

B. No Foods with Non-Kosher Ingredients

Foods that contain non-kosher ingredients may not be served at Sha'arei.

C. Fish

Kosher fish is considered pareve and may be prepared in, and served at, Sha'arei. Only fish that has both fins and scales is considered kosher. Shellfish is not kosher. If there is a question as to whether a particular fish is kosher, we recommend the following website: http://www.crcweb.org/kosher/consumer/fishList.html.

D. Cheese

All cheeses are permitted unless there is an obvious addition of a non-kosher substance added to the cheese. Animal rennet is often included in cheese and this is not acceptable. However, cheeses with vegetable rennet are increasingly popular and are acceptable.

E. Bagels

We consider purchased bagels (such as from New York Bagels or Brueggers Bagels) to be pareve. Bagels may, therefore, be served on Sha'arei platters.

F. Packaged Foods Brought to Sha'arei

Packaged foods brought to Sha'arei must be marked with a *hechsher* – a little symbol by an agency that certifies the product is kosher. The most common of these is the Orthodox Union symbol, which is a U inside of a circle. There are many other kosher certification symbols. If you would like to familiarize yourself with the most common symbols, we recommend the following website: http://www.yrm.org/koshersymbols.htm.

G. Preparation of Foods Outside of Sha'arei's Kitchen

We do not limit the type of kitchens in which non-packaged foods brought into Sha'arei are prepared. When preparing foods at home for Sha'arei events, members are expected to make sure that the food contains no non-kosher ingredients (such as lard, shellfish extracts, etc). If one is preparing a dish from a box (such as brownies), it is strongly encouraged that the package have a *hechsher* symbol (see above III.F.).

H. Prepared Foods Brought into Sha'arei

Prepared food brought to Sha'arei should remain on the owner's dish (on which it is brought to Sha'arei). If it is necessary to place the food on a platter, then a paper/disposal platter should be used.

I. Sha'arei Platters

Only foods that come directly out of packages bearing a *hechsher* may be placed on Sha'arei platters. Prepared foods should not be placed on Sha'arei platters.

J. Snacks for Classrooms and Nursery

Only pareve snacks should be served to the children, and they should be served on paper goods. Packaged snacks must come from packages marked with a *hechsher* symbol.

K. Personal Dishes

People who bring dishes for oneg must bring their dishes home without washing them.

L. Passover

During the week of Passover, in addition to the above-mentioned guidelines, foods classified as *chametz* (leaven), and all products containing *chametz*, are not permitted at Sha'arei Shalom. We are in the process of drafting guidelines for Passover.

M. Cleaning Products

All cleaning products in the kitchen should be marked with a kosher certification symbol. Sha'arei Shalom's preferred line of cleaning products is Seventh Generation.

N. Avoid Common Pitfalls

Animal rennet, sometimes found in cheeses, and gelatin, sometimes found in packaged products, are not kosher and to be avoided.

O. Periodic Kashering of the Kitchen

The kitchen will be kashered periodically throughout the year, and definitely in preparation for Passover. We are in the process of standardizing the kashering procedures.

ENDNOTES

1. Gen 15:6. Unless otherwise noted, all scriptural translations are from the English Standard Version.
2. Heb 11:6.
3. Isa 64:6; Rom 3:20, 28; Gal 2:16.
4. Eph 2:8-9.
5. Heb 1:2.
6. John 3:16; 2 Tim 1:9.
7. Acts 15:11; Rom 3:21-26; 10:11-13; Gal 3:27-29.
8. Matt 5:17.
9. Rom 10:4.
10. Luke 24:46-47.
11. Matt 5:21-48.
12. Exod 20:14.
13. See Acts 15:1-35.
14. Acts 15:20.
15. Rom 7:7-8.
16. Gal 3:24.
17. Acts 21:21.
18. See Acts 21:17-26.
19. Shaul writes glowingly about the Torah in Rom 7:12, 14, 22; 1 Tim 1:8.
20. For example, 1 Cor 9:20-21.
21. Lev 23:40.
22. It is, however, open to interpretation whether the intent is that all seven days of rejoicing include the taking up of the four species.
23. Incidentally, there are also non-messianic Jewish congregations that do wave the lulav and etrog on Shabbat.
24. For a fuller version of our guidelines, see Appendix.
25. The following policy has helped us in formulating our own: http://www.chkehillah.org/kashrut_policy.htm.

WHAT IS OUR RELATIONSHIP WITH THE WIDER JEWISH COMMUNITY?

Tuvya Zaretsky, Th.D.
One of the founders of the Jews for Jesus Ministry,
Director of Staff Development internally,
Chairs the Board for the Jews for Jesus branch in Tel Aviv, Israel

"What is our relationship with the wider Jewish community?" The plural pronoun in that sentence, "our" is understood as referring to the Messianic Jewish community. In my view that is a bit like asking the proverbial fish, "How does it feel to swim in water?" Organizational anthropologist Caroline Turner observed, "The fish is so IN the water that he can't *see* it or describe it. It's all he or she knows; the fish doesn't know there is anything else."[1] We are, after all, members of the same tribe—that wider Jewish community. So, if our belief in Messiah Yeshua is true, then our voice is needed within twenty-first century Jewry.

All culture is composed of things that we learn. At descending levels of meaning those are behaviors, authority standards, the accumulation of personal experiences, and eventually the core beliefs that order our world. My cultural perception says, I am Jewish and I am of the Jewish community. Like the fish in the water, Jewish culture has had a major role in defining my perception of the world. As such, I see Messianic Jews as one facet of world Jewry whether here in the US, in other Diaspora regions, or in Israel. We are of the Jewish community.

Jewish history and studies of developments in Jewish religious thought present a surprisingly diverse gallery of portraits depicting "who is a Jew."[2] Jewish cultures have been shaped by a multitude of historical, biblical, and trans-national experiences. So, we should expect that Messianic *Jewish* identity would be just as diversified and no less an aspect of world Jewry.

I grew up in California in a post-World War II, post-Holocaust Jewish experience. That included immigrant grandparents, personal encounters with anti-Semitism, a synagogue community, assimilationist tendencies, and an anti-Christian secularist outlook. It was a pretty plain vanilla, baby boomer, Jewish experience. Like the fish in water, I was just part of the American Jewish community.

After coming to faith in Yeshua in my early 20s, I wondered how I would deal with Jewish attitudes towards the "J-word"—attitudes that I had expressed before coming to faith. Then, it occurred to me that if other Jewish people knew what I had learned about Yeshua, they would embrace Him too. So, Yeshua-phobia by some in the wider Jewish community had to be culturally acquired. If an argument is to be engaged, it is not with me or with you—with our Jewishness or biblical scholarship—but with the Messiah Yeshua. HE is the issue that rocks the survival instinct in contemporary Jewry.

The next generations of Messianic Jews are growing up in a very different cultural environment. The American Jewish Diaspora is now characterized by intermarriage, secularism, disaffiliation, and religious ambiguity where discussion about God is a real source of embarrassment.[3] Our children, who share faith in Yeshua, will define their Jewish identity according to their own experience. They, like the majority of American Jewry, will likely grow up in Jewish-Gentile families. They find broad-spectrum Jewish culture to be more comfortable, with greater vagueness about religious practices and more emphasis on finding meaning. They are discovering their messianic identity as part of a new American Jewish community.

We might ask, "What is the wider Jewish community's relationship to us—as Messianic Jews?" No doubt, there are Jewish community activists and religious stakeholders in the institutions of American Judaism who prefer to set boundaries for Jewishness in such a way as to exclude Messianic Jews.

Southern California conservative pundit, talk show host, and Jewish educator, Dennis Prager, has spoken out against Messianic Jews for a long time.[4] His declared aim is to divide and conquer Messianic Jews.[5] He wrote, "We have labeled them as a cult and fought their methods of luring Jews to Christianity. We have denied that even Jews-for-Jesus born Jewish are Jews. We have, for all intents and purposes, put them in *cherem* (excommunication). I have long subscribed to this approach." Still, he acknowledged, "They are also not disappearing and our unrelenting war against them has not been particularly successful."[6]

Jewish opinion leaders, like Prager, appear to speak with malicious intent. I think, more often they are motivated by fear—an instinct for Jewish survival that we understand and share. Their understanding of "Who is a Jew?" can be inconsistent and self-serving.[7] I suggest we listen to their arguments for the sake of engagement while rejecting Prager's right, or anyone else's, to judge or nullify Jewish identity.

No one has the right to "validate" your or my Jewish identity. I was born a Jew and I'll die a Jew. No pronouncement or symbolic action of a *beth din* (religious court of Judaism) will ever change that. Only God adequately defines who is a Jew or the Jewish community.

The Apostle Paul rightly said that not even every physical Jew is a Jew in God's reckoning.[8] I suggest that we embrace the biblical theology of a remnant [Hebrew *she'arit*]. The Lord is calling to Himself a faithful remnant from every nation, including our Jewish people.[9] That provides a new perspective of the "wider Jewish community."

We have a different basis for defining Messianic Jews. Only God sets the norms for "authentic" and "valid" Jewish identity. In my view, wider Jewish community opinion leaders misappropriate the right allocated to God alone for validating who is within or outside of the boundaries of Jewish identity.

Therefore, the Messianic Jewish community is already one unique facet of the wider Jewish community. With all of our diverse cultural expressions, Jews are an internationally scattered, multicultural people. Jewishness cannot be defined in ethnocentric terms like *Yiddish-keit* without denying *Sepahardi* or *Mizrachi* cultures. Modern Judaisms do not even properly define Jewishness when the majority of world Jewry is secular or moderately traditional.

Our Messianic faith is the untold Jewish perspective. A rich multidimensional contemporary Jewry is portrayed with surprising variety in a collection of essays titled, *I am Jewish: Personal Reflections Inspired by the Last Words of Daniel Pearl.*[10] It offers complex cultural reflections on identity, heritage, covenant, ethnicity, and purpose. If you are Jewish, you see elements of yourself in the lives of others. Yet, that collection needs at least one more essay—from a Messianic Jew. To use the metaphor one last time: we are many fish in one tank of water.

I am Jewish. We are of the wider Jewish community. And the Messianic perspective has a critical message for the wider Jewish community, which does not regard our Jewishness, but rather our claim that the Messiah has come and He is Yeshua. They need to know that

God has said, through His Son, "I Am the way, the truth and the life. No one comes to the Father but through Me."[11]

I want to conclude with an encouraging observation by Israeli scholar Yaakov Ariel.[12] Ariel is an assistant professor of Religious Studies at the University of North Carolina at Chapel Hill. He is not a Messianic Jew. However, he carefully researched spiritual developments in the American Jewish community and in particular Christian mission efforts that have been in practice among them. His report is fair-minded and may be surprising at some points.

Ariel observed, regarding the modern Jewish mission movement, "For the first time in American Jewish history, propagation of the Christian gospel among Jews proved successful and captured the souls of tens of thousands of young Jews."[13] And of the messianic congregational movement he said, "These congregations proved to be effective in evangelizing Jews, as they demonstrated both the spiritual and communal merits of the Christian evangelical faith and were particularly compelling for those Jews who wished to retain their Jewish identity and continued to identify with Jewish causes."[14] Yaakov Ariel recognizes Messianic Jews as part of the diversity in American Jewish communal life and, in fact, also in Israel. Not only that, he sees positive and effective methodologies that are making the Gospel known to Jewish people.

Messianic Jewry is already in relationship to the wider Jewish community. That is already an existential reality. The question is not about Jewish identity or the authenticity of Messianic Jewish culture. The wider Jewish community needs more experience from a uniquely messianic spirituality, expressed as a relationship with the God of Israel and found in Yeshua.

I believe that the Messianic Jewish component of the wider Jewish community ought to be serving our own people. In my view, the most substantial contribution that can be made is by communicating the Messiahship of Yeshua. That needs to be done in a manner whereby the audience can hear the message and perhaps investigate it further if they choose. There are lots of methods by which to do that. And it is compelling to consider implications of a wider Jewish community that understands the uniqueness of Messianic Jewry.

ENDNOTES

1. Caroline Turner, "Organizational Culture as the 'Water' We Fish Swim In: What's the 'Water' Like in There?" last modified October 27, 2010, www. http://difference-works.com.
2. Some references: H.H. Ben-Sasson. *A History of the Jewish People,* (Cambridge: Harvard University Press, 1976); Cohen, A. Arthur and Paul Mendes-Flohr. *20th Century Jewish Religious Thought,* (Philadelphia: Jewish Publication Society, 2009); Fishman, Sylvia B. *The Way into the Varieties of Jewishness,* (Woodstock VT: Jewish Lights Publishing, 2007); Johnson, Paul. *A History of the Jews,* (New York: Harper & Row, 1987).
3. See for example Schiffman, Lisa. *Generation J* (NY: Harper Collins, 2000).
4. Denis Prager, "Is the Such a Thing as "Jews for Jesus?" in *Ultimate Issues*, Oct.-Dec. Vol. 5:4, 1989.
5. Dennis Prager, "A New Approach to Jews-for-Jesus," June 2000.
6. Ibid.
7. For a thoughtful essay see "Who is a Jew – Questions of Religion, Ethnicity and Identity" by Michael L. Brown, at http://realmessiah.com/read/who_is_a_jew
8. Romans 2:28-29.
9. Isaiah 10:20-22; Romans 9:27 and 11:5.
10. Judea and Ruth Pearl, ed., *I am Jewish,* (Woodstock, VT: Jewish Life Publishing, 2004).
11. John 14:6.
12. Ariel, Yaakov. *Evangelizing the Chosen People: Missions to the Jews in America,* 1880-2000 (Chapel Hill: University of North Carolina Press, 2000)
13. Ibid., 211.
14. Ibid., 243.

OUR RELATIONSHIP AS MESSIANIC JEWS WITH THE WIDER JEWISH COMMUNITY FROM MY PERSPECTIVE

Diane Cohen
President of Congregation Ruach Israel in Needham, Mass.,
UMJC Camp Director

I am a Jewish woman, born Jewish, all Jewish ancestors, married to a Jewish man. I can't speak from any other perspective and I do not discount any other approach. I can only speak to what I know based on my personal experiences.

Having served as president of Congregation Ruach Israel in Needham, Massachusetts, for the past 6 years, I have had the privilege of being able to interface with leaders of the Boston Jewish community as an ambassador on behalf of Messianic Judaism. At this point in the road, I would say the journey has been two steps forward and one step back on the subject of advancement of understanding by these Jewish leaders—at least in the Boston area—of who we are and what we are about. I have had much more success on a one-on-one basis in dialoguing with Jews in non-Jewish community leadership positions regarding their understanding Messianic Judaism as a denomination of Judaism rather than it being a form of Christianity. I have experienced over the last eleven years, since the time I first became a believer in Yeshua, what I perceive as a softening of the hearts of our Jewish brethren, a work I believe is of HaShem and one which makes my role increasingly easier, and encouraging.

Many of you may have heard about the concert that occurred at our synagogue several years ago. When I had the idea to invite a mainstream Jewish band to perform, it probably was very naïve of me since I did not anticipate the extreme negative reaction this seemingly simple plan would generate in the wider Jewish community in Boston. In a way, my being somewhat of a new "believer" is a blessing. I just ask and talk and don't have much defensiveness or fear of the consequences that would temper such requests from someone more experienced in our movement. Even though I'm no longer a newbie, my innocence has been replaced with a strident voice against the injustice we often experience as Messianic Jews and motivates me to continue my goal of educating the Jewish community about Messianic Judaism. The reasons for this are several, as will be developed in this paper.

When I contacted the band, I was very direct with them that our synagogue is Messianic Jewish and sent them the link to our website. Although I didn't think it would be a showstopper (as it literally almost was), I did know we were controversial. From the time of their acceptance of our offer until about a month before the concert, there were some adverse reactions in the Jewish community, including the band's manager quitting, but nothing too difficult for either the band or me to handle. However, once we began to publicize the concert, the band's fan base, which is primarily Orthodox, became very vocal.

Local Jewish colleges and universities as well as the local Jewish community center and local synagogues had not hesitated to put up our flyers advertising the upcoming concert. Another obvious place to advertise was in Brookline, the heart of the Boston Orthodox Jewish community where most of the band's local fan base lives. One of the local merchants there had already allowed our concert flyer to be posted. I went to another popular shop and as I looked at the bulletin board there, I noticed that there were postings by secular organizations. I asked the sales person if I could put up our ad for the concert. The flyer on its face did not designate us as Messianic.

A short time later, a posting appeared on a Jewish Boston listserve that seemed to be a posting by that shop, although we later learned that it was by an individual and not authorized by the store. The post was very condemning of Messianic Judaism and stated that the concert was obviously a sham since there is no way the band would ever do a concert at our synagogue. The post stated, "These organizations use very deceptive tactics to attract our fellow Jews into their lairs."

Needless to say I was horrified. I went to the office of one of the Jewish attorneys I work with who I thought might help me get to the bottom of this. He helped me get onto the Jewish Boston listserve where I posted the following:

> First, let me fully disclose that I am a Messianic Jew. I am president of Ruach Israel and I put up the band concert advertisement at the shop last week. I did so with the permission of the person who was working at the counter. I showed her the ad and she helped me put it up. I had noticed there was an ad for an event at a hardware store so I concluded that the location for the ad was not just for religious organizations.
>
> In fairness to the salesperson, we did not discuss the type of synagogue that was hosting the concert. Since it is not a religious service, but rather, is a concert, the religious denomination of the venue is not relevant to the ad. I don't see many concert ads at synagogues that start with "Temple Whatever, a Conservative shul, is having a concert." However, I apologize for any embarrassment this may have caused the shop. They absolutely did not know that Ruach Israel is a Messianic synagogue when they helped me post the ad.
>
> As for the band, I informed them up front who we are, that we are a Messianic synagogue, and what we believe. They rightly are not interested in our religious beliefs since, after all, we are having a concert, not a service.
>
> I do take issue with the statement, "These organizations use very deceptive tactics to attract our fellow Jews into their lairs." I'm just a Jew observing my faith; may you be well as you do so too.
>
> Diane Cohen
> President, Ruach Israel

The Jewish attorney I work with came into my office to discuss this whole situation. He explained to me that the original posting was not actually by the shop and he and others were embarrassed by it. He and I had some of our first very meaningful discussions about Messianic Judaism at that time. And because my colleague is very involved in that community, he has shared these insights with many others there as well. I realized that concert or no concert, important dialogue was now stirring within the Orthodox Jewish community about Messianic Judaism. Rumors and stereotypes were being dispelled. However, it was not an easy time generally. Below are excerpts of interactions on the listserve:

> Diane,
> Your belief that Jesus is the Messiah is completely antithetical to Judaism. Calling yourself a "Jew" is indeed deceptive.
>
> Richard

> Richard,
> I respect your opinion and you are indeed entitled to it. It might be hard to convince my four Jewish grandparents, my two Jewish parents, including my mother, of course, and my Jewish husband and children that we're somehow not Jewish. And each day as I pray Shachrit and each Shabbat at services, especially during the Torah portion, it's pretty hard to not feel like I'm Jewish. I believe volumes have been written on what it means to be Jewish and I don't believe faith in Yeshua as the Messiah is a definitional standard.
>
> Diane

> Diane,
> You mean it must be devestating for your four Jewish grandparents, two Jewish parents and the rest of the Jewish people that you've gotten yourself wrapped up in a cult. Do you really not suspect in any way that the superficial observance of Jewish law might be a desceptive ploy to get Jews such as yourself to buy into Christianity?
>
> Richard

> Sorry Richard. We'll just have to agree to disagree.
>
> Diane

> Diane,
> In that case, perhaps it would be worthwhile for you to check out http://jewsforjudaism.org/. Unless of course you're afraid of what you may find out.
>
> Richard
>
> Thanks, Richard. I am familiar with that website. I look forward to a day when we Jews can be respectful of each other's differences and truly be able to work together to address issues we face that are the real threats to our Judaism.
>
> I appreciate your passion and I know your heart is with Adonai, our one and only G-d.
>
> Shalom,
> Diane

I received other negative e-mails and learned firsthand what many of you already know—that many in the Orthodox community have very negative impressions of Messianic Jews, to quote them, "We are wolves in sheep's clothing trying to steal Jews" and we're "luring Jews into churches to get them to worship Jesus" and into becoming Christians. There's no middle ground in this thinking—a Messianic Jew is not a Jew; he or she is a Christian using deception to brainwash Jews away from their Judaism.

With that thinking as a backdrop, and the band receiving even more hate mail than me, it wasn't surprising that I received the inevitable message from the band's leader on Thanksgiving weekend that year, just a couple weeks before the scheduled concert, informing me that the band would have to cancel. I wrote to him the following:

> I understand completely your feelings. Yesterday was an amazing day for me as well.
>
> For the first time, I learned about this controversy. There is a Jewish list-serve in Boston that apparently had received a letter stating that someone had put up an ad about the concert and it was written in a very unflattering way with lies about us and horrible accusations. This was brought to our rabbi's attention by one of our congregants.

> I joined the list-serve group so that I could respond and clear the air. The result was very strident interchange from just one writer, actually, and requests from others for how to get tickets. I would not want you to do anything to jeopardize your livelihood. And I understand that there are some in the Orthodox Jewish community that have very strong feelings about this. However, playing a concert is not supporting a theology; it is just playing a concert.
>
> I would urge you to reconsider. I would never expect an Orthodox rabbi to agree with our beliefs. And I respect their beliefs, as I do Reform Jews, Conservative, etc. The air of intolerance is actually what I find it harder to agree with, and the air of uninformed judgment and condemnation as well.
>
> Due to the controversy, you received free advertising in that the list-serve readers were made aware of the concert. In addition, earlier this week, all of the local Reform and Conservative synagogues asked for flyers for your concert. I don't know if you really want a vocal minority to be the last word on your decision.
>
> And in fairness, I can't guarantee what will happen. But this much I know: intolerance is not a part of anyone's religion.
>
> I will await your final thoughts on this very sad situation.
>
> Diane

The result was that the band's leader called me and we discussed the issue at length. He was frankly shocked that I "turned the other cheek" instead of threatening to sue him (a thought which never crossed my mind, of course). We discussed theology. His and his rabbi's issues concerned the resolution of these two questions: first, since the New Testament contradicts the Old Testament (his words), does the NT supersede the OT in importance? And what is the rank of Torah in importance? I explained to him that we look at the New Testament as a continuation of the Old Testament and we look at Yeshua as the living

Torah. We discussed the many passages of the NT that are interpreted as anti-Semitic and contradictory. It was a fascinating discussion. I explained to him our understanding of Isaiah 53. He probed whether we pray to Jesus as Lord (his words). I told him we do not pray to Jesus/Yeshua as separate from God, that HaShem includes Yeshua as part of Himself. I discussed how God somehow put Himself physically on earth to live with us for a while and somehow in a way we can't truly comprehend, Yeshua is God. We discussed the trinity (his words). He shared stories of studying Yeshua in school. It was a great conversation.

Afterwards, he and his rabbi studied Ruach Israel's website (for an hour!). At the end of the day, they concluded the band could do the concert at our synagogue, which in my opinion, was a pivotal moment in Messianic Jewish and mainstream Jewish relations, a day which brought the Jewish community suffering from such a schism over millennia together for an evening of music by a band of great courage and integrity, one which would even jeopardize its own financial wellbeing in order to do the right thing. Men of God. A quote from my journal:

> One by one they came through the door, and finally the band's leader. We hugged and smiled. I asked him if things had calmed down a bit with the complaints, and he said, "I was taught that if you're about to do something really good, oftentimes really bad things come at you, evil to pull you away from the good. Every time I get another one of those complaints, I know even more that what I'm about to do is really good."
>
> The concert was amazing beyond words. The musicians' hearts for kindness, their understanding that love is what brings down the barriers, rang out in words and song.

The concert generated front-page coverage in one of the largest Jewish newspapers in circulation and featured interviews of the band's leader and me. Although the story was not unbiased, the fact that the concert had occurred and that so many Jewish organizations allowed advertising was definitely a step forward in normalizing our relationship with the greater Jewish community. It was a breakthrough in the process.

The concert experience presents a microcosm of the issue, that is, mainstream Judaism generally does not consider Messianic Judaism as a part of Judaism. There can be Jew-Bhus, secular Jews, even Humanistic Jews who may not even believe in God, but these fellow Jews would still be part of the Jewish family and welcome in the local community *mikvah* (where we are not). We Messianic Jews, however, have somehow crossed the religious identity barrier by our embracing of Yeshua, and therefore, have become Christians. So you may ask, so what? After all, the Church has been our brother in this walk and integrally a part of our identity, our nurturing partner to whom in many ways through its support we owe our very existence today.

From my perspective as a Jewish woman who came to know Yeshua after many years of being a part of the Jewish community, the answer is obvious. I am Jewish. I did not convert to Christianity just because I came to a fuller understanding of the Messiahship of Yeshua. Judaism is our common ground. By normalizing the relationship between Messianic Judaism and mainstream Judaism, I, and other Messianic Jews like me, have the ability to dialogue with Jews about our religious beliefs. Our disagreements about Yeshua become infighting and a discussion we can have without threat of assimilation. And as we have these amazing discussions, hearts are softening, minds are opening, and dialogue is occurring, which otherwise would not be possible. As I talk to other Jews, I retain my Jewish identity, which overcomes the barrier they may otherwise feel by discussing the subject of Yeshua. We discuss Him as fellow Jews.

My experience with the Jewish community has been quite different depending on whether I am dealing with the gatekeepers or the lay people. I sometimes analogize this to how it must have been in the time of Yeshua, i.e., His experiencing very different treatment from the Jewish leadership as compared to the Jewish people, generally. Although I continue to have meetings with Jewish leaders, the ability for our synagogue to advertise in Jewish media, for example, has been very limited. When we have had successes in that area, they don't last long as most likely negative feedback from Jewish readers forces those with whom I've interfaced to remove our listings.

On the other hand, Ruach Israel has been a regular supporter of our regional Jewish music festival without repercussion. This result started with my contacting the organizers who initially had many questions about the usual reservations and us. I had decided to contact the organizer based on a quote on their website about the diversity of

Judaism. I called him to probe this point and ask whether Ruach Israel could participate as a supporter of the festival as a synagogue. This suggestion really stretched the fellow's thinking, but as we talked, he couldn't help but hear the merits of the argument, i.e., what does diversity really mean? At this point I was much more savvy about consequences so I warned him that if they accepted us, our meager $500 donation would be nothing compared to the potential loss of big Jewish donors and Jewish organizations that may be offended by our participation. Nevertheless, he was a man of integrity and took us on. We are now in year three of this relationship and he and I continue to dialogue.

Similarly, I have participated in a local Jewish college seminar discussing the plight of Messianic Jews vis-à-vis discrimination at the hands of their own people. I find the raising of this awareness in Jewish circles has been met with great openness and often the same surprise that I first experienced, i.e., how can Jews known for their acceptance of diversity be so judgmental of Messianic Judaism? Again, the rank-and-file Jew rather than Jewish leadership is much more open to this dialogue.

As suggested, one might ask why such connections with mainstream Judaism are so important, despite the obvious one of the ability to educate others about who we are. It's not about acceptance. It's about normalization. Messianic Jews are Jews. At this point in the history of our movement, we are fortunate to be able to reclaim this truth and to be able to live it out in synagogues such as Ruach Israel, and others. By the normalization of Messianic Judaism within mainstream Judaism, over time the result should be more Jews coming to faith in Yeshua since there is more day-to-day opportunity for dialogue on the subject. As hard as this may be for the reader to believe, in my experience, most Jews still believe Jesus/Yeshua started a new religion, i.e., Christianity, even if He at one point was Jewish. Add to that 2,000 years of anti-Semitism. The result is a huge emotional barrier—called "fear" (of assimilation and persecution)—that prevents most mainstream Jews from possibly considering Yeshua, and Messianic Judaism, as part of Judaism, let alone Yeshua as part of the Godhead. On the other hand, once the relationship between mainstream Judaism and Messianic Judaism is normalized, the emotional wall that prevents the majority of Jews (in my experience) from even discussing Yeshua will come down. After that, it is just a matter of time before hearts are softened and beliefs are changed.

I know that in the late '60s and early '70s many Jews came to faith in Yeshua. It must have been a powerfully moving time to be in our movement. Today, at least from my perspective, it seems it's one person at a time, more from the ground up than from the top down. But there is movement. And times, they are a changin'! Last spring, JewishReviewofBooks.com did a review of three books about Yeshua in an article entitled "What a Friend We Have in Jesus," which included reviews of some New Testaments as well as Rabbi Boteach's *Kosher Jesus*. And what about *The Jewish Gospels* by Daniel Boyarin? Are these writings in agreement with us on the theology? Some in part and some not at all. But get Jews talking about Yeshua as a starting point instead of fear of the entire subject, well, that's a good start in my opinion. We crawled before we walked before we ran.

Another good example of the power of normalization is the Messianic Jewish teen summer camp we hold at one of the oldest mainstream Jewish camps in the U.S. Several summers ago we approached that organization about hosting our Camp Or L'Dor at their facility. The looks on the faces of the mainstream Jewish camp leaders were amazing, like not positive! However, we were able to spend an entire day there to meet the rabbi, the camp director, various staff, and talk, and talk, and talk, and listen as well. There is no doubt, at least in my experiences with the camp personnel as well as with the Jewish community generally, that their main perception of Messianic Jews was that we are judgmental of them if they don't believe in Jesus and that we no longer follow Torah. Many of them were unfamiliar with the existence of Messianic Jewish synagogues, or ones with Jewish-type services, but rather, they assumed we now go to churches. I listened to their experiences with Messianic Jews and they listened to my description of Messianic Judaism. Thankfully we were given the opportunity for them to let us come and try it, i.e., to hold our camp there at the same time that they would be running their regular camp for the several hundred Jewish campers also there during the same week. There is no question in my mind that if we were not able to interface with them in a way consistent with traditional Jewish practices, we would not have had the opportunity to utilize those facilities. Thankfully, the vision of our particular camp fits well with a traditional Jewish camp. And as you will see, we did not hide our belief in Yeshua.

We just completed our third summer there and all I can say is that they can't wait to have us back. We have formed deep and meaningful relationships with the camp rabbi and staff. They have attended our Messianic Jewish services and continue to tell us how beautiful they are. They have had our rabbi co-lead services with their rabbi for all the campers, theirs and ours. We have led music and dance for their campers. We have had countless opportunities to share our testimonies with so many people. I arrived this year and our camp liaison, a Jewish former camper, greeted me with, "We're so glad you're here! I can't wait for you to tell your story to Sam. He's interested in discussing Messianic Judaism with you."

It's not always wonderful. But even the challenges are encouraging. The camp director was telling me how he handled parents who were upset that we were allowed to be at the camp. The director explained to them more about us and now the complaining parents no longer complain. As he so wisely told us, "Conversation leads to understanding." Some suggested approaches:

> BE YOURSELF: I am wired to fight injustice. I was a child of the '60s and find that mainstream Jewish prejudice against Messianic Jews offends me. It inspires me to be very direct about who I am and what I believe. I invite dialogue that challenges the listener to recognize hypocrisy: "You're a Jew, a liberal minded person open to diversity, and yet you discriminate against your own people."
>
> BUILD RELATIONSHIPS: I work with a good number of Jewish colleagues at my office. Just by working side-by-side with them over the past 7 years, they have come to know me, to trust me, and to respect me. I have amazing conversations with them about Messianic Judaism, which has only happened due to those deep relationships. I have shared Isaiah 53 at work in a natural way that happens because we work so closely together. At work it is not unusual at this point for colleagues to ask ME about my beliefs, they want to know. I can't help but think that HaShem is greatly at work in their hearts.

BE PATIENT: For many of you, it has been decades of work. And I do believe that something extraordinary occurred in the late '60s and early '70s that caused a supernatural surge in Jewish believers. Today, they are breaking barriers, increasing awareness, softening hearts, and setting the stage for HaShem's mighty hand. In my experience, recently there has been an improvement in some Jewish peoples' understanding of us. It is not unusual for me now to talk with a Jewish person who will actually say, "What is the big deal?" about our being a Messianic synagogue. I've had some Jews be as outraged as I am that we have trouble advertising in mainstream Jewish media. A recent Jewish visitor to our synagogue said she had always been curious about what our services were like. She loved them and said she'd be back. We've had Jewish visitors at Ruach Israel who have commented that our services have something special about them, that they feel the Ruach. I believe we are living in changing times.

PLANT SEEDS: I love how we don't really know how this works, and yet it does. When I first became a believer in Yeshua, I shared my testimony with one of my Jewish colleagues at work who was very shocked. At the time I was also on the board with him at my mainstream Jewish synagogue, so when I "came out of the closet" theologically, words couldn't describe his shock. I moved from Ohio to Boston and we hadn't communicated after that for years. Until he called me several years ago and asked if I could do a workshop on Messianic Judaism for the upcoming National Chavurah Committee meeting that summer. What an opportunity that was to demystify and debunk rumors about Messianic Judaism for Jewish lay leaders and rabbis from all around the country. At the beginning of the workshop the vast majority had stated they would not be comfortable allowing a Messianic Jew to participate in their chavurah. Their opinions were greatly changed by the end of the workshop.

PUSH THE BOUNDARIES: As a lay leader of my synagogue, I love opportunities to reach out to Jewish organizations and let them know who we are and explore how we can interface. I find the more I share the successes we have with some Jewish organizations, the more that other such organizations are encouraged to give us an audience. There is leverage in relating these successes since most do not want to be at the forefront of this issue. After all, this movement is our cause, not theirs. On the other hand, even gatekeepers should be called to task if the boundaries as they are setting them are becoming outdated. Communicating that message is one that I hold dear.

TIKKUN OLAM AND MORE: The more our congregations can do to work with other Jewish organizations to support worthy causes or even socially, the more opportunities our Jewish brothers and sisters will have to understand us. "Conversation leads to understanding." It is the first step, in my opinion, in our Jewish brethren learning about Yeshua and ultimately accepting Him as the cornerstone of our faith. Conversely, our interfacing with the mainstream Jewish community keeps us grounded in who we are. Repairing the world is part of our hard wiring.

The faces of Messianic Judaism are many and I do not doubt there are other worthy perspectives. I can only speak to what I know based on my personal experiences as a Jew. The normalization of Messianic Judaism within the Jewish community will only create that many more opportunities for Messianic Jews and mainstream Jews to interface. Messianic Jews who are able to interact within their Jewish communities as ambassadors of Messianic Judaism have a unique opportunity to educate mainstream Jews about Messianic Judaism. As a result, many Jews today are losing their fear of discussing, and with God's grace, ultimately embracing Yeshua as these opportunities increase through fellowship with their Messianic Jewish brothers and sisters.

WHAT IS OUR RELATIONSHIP WITH THE WIDER JEWISH COMMUNITY?

Oded Shoshani
Pastor of the Hebrew congregation of King of Kings Jerusalem

My name is Oded Shoshani; I was born in Ramat Gan, a suburb of Tel Aviv. Both of my parents were born in Jerusalem as well as the grandparents on my mother's side. I grew up in a secular family that, nonetheless, observed traditional aspects of Judaism such as the kosher food laws.

My parents raised us as Zionists and instilled a love in us for the Land of Israel. My father was wounded in the War of Independence and my mother lost a brother and a sister in the same war. I served in the IDF for three and a half years.

From a young age, the Spirit of God stirred in me a desire to search for the deeper meaning of life, to search for the ultimate goal of why I was alive, to search for perfect love. Immediately following my release from the army, I accepted Yeshua as the Lord of my life. Afterwards I married Sandy, a new immigrant to Israel from the USA. We have been married for over thirty years; we have seven wonderful children that are all walking with the Lord and three grandchildren.

I am a mechanical engineer by profession, and worked for thirteen years as a project engineer in companies that installs plumbing, heating, and air conditioning. In 2002, the Lord began calling me to serve Him in a full time capacity as a congregational leader or Pastor. In January 2004, I was appointed to be the congregational leader of the Hebrew congregation of King of Kings in Jerusalem, a role in which I continue to serve today.

The spoken language of the congregation is Hebrew. We celebrate the Festivals of Israel, we pray for and commit to God all of our youth as they begin their army service, and we have a Sepher Torah that we use for bar and bat mitzvahs. I believe with all my heart that we are seeing the Lord answer the prayers of millennia in the stages of the return of the people of Israel to Eretz Yisrael. In spite of the fact that the State of Israel exists as a sovereign state, we are still in the process of the restoration of the exiles of our people to the Land. I believe that the Lord is not only restoring us to the Land of Israel, but rather that in the Land of Israel, according to ancient promises, He is beginning the process of the pouring out of the Holy Spirit on the people of Israel, the ultimate purpose of which is the salvation of the nations and of the people of Israel.

IDENTITY

In order to be able to discuss the topic, I need to first discuss the issue of our identity. Our identity defines the way we relate to every aspect of life. Identity has several aspects: personal identity (where one grew up, one's immediate family, etc.), social identity, and national identity.

At this Symposium, (and this specific session) we are engaging this subject through the lenses of Messianic Jewish identity. This identity is made up of two parts: Jewish identity and Messianic identity. The two parts have some common and some conflicting values.

Jewish Identity, What Is It?

We could easily spend the rest of our lives until the return of the Messiah dealing with this topic and not arrive at a general agreement because of our diverse answers to this question and the factors that influence our views: traditions, the lands of our Diaspora, different ways and emphases related to Halakic practice, etc.

In any case, we can define some general principles of Jewish identity as identity that is built upon the unique ethnic identity of a group of people that understand their corporate ties to a common ancestor, Abraham, and who share a basic belief in the monotheistic God who revealed his Word in the Tanakh, and who share a spiritual and religious connection with the land of Israel.

Jewish identity has two emphases, one is on the separation from the rest of the nations and the second is the connection of our people with the plot of unique Land called Eretz Yisrael. Throughout our historical existence we have developed very unique identity characteristics:

Characteristics related to our faith (including new bases for theology in order to adapt to the realities of losing our temple, sacrifices, and the priestly service).

Characteristics related to our common social experiences (persecutions, anti-Semitism, and our unique responses to them) and traditions (Jewish humour, specific foods, etc.).

Characteristics related to our history in the Diaspora. A basic part of our Jewish identity has been our yearning and longing for the coming of the Messiah and the restoration of the people of Israel to the Eretz Israel.

Characteristics related to Yeshua. Within this complex of factors are also profoundly negative factors rooted against Yeshua as the Messiah of Israel and against those who represent him, because of the persecutions and the great suffering that has been the lot of our people at the hand of "Christians."

What is Messianic Identity?

Here too, we could spend the rest of our days in an attempt to reach a definition and still not succeed due to the sheer number of streams of Messianic belief that exist: each with differing emphases due to the Reformation and various revivals that have occurred since that time and which have resulted in separation and segregation within the Body of Messiah.

In any case, we can define some basic lines of definition of Messianic identity as an identity that is built upon a general universal basis, in which there is no difference between people and different races. This identity is based upon what Yeshua did on the cross for all humanity. Every believer in Yeshua, whoever they are, is waiting for a new Heaven and Earth in which there will be no sin, death, sickness, or pain, where they can be in the full, unmediated presence of the glory of the eternal God. Believers from all peoples base their righteousness not on commandments and laws, that in themselves cannot save, but upon simple faith in the grace that our Heavenly Father freely gives to all who believe.

Already in these basic definitions we can see the tension between the two identities. In this context of my brief introductory discussion on Jewish and Messianic identity, I want to relate briefly to three texts:

Ephesians 2. This chapter describes what Yeshua has done on the cross in order to remove the enmity between the Jews (circumcision) and God, between the Gentiles (uncircumcised) and God, and between Jewish believers and Gentile believers. This chapter also describes how a way has been opened for us to freely come by the Spirit to the Father, how He has united us as Jewish and Gentile believers to be a holy temple to God with Yeshua as the chief cornerstone. Together with this, the chapter does not abolish the unique ethnic identity and culture of each people, just as the Scripture does not abolish the uniqueness of our gender identities as male and female.

Romans 11. In this chapter, Paul begins by declaring that God has not abandoned his people, the people of Israel. Paul continues by explaining that amongst ethnic Israel there is a faithful remnant (or the elect) that obtained the will of God. The chapter notes how the stumbling of Israel (not of the elect within the people) was a vessel in the hand of God to bring salvation to the Nations. Paul describes the good olive tree, that is the Messiah, and the natural branches, which are the people of Israel, that were cut off from it because of unbelief. Paul continues to describe how the wild olive branches were grafted into the original olive tree, which represents the believers of the Nations, who now take part in the life that comes from the trunk of the tree. The chapter ends with the will of God to restore the original branches, the ethnic people of Israel, those of Jewish descent and identity, according to God's great love and mercy.

Isaiah 11. This chapter describes the Messiah who brings righteousness and world peace, which the Nations seek, the glory that rests upon him, and the restoration of the people of Israel to the Eretz Israel.

As Jews, we are part of the chosen people that carries within it Jewish characteristics, some of which are traditional, such as clothing, food, language, etc. We do well to remember that during the time that we took part in the identity of the people of Israel, we were still broken-off branches and cut off from God. As believers in Yeshua the Messiah, God has chosen us to be restored olive branches that are now re-joined to the trunk. As believers, God has given us one Spirit which we share with our fellow believers from the nations.

The focus of our lives and the centre of our identity has now become the Messiah himself. This focus has to be our central understanding and the means by which we relate to every aspect of our lives: holiness, raising children, marriage, congregational life, and our relationship to the wider Jewish community.

HOW DO I VIEW MY PERSONAL IDENTITY?

Jewish Identity

Despite being born and raised as a Jew in the land of Israel, up until the point that I became a believer in Yeshua, I led a secular life, remote and detached from God. I was both a Jew and an Israeli but my Jewish identity was not clearly defined and was, in many ways, mixed up with my identity as an Israeli. As a secular man, all I wanted to do at that time (up until I became a believer) was to leave Israel for the States for an easier life. This is obviously not my conviction today.

Messianic Identity

After inviting Yeshua into my life, my personal understanding and sense of belonging to the chosen people was brought to fulfilment. I'd arrived at the point that every Jew longs for at the bottom of their heart—that place of knowing God in a personal rather than a religious way. I also experienced (and continue to experience) a sense of belonging and unity with believers from other nations who've invited Yeshua into their hearts to be the Lord of their lives. I do not feel a sense of superiority towards Messianic Gentiles just because I'm part of the people of Israel. In fact, the opposite is true; I feel a great debt and closeness to those who have kept the flame of faith in the Messiah burning for the last 2000 years when my people chose to disengage from Him. I feel a deep sense of gratitude to those of the Gentile nations whose prayers and deeds, hundreds of years before the advent of modern Zionism, made possible the reality that today the people of Israel can live in a sovereign state in Eretz Israel.

Today, as one who celebrates the feasts of the Lord, whose sons have been circumcised, whose children have gone through their bar/bat mitzvahs, I can say that it is through my faith in Yeshua that my identity as a Jew finds its fulfilment.

Israeli Identity

As one born and raised in Israel, in a family that have both fought and paid a high price in the wars of modern Israel, as one educated in the Israeli system both as a Jew and as a Zionist, as one who works and pays taxes to the State of Israel, and as one who has served (and whose children serve) in the Israeli army, I completely see myself as an Israeli.

Because the Jewish people who live in the land of Israel only make up about 40% of the global Jewish community, Jewish Israeli identity is not necessarily one easily understood by Jews of the Diaspora. As an Israeli Jew whose people are a majority in their state, and not a minority, as in the case of the Diaspora, and as one who hasn't experienced anti-Semitism first hand, I feel secure in who I am and don't feel the need to either apologize for or to justify Jewish identity.

Summarising my Identity

In summary, I see myself as a completed Jew because of Yeshua. I see myself as an Israeli Jew who fulfils the age-old hope of faith in the Messiah and of life in a sovereign state in Eretz Israel. I see myself as an active partner in the reforming of the people of Israel in Eretz Israel. There is no anti-Messianic action or declaration that can shatter my sense of security and belonging to the people of Israel and the land of Israel.

OVERVIEW OF THE JEWISH MESSIANIC BODY IN ERETZ ISRAEL

For many years the identity of the Messianic Body in Israel was that of a minority, rejected by the people of Israel. The role played by many non-Jewish organizations in the establishment and growth of the

Messianic Jewish Body of believers in Eretz Israel unwittingly contributed to the sense of estrangement that many of the early Israeli believers felt—in their identity both as Jews and as Israelis.

In the course of the last 30 years there have been several major developments that have changed both the makeup of the State of Israel and, within that, the makeup of the Body of Messianic Jewish believers:

The first of these developments was the large number of immigrants from both the former Soviet Union and Ethiopia who have made Eretz Israel their home.

The second, related, development was the way in which the Israeli State and its inhabitants reacted to these waves of immigration: As a nation we were forced to absorb and receive the newcomers and to provide them with education and employment. This required a willingness to accommodate the "other" and the "different."

The third, also related, factor was the openness amongst these new arrivals to the message of the Gospel.

Another factor is the growing number of children, youth, soldiers and young families who were born into believing families in Eretz Israel and who have chosen to make the faith of their parents their own. In a natural way, the focus of their identity is closer to that of my own simply by virtue of the fact that they were born in the land.

Our children are educated in the Israeli school system and there they are known to come from Messianic Jewish families. Our young men and women are serving in all kinds of army units, and also in the army it is clear that they are part of the Messianic Jewish movement. In many cases the Messianic soldiers reflect a moral and ethical lifestyle that is rare in our culture, and for this they are esteemed. This contributes further to the legitimization of the Jewish Messianic movement in the eyes of the people of Israel. For many of these young people, the sense that they are a part of the re-forming of the people of Israel is an integral part of their identity as believers.

One should not ignore the impact that numerical growth has had on the Body of Messianic Jewish believers in the land: from around 300 believers in the beginning of the '80s to around 15,000 believers today. As numbers have grown so has our self-confidence—we are no longer an indistinguishable minority. The number of ministries in our midst has expanded through those reaching out to the poor and needy, leadership development programs, diverse discipleship programs, diverse evangelism programs, business development programs, theological development programs, and the list goes on.

WHAT IS OUR RELATIONSHIP WITH THE WIDER JEWISH COMMUNITY?

When asked to present this topic I was posed with several questions:

How do we Balance Witness and Participation?

I have already described my life in Eretz Israel and the application of my Jewish Messianic Israeli identity. As I live my life, I naturally share every aspect of it with those around me, discussing our kids who attend Israeli schools and our young men and women who serve in the Israeli army. We encourage our young people to pursue academic studies in order that they might fulfil their God-given potential in professions that allow them to influence Israeli society.

Our lives are intertwined with those of our neighbors and colleagues and, in most cases, it is clear to them that we are Messianic Jews. We both fulfil our duties and receive our benefits from the State. As all Israelis, we are coping with financial difficulties and like our neighbors, we have lived for a long time under diverse threats of war. Our participation in the daily life of Israel and in the lives of our Israeli neighbors, colleagues, and friends is a given part of who we are.

Likewise our witness is an integral part of our life. In schools our children naturally share their faith, our soldiers share their faith naturally in the relationships they have during their periods of service, and in the workplace faith is expressed and shared on a daily basis. This kind of daily witness is effective as non-believers observe our faith expressed through our works. Obviously there are other ways in which one can witness: there are several websites for seekers, diverse evangelism campaigns, mailing campaigns, etc.

What are Some Practical Ways to Relate to the Wider Jewish Community?

I've already touched on the answer to this questions but I'd like to add two further points. Ministries that answer to humanitarian needs, such as food/clothing distribution, helping families that suffer violence and abuse, holocaust survivors, drug addicts, and human trafficking, often deal with problems that Israeli society would rather ignore and that the State struggles to deal with effectively. These kinds of ministries demonstrate the essence of our faith in a practical way and open doors that words on their own cannot.

Many Israeli Jews carry bitterness in their hearts towards Gentiles (in particular towards Messianic Gentiles) for the persecution that they have suffered at their hands over the centuries. Messianic Gentile organizations that serve Israeli Jews help break down the prejudices that exist and open hearts to the message of Yeshua.

Do we Need Boundaries in our Relationship with the Wider Jewish Community? What Would They Be?

In each of the aforementioned areas (daily life, school, work, army) believers are faced with all kinds of pressures such as job loss, non-renewal of passports, etc. Our identification with the state of Israel cannot be placed above our allegiance to Yeshua and should not cause us to either hide the fact that we are believers nor, in any way, water down the gospel. Obviously this doesn't negate the need to share the gospel with sensitivity and in no way does it justify ramming the gospel down people's throats.

CONCLUSION

Our relationship with the wider Jewish community is grounded in, and determined by, our personal and corporate identity. I am an Israeli Messianic Jew whose identity is centered on Yeshua and my understanding of my identity affects every area of this relationship. I would like to conclude with the following verses:

Isaiah 2: 2-4 (NIV)

> *2 In the last days the mountain of the Lord's temple will be established as the highest of the mountains; it will be exalted above the hills, and all nations will stream to it.*
>
> *3 Many peoples will come and say, "Come, let us go up to the mountain of the Lord, to the temple of the God of Jacob. He will teach us his ways, so that we may walk in his paths." The law will go out from Zion, the word of the Lord from Jerusalem.*
>
> *4 He will judge between the nations and will settle disputes for many peoples. They will beat their swords into ploughshares and their spears into pruning hooks. Nation will not take up sword against nation, nor will they train for war anymore.*

My heart's desire is to glorify Yeshua in the midst of my people. If we are to hasten His return it's imperative that the worldwide Jewish messianic Body work together, in spite of our differences. We should develop personal and work relationships between the different organizations and congregations, look for ways to co-operate and reduce operational costs, develop and implement strategies to reach our people, and encourage Aliyah. In this context it is viable that we also work together with other non-Jewish Messianic organizations as one body.

GENTILES WITHIN THE MESSIANIC JEWISH COMMUNITY

Jeffrey A. Adler
Master of Divinity Degree, Rabbi of the Messianic Jewish Congregation Sha'arey Yeshua in Indianapolis, Indiana, Formerly held offices in the Messianic Jewish Alliance of America and the Union of Messianic Jewish Congregations

It might help us in dealing with this issue to look back at the call of Israel. Abraham was called to leave everything he had known to follow the God he could not see to a place he had never been, abandoning all security for himself, his servants, and, even more, for Sarah. All this was done for the purpose of his being blessed and being a blessing—or we might say be blessed by being a blessing: "through you all the families of the earth will be blessed." Abraham would represent his God, despite being without might or power of his own, yet having the intimate and personal oversight, protection, favor, and provision of the Creator of the Heavens and the earth. He would be the delegate of the Divine One to a broader world that since the Fall in the Garden had not a clue as to what to expect from the Holy God. In God's dealings with Abraham and his fledgling band, He established that He would show mercy, faithfulness, rachamim (parental compassion), and power, among other infinite qualities, to those willing to enter into a covenantal relationship of complete trust. The world, now made up primarily of a people to be known as Gentiles, needed to see the character of God acted out, demonstrated in real time and real events, and so it happened. God showed His power and might through the events so eloquently portrayed on the pages of the Tanakh—the birth of Isaac, the wisdom given to Joseph, the plagues on Egypt and subsequent Exodus, the supply of manna and water from the rock, the parting of the Jordan, destruction of Jericho followed by the Conquest of the Land, the triumphs of David, et cetera. Even when the people turned away, God's "soul could bear no longer the misery of Israel" (Judges 10:16). Hence, He raised up deliverers such as Barak,

D'vorah, Gideon, Shamgar, et al. Bear in mind the stirring promises of passages like the great statements of Deuteronomy 7:6-9:

> For you are a holy people to the Lord your God; the Lord your God has chosen you to be His own treasure out of all peoples that are upon the face of the earth. The Lord did not set His Love on you, nor choose you, because you were more in number than any people—for, you were fewest of all peoples—but, because the Lord loved you, and because the Lord would keep the oath which He swore unto your fathers, has the Lord brought you out with a mighty hand, and redeemed you out of the house of bondage, from the hand of Pharaoh, king of Egypt. Know, therefore, that the Lord your God, He is God, the faithful God, that keeps covenant and mercy with them that love Him and keep His commandments to a thousand generations.

It should not surprise us if many who recognize this God as the God of the Jewish people would want to identify as closely as possible with His people. The texture of the world causes many of us to feel small, obscure, unimportant, unnoticed, and powerless. A God like the one just described is so appealing. What would it be like to be one of His very own?

Even the call to humility could be understood to be telling Israel not to allow pride to obscure the role of the nature and character of the God of Israel from the eyes, not only of their own future generations, but, also, of the nations, who need to trust in Israel's God. This can be seen in passages such as Deuteronomy 8:11-18:

> Beware lest you forget the Lord your God . . . lest when you have eaten and are satisfied, then your heart be lifted up, and you forget the Lord your God, Who brought you out of the Land of Egypt, out of the house of bondage . . . and you say in your heart, 'My power and the might of my hand has gotten me this wealth. But, you shall remember the Lord your God, for, it is He that gives you the power to get wealth, that He may establish His covenant which He swore to your fathers, as it is today.'

Having said all this, we, as the Messianic Jewish community, must humbly realize that we, as an avant-garde of the future believing remnant of Israel, carry the standard and responsibility of serving as the collective witness of the faithful rule of the Lord before the greater world. As such, our response to the Gentiles among and around us must be handled with some sensitivity and dexterity. The Gentile world, born again and not, still has a need to see the faithfulness of God to His covenant in action. There is a very real danger that the survival of Israel will be perceived merely as the survival of culture and philosophy, rather than the rule of God over all. The use of the Pual stem, *yulad,* in Isaiah 9:6, testifies to the demand for God to exert divine force to carry out His plans, even in the gifting of Messiah's birth. The real message of Israel is less about cultural and religious tenacity and more about divine stamina and resilience, but this message still desperately needs to be communicated.

Bearing in mind that the Messianic Jewish community has in the forefront of its collective consciousness the need and focus to reach our own Jewish community for Messiah Yeshua, we need to maintain a genuine Jewish expression of faith in Yeshua. Since the Jewish community is largely suspicious of our congregations as some sort of church-financed, church-directed, and church-controlled front that is not really Jewish at all, thinking it is merely some sort of sham with Jewish trappings meant to bait an evangelistic mousetrap. There is a genuinely felt need to maintain a viable Jewish face that has an integrity of real Jewish identity. Some feel a need to limit Gentile inclusion to a bare minimum. Some fear the temptation to welcome Gentiles for their financial and administrative support, rather than welcoming them sincerely as partners in ministry.

It is wise to recognize that, while many Gentile Christians might be interested in Messianic ministries of various sorts. This may be because of a desire to reach Jewish friends, relatives, neighbors, business associates, et cetera or for personal enrichment of their faith through exploration of its biblical, Jewish roots due to a fascination with Jewish heritage, such as feasts and festivals. Only certain ones, however, would have a desire for a long-term residential relationship with such ministries. It is here where we might wish to place our focus—on the issue of personal sense of calling.

First of all, we all recognize that not all of us in Jewish ministry have the same personality, temperament, skills, style, motivations, giftings, et cetera. Some work better with more traditional Jewish people, some with mixed marriages, some with professionals, and so forth. Some of us attract certain types of people, functioning better in particular types of settings and formats. Some need more of a team approach, at least in certain circumstances. This needs to be recognized as provision, even fathering, by the sovereign hand of the Lord. In this light, some of us are going to attract more Gentile teammates than others. Others of us are going to draw out Jewish people who might be frightened or uncomfortable—at least initially—by the presence of Gentiles, fearing this might be indicative of a less than Jewish identity should they decide to commit themselves to Messianic faith. These perspectives seem so natural to those in possession of them that it would almost seem that everyone should operate the same way. But, there is still that element of divine calling. All need to be reached, and so, God equips different individuals to reach the different types of Jewish people.

However, God is not so cold, calculating, or manipulative, merely exploiting His children/servants in such ways. Psalms 37:4 says, "Delight yourself also in the Lord, and, He shall give you the desires of your heart." "Desires" here is a rendering of the Hebrew noun *mishalot*, derived from the verb *shaal*, to pray. It refers to cravings sent from God, cravings so intimate and personal that they become part of the relational context between Him and us that we find them at the core of our lives. It was these that caused Adonai to say to Jeremiah, "I have gifted you as a prophet to the nations," in spite of all man's angst and trauma. It was the *mishalot* in Paul that led him to state, "Woe to me if I preach not the Good News," not that God would kill him, but, that he could not be himself if he failed to carry out his calling.

As servants of the Lord, we also have a role in helping the people who come to us determine their *mishalot*—including the Gentiles. We need to help discern whether they have a sincere calling—a *mishalah*—to join us as true partners, or not. There are some who, having become disenchanted with their own identity, merely wish to dump it for another. Jewishness may look exotic and alluring, but, if their involvement is not Holy Spirit-directed, they will be a liability to themselves as well as to the ministry. Their motivation is personal pain, not divine direction.

There are, however, Gentiles who genuinely find their sincere calling in involvement and identity within the Messianic Jewish community. Recently, one of our non-Jewish women was asked by an elderly Jewish woman why she, as a Gentile, was involved with a

Messianic Jewish congregation. This Jewish woman had been given a very questionable response by another person, and was highly disdainful of us as a result. The non-Jewish woman responded that the God of Abraham, Isaac, and Jacob is God. The elderly woman was so impressed by the maturity and sincerity of the response that she has become very open to the younger one. This Gentile woman, with one statement, communicated the integrity of message of the Jewish scriptures in a way only a Gentile could.

When all has been said, there are avenues open to Gentiles in relating to the larger Jewish community not available to us who have been born naturally into the Jewish world. Paul had this in mind in his famous Romans 11:11 letter when he spoke of the ministry to Gentiles being a provocation to Jewish jealousy. While the exact meaning of this concept has been the topic of some debate and discussion, certainly, the love of Gentiles for Israel's people, heritage, and God would certainly expose a deficit of appreciation in the eyes of many Jewish people for their own heritage. That, against the background of so much anti-Semitism by Gentiles down through the centuries stands in stark contrast and can certainly grab attention, at least raising attention as to why and how this came about in this person.

Ezekiel 47:21-23 makes a profound statement about the role of Gentiles in the Kingdom Age: “So, you shall divide this land unto you according to the tribes of Israel. And it shall come to pass, that ye shall divide it by lot for an inheritance unto you and to the strangers that sojourn among you, who shall beget children among you; and they shall be unto you as the homeborn among the children of Israel; they shall have inheritance with you among the tribes of Israel. And it shall come to pass, that in what tribe the stranger sojourneth, there shall ye give him his inheritance, saith the Lord God.” Here, Gentiles have obviously chosen to live amongst Israel to the point of establishing their homes and rearing children. They submit themselves to the culture, economy, and education—the very life of Israel. This is speaking of those Gentiles with a particular motivation to select such a life and home, to the point that God's statements here go so far as to protect their interests and rights. From a Biblical perspective, I believe we must refer to this motivation as a sense of divine calling.

In summation, I believe that we should recognize that not every Gentile is called to live among us, identifying with us and our lives and communities, and that many who claim to wish to do this may well be desirous of an unhealthy escape from their own identity. Also, we should acknowledge that the Messianic community is not desirous of denigrating other cultures and ethnicities, instead recognizing that those other identities are just as gifted from Adonai as ours. Further, we also need to recognize that there are also people who have a genuine call, a *mishalah*, if I may borrow the term from Psalm 37:4, to be among us as more than occasional visitors. If we were to deny them, we would, from a pastoral perspective, be doing them, our ministries, and even our communities a great disservice.

We seek constantly to develop a viable strategy to carry out the tasks presented to us by the Lord. The danger, as the previously cited passages from Deuteronomy 7 and 8 warn, is in not giving priority to the supreme role of the Lord Himself over our own perspectives. If the Divine Composer has written parts for the instrumental gifts of Gentiles, not including them in the orchestra of the Messianic community, would, if not causing the sounding of some sour notes, at least deprive the world of some of the sweetest notes of His symphony.

GENTILES AND JEWS TOGETHER IN ANCIENT ROME AND NORTH AFRICAN CARTHAGE

Jeffrey L. Seif, Ph.D.
Served as Professor of Jewish studies
at a number of academic institutions,
Project Manager and VP of the Messianic Jewish Family Bible Project,
Leads the Sar Shalom Congregation in Dallas, Texas

What is the role of Gentiles in the Messianic Jewish community? Good question. In the interest of tendering an answer, let's consider the following: What was the role? What was the nature and structure of the relationship between Gentile Jesus-believers and Jewish Yeshua-believers in the early days of the Messianic Jewish movement? Why were Gentiles attracted to Jews, to Judaism, and to Messianic Judaism? Did kindly disposed Gentiles join and participate in the movement as Jews? Were they received as new Jews, as quasi-Jews, or as non-Jewish associates? Gentile infatuation and participation with things both Jewish and Messianic Jewish will be the object of our attention in this paper—and this could serve as a backdrop to our discussion.

JEWISH AND GENTILE INTERACTION IN THE ANCIENT ROMAN WORLD

The term "Philo-Judaism" harks to the infatuation some non-Jews have with Jews and Judaism. The ancient Jewish historian Flavius Josephus observed how many Gentiles "adopted Jewish customs and manners" (*War* 2.463) and that Jews were "constantly attracting to their religious ceremonies multitudes of Greeks" (*Wars* 7.45). Elsewhere he said—and perhaps not in hyperbolic fashion: "[T]here is not one [single] city, Greek or barbarian, to which our [Jewish] customs . . . have not spread" (*Against Apion* 2.282). Particularly, says he, "*[in] the whole of Syria . . . each city has its Judaizers*" (Italics mine; *War* 2.262-63). What "Judaizers" meant is another matter. That aside, elsewhere

Flavius Josephus states: "In Damascus [Syria] men noted how 'wives had all become subject to the Jewish religion'" (*War* 2.559-60). For his part, Dio Cassius said Jews were "converting many of the natives to their [Jewish] ways" (*Roman History* 57.18.5a). Tacitus similarly spoke of "those who come over to [the Jewish] religion" (*Histories* 5.5). Lending even more credence to Jewish attractiveness and speaking perhaps in a disparaging manner with regard to it, Horace said: "We, like Jews, will compel you to join our throng" (*Satires* 1.4.142-143).

Epigraphic evidence in Asia and Rome speaks of "proselytes"[1] in higher echelons who appreciated the Jewish world and ways. Veturia Paula, for example, was remembered as "a proselyte for 16 years under the name of Sarah, mother [or patroness] of the synagogues of Campus and Voluminus." Julia Severa was a patroness of the Jewish community and known to have financed a synagogue in Phrygia. (Her son, L. Servenius Cornutus served in the Senate under Nero in 73 CE and was legate to the proconsul in Asia. Another relative L. Iulius Severus served as a consul.) According to Josephus, other Jewish-friendly friends in high Roman places include Emperor Nero's mistress Poppaea Sabina who "pleaded on behalf of the Jews." Titus, the elder son of Vespasian—both of whom participated in the "sack" of Jerusalem—took a Jewish woman named Bernice as his mistress with him back to Rome after the war—which would give him a Jewish-friendly voice in the bedroom, at the very least. Lastly in this regard, Professor Magnus Zetterholm, in his *The Formation of Christianity in Antioch*, alights upon Judaism's presence and influence in culture by referencing St. Augustine citing Seneca: "*The customs of the accursed [Jewish] race have gained such influence* that they are now received. The vanquished have given laws to the victors."[2] That Gentiles were attracted to Jews and Judaism is obvious. But why were they?

JEWISH AND GENTILE INTERACTION IN THE ANCIENT ROME

Valerius Maximus reported in 139 BCE that Jews invoked the ire of Romans and that Cornelius Hispanus/Hispalus had them expelled from Rome for "peddling their ancient wisdom" and "for attempting to transfer their sacred rites to the Romans" (*Val. Max.* 1.3.3).[3] Seneca is on record describing Jews as a most pernicious people (*sceleratissma gens*). Because he nowhere else speaks directly of Jews in his vast writings—save for this extract culled from St. Augustine's *City of God*—one cannot say that Seneca was particularly obsessed with Jews and given to their slander. The satirist Juvenal took on Jews for adherence to dietary laws, Sabbath, circumcision, and the like but construed the practices to be "more laughable than dangerous."[4] For his part, Tacitus was tolerant of Jews, but "angrier at the converts than at the Jews . . . who have disserted their native gods, ancestral traditions, homeland and families."[5] He noted, as well, that Jews had a passion for reproduction—a matter that will be considered below.

In his *Diaspora: Jews amidst Greeks and Romans*, Dr. Erich S. Gruen, professor emeritus in the Department of History, University of California, says the population of Rome "exploded" in the first and second centuries BCE, resulting in "Jewish communities . . . in the late Republic and early Principate, with modern estimates of a Jewish population ranging from 20,000-60,000"[6] people.[7] After calling for and assessing Gentile views of Jews in his section, "The Jews of Rome," Professor Gruen concludes:

> Romans in the private sphere had little reason to trouble themselves over the Jews. Writers scoffed and laughed. The weird ways of the Jews provided a source of amusement, even amazement. However, they did not lead to bile, and they did not provoke hostilities. The preserved comments, even in the aftermath of the [Jewish] Revolt, convey mockery rather than malignancy.[8]

Though anti-Jewish statements appear in the Roman press, every now and again, Dr. Gruen isn't minded to make too much of it—and rightly so. For, at the street-level, it could be argued that Jewish ideas made headway. Roman women were increasingly attracted to Judaism and its daughter religion—Messianic Judaism.

"The early church was so especially attractive to [non-Jewish] women," says Professor Rodney Stark, "that in 370 [CE] the emperor Valentinian issued a written order to Pope Damascus I requiring that Christian missionaries cease calling on the homes of pagan women."[9] For reasons that will be unpacked below, Dr. Stark believes "women enjoyed far higher status" in Jewish and Messianic Jewish homes and communities in Rome as elsewhere "than did women in the Greco-Roman world at large."[10] For reasons that will become patently obvious, this higher status and consequential better treatment drew non-Jewish women into the Jewish fold and into the Messianic movement's ranks.

Writing around 200 CE, in his *The Roman History: The Reign of Augustus,* the Roman historian Dio Cassius notes there was an "extreme shortage of females" in Roman culture. Dr. J. C. Russell concurred and, for his part, posited that there were 131 males for every 100 females in the city of Rome and 140 males for every 100 females in Italy. Why the disparity in numbers, and what does this have to do with Jewish attractiveness?

In *The Ancient World: Manners and Morals,* Dr. Jack Lindsay notes how even in large and reasonably wealthy families "more than one daughter was practically never reared."[11] Why not? This diminished number of Roman women, according to Dr. Stark, can only be attributed to some engineering of human life, or "tampering" with it, as Dr. Lindsay put it. With no offense to culture and morals, *many, many baby girls were left to die at birth in Greco-Roman culture*—as were males with deformities. Undesired baby girls were left to die at dumps at the edge of Roman cities. Most did; some, however, were picked up and raised as prostitutes.

Seneca viewed the disregarding of unwanted children as "reasonable" and "commonplace."[12] Plato and Aristotle recommended infanticide as a legitimate state policy and lent their credence to the pagan practice as a result. Torah-minded Jews disdained the murderous practice and were game to criticize it. In *The Histories* 5.5, Tacitus construed the Jewish notion that it is "a deadly sin to kill an unwanted child" as one of the Jews' "sinister and revolting" ways of thinking.[13] Testifying to the horrific pagan views, while positioning Jewish practice over and against them, Josephus notes: "The [Jewish] law, moreover, enjoins us to bring up our offspring, and forbids women to cause abortion or to destroy it afterward; and if a woman appears to have done so, she will be a murderer of her child." Torah forbids the murderous brazen disregard for life in the Ten Commandments. In *Sentences of Pseudo-Phocylides,* an Alexandrian Jew similarly advises: "a woman should not . . . throw it [i.e. her newborn baby] before dogs and vultures of prey." In *First Apology*, Justin Martyr expresses this sentiment with: "It is wicked to expose even newly-born children . . . [for] we would then be murderers."[14]

As noted, Pagans by contrast disregarded their unwanted children—*girls particularly*—whereas Torah-bound Jews eschewed the immoral practice. Mindful of this, Dr. Rodney Stark surmises: "*The views of family . . . sustained by Christians revealed the Jewish origins of the movement* . . . [those views] being 'very family oriented'[15] at the core." Messianic believers' refused to condone female infanticide. Coupled with Judaism and Messianic Judaism's stalwart disparagement of divorce, marital infidelity, fornication, and polygamy, *it is not hard to understand how non-Jewish women could and would become attracted to the Jews*. Life-loving and nurturing were accentuated. Fidelity without divorce was held out to be the norm in the Jewish counter-culture and was expected of every Messianic adherent as well.[16]

Not only that, believers' marriages were entered into on better terms than what tended to prevail in the broader culture. The fortunate Roman girls that made it past the disgraceful abandonment were typically married off to older men before puberty. In "The Age of Roman Girls at Marriage," in *Population Studies*, Dr. Keith Hopkins informs through Plutarch: "Romans gave their girls in marriage when they were twelve years old, or even younger," something Plutarch said caused "the hatred and fear of girls forced [into sexual relations] contrary to nature."[17] Dio Cassius said much the same, that "girls are considered . . . to have reached marriageable age by their twelfth year."[18] According to Dr. Hopkins, ten percent of pagan girls were married by age ten, with forty-four percent marrying by age fourteen, most often with men much older and with the unions consummated at once, despite the tender age of the girls. Women in Messiah-believing communities tended to marry later.

Though not particularly respected in the broader Greco-Roman culture, babies, girls, and older women arguably fared much better in the Messianic Jewish subculture. Therein, not only were believing men more predisposed to value their marriage partners with exhortations in the Scriptures to "love their wives," but, should women fall upon hard times when untimely death seized their husbands, the Messianic community felt it incumbent to assist the unfortunate widows—their "sisters" in a communal sense. This harks back to James' noting that assisting widows represents religion that is "pure and undefiled before God," and thus at its best.[19]

Arguably, the valuation of female life in Jewish communities, over and against the devaluation of female life that prevailed in the regnant culture, prompted not a few women to cast their approving gazes toward the Yeshua/Jesus movement. In *The Body and Society: Men, Women and Sexual Renunciation in Early Christianity,* Dr. Peter

Brown observed how "'women were prominent' among upper class Christians."[20] That women were prominently represented in the believing community's ranks—way in excess of the women that presented in the broader culture where they were outnumbered 140:100 in Italy—created an unanticipated "surplus of women" in the Messianic movement and at a time when the world was used to there being a "vast surplus of men,"[21] not of women. This created something of a problem.

In about 200 CE, Callistus, Bishop of Rome, "upset many of his fellow clerics when he 'ruled that Christian women could live in just concubinage,' without entering into marriage"[22]—what we would call fornication. Why would a bishop provide a mechanism for such things? Professor Harnack opines, "[T]hese circumstances arose from the . . . problem[s] facing upper-class women whose only marital option within the Christian community were to men of far inferior rank . . . [H]igh born women would have lost many legal privileges and [the] control of their wealth."[23] Wanting to provide a means for this growing inventory of women to secure the personal benefits of believing marriage, without imposing the legal obligations of marriage that would reduce their standing, the bishop opted for another arrangement. Irrespective of what one thinks of his position—or the women—clear is the fact that a Torah-based culture was gaining headway in a bankrupt world.

Dr. Stephen Spence posits, "Jewish features underlie a large part of the Roman [Gentile] Church." This, according to him, is "explained by its proximity and familiarity with Jewish traditions, which lead some to believe that Christianity in Rome began within the well-established Roman Jewish community."[24]

Though the notion that Roman Christianity evolved from a Jewish matrix may appear novel at first blush (especially for those inclined to think of a Roman Catholic Church as the original), a careful consideration of the sources supports the thesis *that ancient Roman Christianity came by way of Judaism and Messianic Judaism*, given the appeal of the egalitarian and redemptive natures of the respective Jewish movements. Jewish culture was virtue-rich; pagan culture operated with a virtue deficit. Greco-Roman utilitarianism humbled and dehumanized human beings—even the citizens of the empire. Reducing non-citizens of lesser race, class, and gender to less-than-hoped-for lives, the doomed unfortunates were socialized into accepting their unfortunate lot. Many knew they were little more than utilities to be used and abused in the gladiatorial games, to be harvested as slave-stock for the mines, and to be used as human chattel to serve the various needs and interests of oppressive overlords, as agricultural slaves, as sex-slaves of both sexes, or both, or whichever. Though this ubiquitous dehumanization tended to prevail in the larger culture, and on quite a grand scale, the Torah-based sub-culture within the regnant culture cast a loftier moral vision, where *all people*—irrespective of their race, class, or gender—had inalienable, God-given dignity and rights. That these "rights" extended to women in the decidedly patriarchal culture may well account for why women from all classes were attracted to the synagogue originally, and then why many women preferred Judaism's daughter religion as it got a foothold in ancient Rome. Much as Christian life (so called) was impacted by Jewish life, so too was Christian death.

In *The Jews in Late Ancient Rome: Evidence of Cultural Interaction in the Roman Diaspora*, Professor Leonard Victor Rutgers concludes that Jews and Christians shared much in common.[25] A careful assessment of archeological findings in ancient Rome and Venosa similarly prompted Professor Eric Meyers to note in his "Report on the Excavations at the Venosa Catacombs" that: "Jewish and Christian burials reflect an *interdependence* and [a] closely related community of Jews and Christians in which *clear marks of demarcation were blurred* until the third and fourth centuries."[26] With this in mind, Dr. Rodney Stark goes on to parrot Dr. Meyers again noting that it was "only when a triumphant Christianity began, late in the fourth century, to pour money into Palestine [sic] for church building and shrines, was there any serious rupture with Jews."[27]

JEWISH AND GENTILE INTERACTION IN THE NORTH AFRICAN CITIES OF CARTHAGE AND CYRENE

Jewish experience in North Africa is lost to moderns—as is ancient Messianic Jewish experience on the whole. Difficulties with reconstruction notwithstanding, herein, we will call upon extant sources and briefly consider Jewish peoples and communities in North Africa and see what we can learn about Jewish and Gentile believers' experiences.

JEWS, MESSIANIC JEWS, AND GENTILE CHRISTIANS IN CARTHAGE

Dr. Stephanie Binder of the Department of Classical Studies at Bar-Ilan University in Israel brings strong Jewish connections to bear on ancient North African Christian experience. In her post-Trajan, post-war "Jewish-Christian[28] Contacts in the Second and Third Centuries, C.E.?" Professor Binder took up the matter of Jewish and "Christian" interactions in African antiquity.[29] She was particularly concerned with whether ancient Christians and Jews were "either different and isolated from each other or similar and intermingled, in the late second and early third centuries C.E." in Carthage and elsewhere.[30] Her assessment of both the principal sources and the scholarly discussions on those sources yield an affirmative "yes"—that indeed *the Jewish and so-called "Christian" communities were much more connected than disconnected.*

After referencing Dr. Timothy Barnes who says: "no one really knows how Christianity came to North Africa,"[31] Dr. Binder notes others, like Dr. Rene Braun, who suspects that *Christianity came to North Africa through the Jewish community.*[32] After observing through Dr. J. C. Fredouille that the "African church seems closer to the East than the Occident"[33] (i.e., the "West"), and Dr. J. B. Rives who says "African liturgy is more like that of the East than that of Rome,"[34] and Dr. W. H. C. Frend who notes that "Christianity surely arrived through the Jewish community and from Eastern influences,"[35] she then offers her reasons for reasonable connections, based on how the North African church leader Tertullian's thought processes follows Judaism's *Mishnah Avodah Zarah* on matters of festivals, immorality and idolatry, baths, games, garments, saying the names of pagan gods, schoolmasters and teachers, swearing by the names of pagan gods, outsmarting the Law, and then dealing with things dedicated to idolatry.[36] After comparing and contrasting similarities between the *Mishnah*'s responses to these matters alongside Tertullian's decisions on them, Dr. Binder argued that the great church leader Tertullian "lived in close proximity to a Jewish community, founded his arguments on sources that he shared with this community, in the same cultural environment, and reached very similar conclusions."[37] Those interested in her sweep of the aforementioned issues can refer to her monograph. Believing that one illustration will suffice, we will now pick up on a theme noted previously and consider how both the rabbis and the African church leader Tertullian looked at festivals and sacred space.

The *Mishnah* says: "And these are the festivals of the idolatrous: the *Calends* and the *Saturnalia* and the *Kratesis*" (*Avodah Zarah* 1.3). Archaic as these expressions are, an explanation is warranted at the outset. "Calends" was used in antiquity to note the first day of a month—and seems to have particularly been used to denote the 1st of January, or the beginning of the Greco-Roman year.[38] "Saturnalia," for its part, was an extremely popular Roman holiday, as well, one held in honor of Saturn (or Cronos), the youngest of the Titans and the father of the major gods celebrated by the Greeks and Romans. Foremost among Saturn's sons was the famous Zeus. "Saturnalia," the holiday in his honor, was inaugurated to lift spirits in the wake of a Carthaginian defeat in mid-December. Popular, it grew into a weeklong celebration, one accentuated by special foods, clothing, and benefits—with special benefits even extending to slaves. Much as Santa is said to go "Ho, Ho, Ho," the greeting for the mid-to-late-December Saturnalia holiday was "*Io, Saturnalia,*" or "e-o," with "e-o" being a Latin expression similar to Santa's "ho." Lastly, according to Dr. Peter Schafer in *The Talmud Yerushalami and Graeco-Roman Culture, III: Texts and Studies in Ancient Judaism*, the term *Kratesis* was presumed from the rabbinic point of view to hark to the founding and beginning of Rome, with Romulus and Remus, and the subsequent ascensions of the ruling emperors. *Kratesis* thus commemorates the beginning of civilization (*natalis urbis*) and in some sense, to the regnant culture's majestic, mythic, and seemingly mystical power.[39] In sum, the aforementioned holidays hark to legendary triumphs in Greco-Roman mythology and history.

Avodah Zarah 1.3 put it succinctly and with a warning: "These are the festivals of the idolatrous: the *Calends* and the *Saturnalia* and the *Kratesis.*" So much for the Jews. In his *De Idololatria* 14.4, the church leader Tertullian similarly exhorts North African Christians to avoid "*Saturnalia et calends Ianurias*"—i.e., the mid-December feast to Saturn and the new year's celebration which comes on its heels.[40]

Associated gift giving was to be shunned by both the Jewish and Christian communities. Tertullian wanted Christians to avoid receiving gifts, as per *De Idololatria* 14.6, much as the Jewish sage Resh Laqish wanted Yehuda the Prince to dispose of a gift received from a *min* (heretic—used at times to refer to Jewish believers in Yeshua/Jesus) as a new year's gift in *Babylonian Talmud Avodah Zarah* 6B.[41] How ought one to account for the similarity in thinking, here as elsewhere?

Tertullian's familiarity with Judaism may well be attributed to his having himself once come "near to conversion to Judaism," as some allege.[42] This is no forgone conclusion, however. Dr. Michael Rydelnik, professor of Jewish Studies at the Moody Bible Institute, accepts the idea that Tertullian had not had "any personal knowledge of his opponents and their religion,"[43] i.e., Judaism, an idea he parroted from Williams in *Adversus Judaeos*.[44] (I prefer the notion that he did have personal knowledge.) This discussion aside, that Tertullian's Carthaginian Christians were "found in synagogues" and that they had to be "encouraged to preach to Gentiles *too,*" in *De Fuga* 6.2-3,[45] speaks of common ground, natural degrees of familiarity, and mixed associations—something the churchman wanted to weaken and/or break up outright.

Though Tertullian takes on Jews in his *Adversus Iudaeos*, this is but a "stereotyped invention"[46] of Jews—not the real-world Jews of his day. That "he does not attack or evenly openly refer to his Jewish neighbors" in Carthage leads Dr. Binder to argue that he wrote his strident opposition to "prepare Christians' encounters with Jews of the city and wants them to have proper arguments in hand."[47] Spirited disputation is thus not to be construed as being tantamount to disdain. He postulates: "Tertullian [actually] benefited from Jewish associations and inspiration while writing his treatise"—i.e, *De Idolotatria*.[48]

How Tertullian came upon and applied Jewish notions is a matter of conjecture. Did he get them from Jewish believers in Yeshua/Jesus? Did he get them from his own Jewish associations? We do not know. We do know, though, that Jewish presence and influence is evidenced in Carthage, North Africa. Dr. Binder's best argument to this effect is that "social, ethnic and religious cosmopolitanism in Carthage [would have] prevented total separation between Jews and Christians,"[49] and, not only that, but the communities could have been so close that "there might [even] have been uncertainty about what makes a Christian different from a Jew."[50] "The only definitive conclusion that can be inferred from the study," according to Dr. Binder, "is that when Jewish and Christian communities co-existed in the same place—even though their respective leaders worked hard to maintain a clear theological boundary—on the interpersonal, individual, and social levels, they *were still intertwined and shared their ideas and religious experience.*"[51]

ENDNOTES

1. Emmanuel Testa, The Faith of the Mother Church: An Essay on the Theology of the Judeo-Christians (Franciscan Print. Press, 1992), 13.
2. Magnus Zetterholm, *The Formation of Christianity in Antioch* (London: Routledge, 2003), 127 (my italics). Evidence of non-Jews joining Jews is attested by the size of the "Court of the Gentiles"—by far the largest area on the Temple Mount. Just to the south, in the "City of David," one could not help but have noticed the largest facility there, one that handily protruded in the city's first century CE skyline. Built in the style of the Parthian Empire—an architectural feature very much in vogue in the Levant—was the Adiabene Royal Palace(s). Josephus noted this in *War* 5.352-353 and 6.356. Visitors to Jerusalem today, who happen upon the 1:50 scale model of the old city, are similarly drawn to the palace situated just next to David's old residence in the city that bears his name. The palace takes a full half of the hill of the City of David. It was brought to life in modernity by archeologist Dr. Mikhael Avi-Yonah's reconstruction, which is used in the aforementioned model. Noteworthy for our purposes here is the fact that the palace was built by Queen Helene of Adiabene who, with her sons, converted to Judaism in 36 CE and took residence in Jerusalem. The name "Adiabene" is derived from the Syria-Aramaic *Hady'ab* or *Hday'ad* and references an ancient kingdom nestled between Mesopotamia's Tigris River, just to the east of Syria at the edge of the Levant.
3. Ibid., 16, 260.
4. Ibid., 45.
5. Ibid., 46-47.
6. Erich . . . S. Gruen, *Diaspora: Jews amidst Greeks and Romans* (Cambridge: Harvard University Press, 2002), 15.
7. Jews who settled in the district of Trastevere, Rome, were said to have originally been prisoners of a sort—prisoners of war, particularly, or folk who were enslaved and then manumitted. Some others seem to have been free men, who came because of the social and commercial allure of the imperial city.
8. Ibid., 53.
9. Rodney Stark, *The Rise of Christianity: A Sociologist Reconsiders History* (Princeton: Princeton University Press, 1996), 95. He is the principle source for this section, a considerable part of which was culled from "The Role of Women in Christian Growth."
10. Ibid. Stark leans upon Robin Lane Fox, *Pagans and Christians* (New York: Knopf, 1987); Henry Chadwick, *The Early Church* (Harmondsworth, Middlesex: Penguin Books, 1967); Adlof van Harnack, *The Mission and Expansion of Christianity in the First Three Centuries.* Translated by John Moffatt. 2 Volumes (New York: G. P. Putnam's Sons, 1908).
11. Jack Lindsay, *The Ancient World: Manners and Morals* (New York: J. P. Putnam's Sons, 1968), 168. Of six hundred families with inscriptions left in Delphi, only six reported raising more than one daughter—thus only 1%. Astounding! Troubling, is it not?

12. Stark, 118.
13. Ibid., 118.
14. Ibid.
15. Ibid., 124 (my italics).
16. Ibid., 104.
17. Ibid., 107.
18. Ibid., 106.
19. That the lesson was not lost to the ancients is attested in Eusebius' writings, where Cornelius the Bishop of Rome wrote to Fabius the Bishop of Antioch in 251 CE and said that more than 1,500 widows and distressed persons were in the care of the local congregation, which may well have amounted to about 30,000 by that the time of the writing.
20. Ibid., 99.
21. Ibid., 101.
22. Ibid., 111.
23. Ibid., 112.
24. Stephanie Binder, "Jewish-Christian Contacts in the Second and Third Centuries, C.E.?" The Case of Carthage; Tertullian and the Mishnah's Views on Idolatry," in Dan Jaffee (ed.), *Studies in Rabbinic Judaism and Early Christianity: Text and Context*, (Boston: Brill Academic Publishers, Inc., 2010), 220.
25. Leonard Victor Rutgers, *The Jews in Late Ancient Rome: Evidence of Cultural Interaction in the Roman Diaspora*, (Boston, Brill Academic Publishers, Inc., 2000), 260-268.
26. Eric M. Meyes, "Report on the Excavations at the Venosa Catacombs 1981." In *Vetera Christianorum* 20:455-459; culled from Stark, 69 (my italics).
27. Ibid., 68.
28. Meaning Jewish *and* Christian contacts as opposed to Jewish-Christian individuals, a term oft employed when referring to Jews who believe in Yeshua/Jesus.
29. Stephanie Binder, "Jewish-Christian Contacts in the Second and Third Centuries, C.E.?" and "The Case of Carthage; Tertullian and the Mishnah's Views on Idolatry," in *Studies in Rabbinic Judaism and Early Christianity: Text and Context,* ed. Dan Juster (Leiden/Boston: Brill, 2010), 187-230, the primary source for the arguments noted below, from who the others' voices were extracted.
30. Ibid., 187.
31. T. D. Barnes, *Tertullian* (Oxford: Clarendon Press, 1985), 68.
32. R. Braun, *Approaches de Tertullian: vingt-six etudes sur l'auteur et sur l'oeuvre* (Paris: Institut d'etudes augustiniennes, 1992) 2.
33. J.-C. Fredouille, *Tertullian et la conversion de la culture antique* (Paris: Etudes augustiniennes, 1972), 271.
34. J. B. Rives, *Religion and Authority in Roman Carthage from Augustus to Constantine* (Oxford: Clarendon Press, 1995), 225.
35. W. H. C. Frend, *The Rise of Christianity* (Philadelphia: Fortress Press, 1984), 348 and "A Note on Tertullian and the Jews," in *Studies Patrista* 10 (1970), 292.
36. Ibid., 197-217.
37. Binder, 217.

38. Ibid., 198.
39. Peter Schafer (ed), *The Talmud Yerushalami and Graeco-Roman Culture, III: Texts and Studies in Ancient Judaism* (Tubingen: J.C.B. Mohr / Siebeck, 2002), 342.
40. Binder, 198.
41. Ibid.
42. Ibid., 218.
43. From his "The Ongoing Importance of Messianic Prophecy for Jewish Evangelism in the New Millennium," in Darrell L. Bock and Mitch Glaser (eds.) *To the Jew First: The Case for Jewish Evangelism in Scripture and History* (Grand Raids: Kregel, 2008), p, 273.
44. See also p. 350, n. 47.
45. Ibid., 226 (my italics).
46. Ibid., 219.
47. Ibid.
48. Ibid.
49. Ibid., 221.
50. Ibid., 222.
51. Ibid., 227 (my italics).

THE UNIQUE PLACE OF GENTILES IN MESSIANIC JEWISH CONGREGATIONAL LIFE

Richard C. Nichol, Ph.D.
Rabbi of Congregation Ruach Israel in Needham, Mass.,
Director of the Rabbinical Ordination,
Messianic Jewish Theological Institute
President of the Messianic Jewish Rabbinical Council (MJRC)

While on vacation this past summer, my wife and I purchased a three DVD set of TV commercials dating from the 1950s to the present. Some of these old ads we had never seen. But, we had fun when an old ad played that we remembered from our childhoods. Here is one that brought a nostalgic smile to our faces: "Certs is a breath mint. Certs is a candy mint. You're both right. Certs is two . . . two . . . two mints in one!"

It can be argued that Messianic Jewish congregations by their very nature are "two . . . two . . . two faiths in one!" With breath/candy mints the identity issues are thoroughly benign. But, among us, the fact that we claim to remain faithful members of the household of Israel, while simultaneously asserting continuity with the historic community of believers in the Risen One, has very special challenges. And because we lay and professional Messianic Jewish leaders seek to bring other men, women, boys, and girls into our spheres, we feel acute responsibility for coming to mature and responsible conclusions about how to relate to these trusting souls.

God in His providence has brought non-Jews into our congregations. Should they be there? Should they all be there? How do we instill a healthy sense of spiritual identity among these good folks, most especially for their children's sake? As we seek to be helpful to the non-Jews attracted to our communities, how do we honor and respect the legitimate sensibilities of the larger Jewish community—a world to which most Messianic Jewish leaders claim allegiance? How do we help non Jewish participants in our communities maintain a positive mindset to the historic Church, guarding their possible future re-entry into the worlds of their childhood memories should they choose to leave our assemblies? To put the matter in broad theological terms, how do we fulfill our callings as those who take seriously both the *particularity* of our calling as Jews and the *universalism* of the Gospel message when it comes to non-Jews in our midst? This challenge is not ours alone.

Largely because of the dramatic rise in intermarriage rates and the general blurring of religious and cultural boundaries in Western society, more non-Jews are showing up at traditional synagogues, particularly among the more liberal branches of Judaism. This has become a topic of discussion. For example, the Reconstructionist movement had assigned a task force to determine appropriate behavior in synagogue life for unconverted non-Jews. The Summary of Opportunities and Boundaries Report[1] offers specific recommendations to member synagogues regarding who may make a Torah *aliyah*, who may become a member, who may lead a worship service, and other matters. The point here is that we Messianic Jews are not the only Jewish leaders struggling with the issue.[2]

Nor is the challenge we face really new. Dr. Jeff Seif has provided our Borough Park family with a detailed analysis of Gentile Christian's shared worship with early Jewish believers in the early centuries of our era. Though we have little documentation, we can easily imagine that discussions akin to those we find in the Book of Acts, chapters 15 and 21, continued long after the passing of James, Paul, and Peter.

In more recent times, papers and position statements have been offered. In 1987, Larry Rich contributed a paper at the Lausanne Consultation on Jewish Evangelism (LCJE) entitled, "The Role of The Gentile in a Jewish Congregation." As Chairman of the Union of Messianic Jewish Congregations Theology Committee, I authored a position paper on Gentile conversion to Messianic Judaism which was adopted by the Union's delegates and can be viewed on the Union of Messianic Jewish Congregations (UMJC) website.[3] More recently, the members of the Messianic Jewish Rabbinical Council (MJRC) have endorsed a number of specific policies specifying some of the appropriate boundaries of participation by non-Jewish members and attendees in our member synagogues. It seems that wherever Jews who embrace Yeshua have gathered, the issue of non-Jewish participation has been in the air. But differing theological outlooks and cultural connections have resulted in different approaches.

PART 1- A TALE OF TWO THEOLOGIES

In the Diaspora, we discern two overarching visions of the nature of the Messianic congregation. Two ecclesiological models emerge, each with differing starting points and therefore, differing implications for non-Jewish involvement in maturing Messianic Judaism. We will refer to these as the Bilateral Approach (BA) and the Missiological Approach (MA). It is important that we understand some of the underpinnings of each approach for at least three reasons.

First, the likely future of the Messianic Jewish enterprise will be controlled in part by which of these stances our movement adopts. Practical out workings inevitably follow theology—and of course, theology is then influenced (sometimes too much) by the "on the ground" realities facing a religious community. But we can say with confidence that the conclusions Messianic Jewish leaders reach in answer to the questions surrounding Gentile participation will have profound effects in the future. The cement is already hardening so that now really is the time to take stock.

Second, theologies have collective psychological meaning beyond the actual words on paper found in doctrinal statements, position papers, etc. BA and MA orientations create overarching value systems that are communicated powerfully in myriad ways in our interactions with one another and with congregants. These systems are powerful. We must be willing to present our presuppositions, our methodologies, and our conclusions for sympathetic, honest peer review if we are to have hope that we deserve God's smile on our efforts.

Third, though I strongly favor one of the models presented below, I submit that we have much to learn from one another. No single theological system can embody all the important truths that must govern successful endeavors for Heaven's sake. As leaders we are mandated by HaShem to love truth so much that we are willing to live with dynamic tension, paradox, complexity, nuance, mystery, and even uncertainty. More difficult still, we are mandated to be willing to change when new compelling data is presented by those who view the situation differently than we.

However, before diving in, some qualifiers are in order. First, among Diaspora Messianic Jewish congregations, the two models, BA and MA, can be identified. However, as in the case of people holding to differing political philosophies, most fall along a continuum, a spectrum of belief and practice where some sensibilities may align with "the other side" more than the declared party: prolife northern Democrats, gay rights-supporting Republicans, you get the picture. To bring the matter into our sphere, BA oriented congregations tend to gravitate more to a traditional Jewish over an Evangelical Christian starting point. As a BA practitioner, this is my orientation at Congregation Ruach Israel. However, our synagogue intentional outreach is becoming more and more important as the years go by. We want to win Jews to Yeshua and we spend a lot of time thinking about how to do this effectively. In this sense we tend in a more MA direction. Similarly, we do a great injustice to MA oriented congregations and missions if we imagine that these are unconcerned with Jewish life. Some leaders may be far too unconcerned in my view. But others really care.[4]

Second, despite real differences, some quite pronounced with far-reaching implications, adherents of missions oriented communities and bilaterally oriented ones have a great deal in common. *Many of us have put everything on the line for the sake of the risen Messiah and his kingdom.*

A parallel from American history: Thomas Jefferson had a vision for ideal American life, which epitomized the virtues of the hard working, land owning farmer. He distrusted the Yankee businessman, seeing only corruption and conspicuous consumption, as the sad end of a society dominated by their alleged values. Another founding father, Alexander Hamilton, saw things differently. His view stressed the importance of amassing capital if the new republic was to have any future at all. A national bank and a thriving business community, these were keys to the future viability of the United States in his view. These men argued, even argued vigorously. But both signed that Declaration of Independence, putting each of their lives, fortunes, and sacred honor on the line.

Third, many Messianic leaders would have trouble identifying completely with either of the models we will be discussing. They will see themselves as favorable to aspects of each and will not want to feel "pigeon-held" by those claiming neatly drawn categories. Let's be clear that in most any human endeavor, people accept ideas along a spectrum. Very few are die-hard exponents of plans and agendas that leave no room for others. Those who claim to live and breathe with such consistency, we suspect, are a bit out of touch with how they actually live. Of course, without the willingness to generalize, there can be no progress toward truth. We must generalize if we are to learn anything. So, as we discuss these theological models and their implications for Gentile participation, just relax with the possible overstatements as we examine ourselves and our place in the ecclesiological sun. Now let us consider these two different views of the very nature of a Messianic Jewish congregation and their implications for non-Jewish participation.

The Heart of Bilateral Ecclesiology

Mark Kinzer has written a book
Weaving for us no ordinary look
At the deeper artistry of our Echad
One people, yet two, in the heart of God.

Long before the publication of *Post Missionary Messianic Judaism* by Dr. Mark Kinzer, I knew that claiming connection to the Jewish world had to be deeper than the merely cosmetic. Even as a fairly young believer, I intuited that wearing *kippot*, saying "Yeshua" instead of "Jesus," etc. required some level of justification beyond mere comfort and familiarity. Some kind of theological rationale was necessary if I were to live a bit differently than believers in my world at Ithaca College and later at the Biblical Theological Seminary. Early on, I settled on a simple idea, which today still has relevance, though in a more sophisticated form: *"Jesus was Jewish. If being Jewish was good enough for him, it's good enough for me."*[5] As the years rolled by, I began to see the incompleteness of my apologetic. Jesus was then and we live now. Almost two thousand years of Jewish and Christian history and identity formation had occurred. I needed deeper reasons for laying claim to time-honored Jewish identity markers. This came in the form of another argument, this one the fruit of the wise reflection of missiologists at Fuller Theological Seminary in Pasadena, CA.

These professors saw that historic Christianity has been severely damaged by a mission enterprise, which did not adequately appreciate the cultures of targeted people groups. Why should not Congolese believers use their traditional drums in worship? Why should they feel they have to dress like white English Anglicans to express their worship? By implication, I could act Jewish because "Jewish" was my culture.

But again, after more years of reflection, this rationale no longer seemed to bear the weight of a consistent rationale for serious Jewish life for Jewish believers. First, Jewish religious symbols such as a Torah scroll or tallit were *sacred* symbols sustained by the blood of Jewish martyrs. Comparing such "cultural" elements to the more mundane aspects like dress, housing styles, and a preference for bagels over baklava seemed superficial. Second, features of Jewish religious life are expressions of biblical ideas, fruits of the reflection of a chosen people. Somehow the specifics of Korean or Eskimo or French culture, even religious culture, seemed to fit in a different, less weighty category.

Another sensibility, very much related to the above, had informed my inner world as a believer, though in a muted voice during the early years of my sojourn with Yeshua. It is the voice of concern about the very survival of the Jewish people. Alan Dershowitz expresses the current reality facing the Jewish people in the Western World: The problem is easily defined: the Jewish presence in America is shrinking so quickly from assimilation, intermarriage and low birthrates that American Jewish life as we know it may cease to exist by the third quarter of the twenty-first century.[6]

I remember the electrifying TV images of the Six Day War in June of 1967. Israel seemed an inch away from annihilation when all those Arab armies attacked. Though not pointing to an external attack threatening Jewish survival, Dr. Dershowitz's comments have some of that resonance.

Enter Mark Kinzer along with other friends, Stuart Dauermann, Michael Schiffman, Paul Saal, and others. Mark has articulated a theologically based rationale for Jewish life in Messiah Yeshua that speaks to the issues raised above and speaks directly to our subject of Gentile participation in Messianic Jewish assemblies.

Here are the basic axioms of BA as contoured by Mark and extended by others. As we shall see the implications for how non-Jews relate to Messianic Jewish congregations are far-reaching: God is the God of history and his presence in history continues with the Jewish people—the physical descendants of Abraham, Isaac, and Jacob—to the present day. Kinzer writes:

> The historical narrative embodied in scripture has a unique revelatory status. Nevertheless, its validity is called into question if the Lord of history to which it bears witness withdraws from history when the narrative ends.[7]

This important observation translates into a view of Messianic Judaism, which is necessarily tied to the ongoing Jewish story and not merely to snapshots of God's dealing with Israel in the biblical period. God has been actively present in the Jewish experience through the Talmudic period, the Middle Ages, the modern era, and until this very day. Kinzer infers that despite the community's color blindness to Yeshua, its liturgical development, ethics, and modes of self-preservation imperfectly but meaningfully reflect the divine will. This is because Yeshua, the greater Joseph, has always and will always reside even among his unsuspecting brothers and sisters. He explains:

> Jews who have not believed in Yeshua but who have loyally sustained a continual communal Jewish presence in the world through hours of deepest darkness are heirs of God's covenant with Israel.[8]

It is important to point out that Dr. Kinzer is not referring here to the eternal destinies of individual Jewish people but to the ongoing vitality of God's relationship with the corporate body of the sons and daughters of Abraham, Isaac, and Jacob.[9]

Kinzer, reflecting on the New Testament text, finds this strong sense of Jewish identification reflected in the teachings and example of Yeshua and in the teaching and examples of his earliest Jewish followers:

> Yeshua and his followers were born and reared within a Jewish world where such practices (i.e., circumcision, Sabbath observance and holiday observance and dietary laws), commanded in the Torah, were presumed rather than disputed. Fierce disputes arose over *how* these commandments were to be interpreted and applied – but not over whether they were to be interpreted or applied.[10]

Summarizing the picture in the New Testament, he says: "We concluded in our previous chapter that the New Testament considers Jewish practice normative for Jews who believe in Yeshua, though not for Yeshua-believing Gentiles."[11]

Jewish practice for Jewish believers remained normative (though the particulars are hotly debated) because God is faithful to his covenant with the Jewish people. Even the sin and blindness of segments of the community cannot rob us of God's covenant faithfulness. Commenting on a passage of Scripture that has provided much ammunition for the supercessionist impulse in the Church, Kinzer writes:

> The second text to be considered has a more tragic history. It contains the words of the Jerusalem crowd after calling for Yeshua's execution: "His blood be on us and our children" (Mathew 27:25). As we noted in chapter 1, most past Christian commentators saw the crowd, representing the Jewish people as a whole, as uttering an effective self-imposed curse that explained—and justified—the history of Jewish exile and suffering. This verse was thus the linchpin in charging the Jewish people with deicide—the murder of God. If this interpretation is accepted, then our hypothesis regarding Matthew's view of the Jewish people as a whole is refuted. God may still take special concern for the Jewish people, but only for the purpose of meeting out special punishment for their uniquely abhorrent crime.

However, most contemporary exegetes rightly reject this anti-Jewish reading of Matthew 27:25. They recognize that the crowd who utters these words represents, not all Jews everywhere, but only the Jews of Jerusalem or of the land of Israel and that "our children" refers, not to all their descendants forever, but only to the next generation, which would experience the catastrophe of the war with Rome in 66-70 CE. Matthew and his initial audience were Jews and they still identified with the Jewish people as a whole. However, like Jeremiah or Ezekiel, in their own time, they also believed that the suffering of Jerusalem was divine judgment, related to Jerusalem's failure to respond properly to God's appointed messengers.[12]

Reflecting on the above, a picture begins to emerge. If the God of history is still vitally involved in the life of his *segullah*—the precious, chosen people, the Jews—if the New Testament picture of assumed expectations of Jewish believers supports ongoing participation in Jewish life, or if, even the rejection of Yeshua by the majority of communal leaders and a (possibly) hand-picked crowd does not obviate his love for his chosen nation, then we modern Messianic Jews should give careful consideration to the practical outworking of God's providential presence among our people. This would include a consideration of boundary markers. You can't have "a people" without them.

A key extension to Israel's enfleshed reality and the Messianic Jew's participation in that reality is the role of Torah, the commandments of God, mediated by Moses and given to the Jewish people as a means whereby the "goy Kadosh"—the holy people—are nurtured and sustained through the centuries. It is beyond the scope of this paper to fully explore the meaning of this important commitment of the BA perspective. However, it is interesting to note that Jewish church leaders and scholars from around the world are beginning to see the importance of Torah as an identity maker even for Jewish believers who identify with the historic churches—Catholic, Orthodox, and Protestant—and is made evident in the complete text of the July 3, 2012, statement by the Helsinki Consultation on Jewish Continuity in the Body of Messiah.

Digging more deeply into the very nature of the Jewish experience, we see an important observation with far reaching implications for our subject of Gentile participation in Messianic Jewish congregations. It is an observation, which, on the one hand is entirely obvious, while on the other is obscured in its implications by its sheer familiarity. Often, the best hiding places are in plain sight. It is an idea that lies at the heart of bilateral thinking and can be called, "Israel as an enfleshed reality." Michael Wyschogrod, an Orthodox Jew and philosopher in his work *Body of Faith* has inspired Kinzer, R. Kendall Soulen, and others. He comments on this all-important idea:

> The election of the people of Israel as the people of God constitutes the sanctification of a natural family. God could have chosen a spiritual criterion: the election of all those who have faith or who obey his commandments. The liberal mind would find such an election far more congenial. But God did not choose this path. He chose the seed of Abraham, Isaac, and Jacob. There are of course, religious and ethical demands made of the elect. When they do not live up

> to these demands, they are punished. But the essential belonging to the people of election is derived from descent from the Patriarchs. The election of Israel is therefore a corporeal election. One result of this is that the Jew cannot resign his election. Were elections based on faith or ethics, a change in belief or conduct would terminate the election and the responsibilities connected with it. But because the election of Israel is of the flesh, a Jew remains in the service of God no matter what he believes or does. The Jewish body as well as the Jewish soul is therefore holy, a truth that was well understood by those enemies of God who knew that they had to murder the Jewish body along with the teachings of Israel.[13]

Israel, the Jewish people, are first and foremost a physical family. Culture, religion, and language surely have functioned as important areas of commonality through the centuries, but having Jewish flesh—Jewish lineage—is the communal super glue that binds the Jewish people together. So strong is this bond that according to Wyschogrod's informed understanding of traditional Halakhah, a Jew cannot escape from being a Jew. (So, the next time a Jewish family member tells you that as a believer in Yeshua, you're not Jewish anymore, just quote Michael Wyschograd to her.)

The physicality of Jewish identity has at times enraged the nations who have turned that body into a punching bag, but even Jewish believers can miss the implications of Wyschogrod's simple but profound observation. Why? Because we tend to define ourselves in terms of faith, commitment, beliefs, and culture rather than as physical family. We almost instinctively gravitate to Romans 2: 28:

> A man is not a Jew if he is only one outwardly, nor is circumcision merely outward and physical. No, a man is a Jew if he is in inwardly, and circumcision is circumcision is circumcision of the heart, not by the written code.

Of course, in context, this passage in no way challenges the principle of the primal physicality of Jewish identity, but it does have a different rhetorical purpose in Paul's letter to the Romans.[14] However, our

Messianic Jewish world, influenced by long Church tradition, has lived with a cloud of self-doubt in this matter. Making it even more difficult to sport an "Abraham, Isaac, Jacob, and I wear the same genes" T-shirt is the sad reality of racism. The Nazi perversion of the importance of physicality as a critical binding agent of people-hood, along with the memory of American slavery and countless other examples of abuse, has inordinately put us on the defensive. But the substructure of BA—the bilateral model of congregational development—is necessarily influenced by Wyschogrod's observation. With it comes an element of particularity that necessarily translates into heartfelt attitudes and specific beliefs regarding the role of non-Jews in our synagogues.

In recent years, God has raised up a growing body of Christian theologians who seem to "get it" regarding the importance of Jewish particularity for the sake of the entire world's future. R. Kendall Soulen is one of these. Advocates of the BA orientation to Messianic Judaism find themselves inspired by his words:

> Human beings can say no to their "supernatural" identities as Jews and as Gentiles, and in this way can close themselves to God's consummating work. In the extreme case this can take shape as the effort to eradicate Israel's body. But short of this, the fact of Jewish and Gentile identity cannot be effaced. The *ineluctable character of these dimensions of human identity* [emphasis mine] attests to the depth and resolution of God's consummating engagement with creation. As the Redeemer of Israel, God acts in fidelity not only to Israel, but to the totality of the human family's created and covenantal identity.[15]

When we think of the descriptive "bilateral," images easily come to mind: the sides of an isosceles triangle; the human body with two lungs, two ears, two arms, and two legs; or a seesaw in the playground. Even Yeshua's body stretched out on the cross can be imagined bilaterally. Two equally balanced sides, bound to each other and together forming the whole is the basic idea of the word "bilateral."

The word "ecclesiology" in its broadest definition is the study of the Church—its structure and composition. Bilateral ecclesiology then, is an understanding of the nature of the Church—the community of Yeshua—that proposes a two-sided structure: its Jewish and non-

Jewish expressions. Speaking of the bond between the historic Church and Synagogue, Kinzer sees a truly organic connection as well as uniqueness:

> It is time to challenge the notion that Christianity and Judaism are two separate religions. We should heed the advice offered by Karl Barth a half-century ago: "The Church must live with the Synagogue, not as fools say in their hearts, as with another religion or confession, but as with the root from which it sprung. Some Christian thinkers are beginning to catch up with Barth. Thus, Richard John Neuhaus writes, 'It is misleading, I believe, to speak of two peoples of God or two covenants, never mind to speak of two religions.'"[16]

The two peoples of God are actually one people, yet differentiated from each other. The idea of BA is that this shared life and differentiation should be expressed as the very core of Messianic Judaism's self-definition and communal formation.[17] I have coined a phrase that seeks to capture the organic connection between these two faiths: "*Christianity* is *acculturated messianism for the nations.*"

> **Christianity** - the faith in Jesus held by millions of people throughout the centuries. Predominantly it has been made up by the non-Jewish peoples of the world, though a continual flow of Jews have been counted among the faithful.
>
> **Acculturated** - expressing their worship in the variegated forms of Catholic, Protestant, Orthodox, French, Italian, Eskimo, Pentecostal, Mennonite, etc.
>
> **Messianism** - Jesus is the great shepherd and hope for those who love him—a faith rooted in the Hebrew Scriptures and issuing forth from the people of Israel.
>
> **For the nations** - Mexican, Native American, German, Eskimo—the peoples of the world, united with, but distinct from Israel.[18]

So, paraphrasing the 1960s commercial, "You're both right. Self-identified Messianic Jews and the Gentile church represent two, two,

two communities in one!" Borrowing Kinzer's terminology, the church is a differentiated reality: "one ecclesia expressed as two ecclesai."

Though practitioners of BA have not stated a comprehensive evaluation of the Christian church, some general convictions have emerged. The Christian church is no second-rate community. Despite its weaknesses (anti Semitic tendencies, participation in religious wars, support for darker aspects of colonialism, etc.) it retains its holiness by virtue of Yeshua's living presence. This positive view of the Church has profound implications for how Messianic Jewish leaders should view Gentile visitors, especially those who claim to have had bad experiences in their churches. See below.

The Church is not merely an invisible body of the truly saved[19] but, like Israel, is a visible body of baptized believers. This understanding creates a more positive appreciation for the historic Christian bodies such as the Roman Catholic and Orthodox communions.[20] By analogy, the people of Israel are not "an invisible body," but a trans-generational, on-the-ground reality.

Though BA oriented Messianic Jews are developing an ever-greater appreciation for the larger Church, special appreciation should be reserved for the Evangelical Christian Church, sometimes referred to as the Free Church. Because of its atomistic governmental structure conducive to experimentation with Jewish-style congregations, its pre-millennial commitments leaving important space for the nation of Israel, and its practical support and help, the Evangelical community has been and continues to be absolutely essential to the development of maturing Messianic Judaism.

God's ultimate purposes for our world (no more war, cancer, or pain and all of creation brought forward into the joyful state promised long ago) will come about through Jewish people and the nations, joined together in Yeshua. "In that day the Lord will be one and his name one!" The consummation of God's overarching plan for planet Earth will come about as both Israel and the nations embrace their roles in what R.K. Soulen calls "an economy of mutual blessing." Borrowing C.S. Lewis' eschatological image, I like to think of it as a great dance—with partners.

We can now distill some of the key features of BA Messianic Judaism and Messianic Jewish congregations from the discussion above. Again, we must consider these broader issues if our discussion of the role of Gentiles in our midst is to be credible and coherent.

The Messianic Jewish Congregation as a Little Piece of Israel

The BA congregation is a unique kind of synagogue and not a culturally attuned church. This principle is axiomatic because it speaks to the very nature of Messianic Judaism, and by implication, means that it must be made up primarily of Jews.

Though its self-identification is primarily Jewish, Yeshua takes his place as central to the Messianic Jewish experience. Kinzer insists that:

> Messianic Judaism involves more than the subtle tweaking of an existing form of Jewish life and thought—adding a few elements required by faith in Yeshua and subtracting a few elements incompatible with that faith. Instead, the Judaism we have inherited—and continue to practice—is entirely bathed in the bright light of Yeshua's revelation.[21]

We are glad that Kinzer is so forthright on this point.

Messianic Jewish congregations must also live out their profound spiritual connection with believers on "the other side of the isosceles triangle." That is the living reality of unity of which believers must find concrete expression.[22]

The divine-human partnership assumes that Jews have a covenantal responsibility to assure the future of the Jewish people. Though among the various Jewish denominations specific answers to questions about how to best ensure that "Am Yisrael" truly will "chai," all agree that every Jew must do her part. Among bilateral practitioners, the role of kashrut, holy day observance, and Shabbat are seen as important factors in the equation.[23] However, these are not enjoined upon non-Jews, even those in the Messianic Jewish synagogue. The expectation that they will support the community's values in these areas has much to do with creating communal cohesion, but is not a function of a Torah-mandated covenantal commitment that Gentiles bear.

Boaz Michael, the Director of First Fruits of Zion, paints a somewhat similar picture in his most recent book, *Tent of David—Healing the Vision of the Messianic Gentile:*

> First Fruits of Zion teaches a distinction between the obligations of a Jewish believer and the obligations of

> a Gentile believer. Not all the commandments that apply to Jews equally apply to Gentiles. This means that Gentile believers who have not taken on those commandments of the Torah that do not pertain to them specifically as Gentiles are not wallowing in sin or rebelling against God. They might be missing out on the disciplines and godly intentions of these commandments, which bring great structure and blessing to one's life—but they are not living in defiance and rebellion towards God. Gentile Christians are not, in fact, obligated to all of the commandments in the same way that the Jewish people are. The apostles chose not to obligate the Gentile believers to certain "sign" commandments and specific markers of Jewish identity which were enjoined specifically upon the physical nation of Israel, the Jewish people: circumcision, Shabbat, festivals, mezuzah, tefillin, tzitzit, kashrut, and the Levitical functions. While Gentile believers should be encouraged to participate in most of these mitzvot on some level, it is not on a level of a Jewish person's responsibility for covenantal fidelity. Besides, these aspects of Torah can really only be kept properly within the context of a Jewish community and culture.[24]

These helpful thoughts represent a shift in thinking among the FFOZ leadership from an earlier view that did seem to mandate Torah observance for non-Jewish believers. Boaz and his team deserve much credit for being willing to lose much financial support and esteem among their core constituency for the sake of Torah's demand for honesty and integrity. Their example can inspire us all irrespective of our convictions on the particulars of FFOZ's theology.

Gentile believers, including the vast majority who attend our congregations, do not become Jews when they trust Yeshua. When they enter the "deep Jewish space" of a Messianic Jewish congregation, they should have a supportive role, as we will discuss below.[25]

Though a Messianic Jewish congregation will in the vast majority of cases have non-Jewish participants, the numbers should be relatively small.

It may sound shocking at first, but the truth is that an activity, which may rightly be viewed as a sin in the church, can be a mitzvah—a truly good deed—in the synagogue, including a Messianic Jewish synagogue. Of course, we are not talking about theft, adultery, or idolatry. These are just sinful, period. However, when it comes to distinctions between Jews and Gentiles in their respective roles in the assembly, the situation will be different. In a church, to demand that a particular group of people may not come forward to read a passage of Scripture publically would certainly seem improper.[26] Or to suggest that members of a particular ethnic group might find a more appropriate home in another congregation sounds like the kind of racism practiced in many white congregations in the South until the 1960s. But, for a synagogue to create internal boundaries for the sake of a God-given mandate to remain a unique, holy people could actually be a mitzvah, even an act of real self-sacrifice for the sake of Heaven.[27]

We are touching here on the very nerve center of the issue that confronts Messianic Jewish leaders today. Each of us is asked by the very nature of our being Jews who follow the Jewish Messiah: "Are our assemblies primarily synagogues—little pieces of Israel, expressions of a uniquely called and covenanted people? Or, are our assemblies primarily churches, that is Jewish-oriented expressions of the multi-ethnic community of Messiah?"[28] The answer we give has everything to do with how we envision the role of non-Jews in our midst.

We have looked at the bilateral approach (BA) to Messianic Judaism. We will now turn our attention to what I will call the Missions Approach (MA) to building congregations with a Jewish ethos and with Messiah Yeshua at center stage.

The Messianic Jewish Congregation as a Jewish-Sensitive Community of Believers

Our subject is the role of non-Jews in Messianic Jewish congregations. However, lest we settle for a superficial treatment that merely catalogues a list of practical strategies disconnected from any theoretical framework, we must seek to understand the deeper structures that undergird the Messianic Jewish enterprise. Only when we understand the basic paradigms will we be able to develop a responsible outlook regarding those from among the nations whom we welcome into our congregational midst.

It should first be noted that the Christian missions to the Jews in the 19th century gave rise to idea that Jewish believers should have the freedom to create their own communities. Mitch Glaser comments:

> It is a mistake to think that Messianic congregations are a new idea and that traditional missions did not start Messianic congregations. For example, CMJ (also known as the London Jews Society, LJS) established a large mission station and center in Warsaw . . . The congregation outside of Bucharest led by Isaac Feinstein, who served with the Norwegian Israelite Mission, is well known by students of the period.

Glaser notes the motivations for starting such congregations:

> The congregations addressed a number of concerns. First, it was understood that congregations were to be an effective means of evangelism. Secondly, they were created as a source of fellowship for Jewish believers, especially those uncomfortable in attending an Evangelical church.[29]

A touching expression of the support for the concept of Jewish believing communities or congregations comes from Rev T. Lindhagen and offered at the International Jewish Missionary Conference in Stockholm in 1911:

> It cannot be denied that up to now the relation of Jewish Christians to their people has been far from altogether satisfactory. The reproaches that have been leveled against them are unfortunately only too well grounded (!) It is quite true that there are Jewish Christians and missionaries to the Jews who make an altogether vicious use of Paul's words to the Galatians, "There is neither Jew nor Greek" . . . It is equally true that the Gentile church has helped to estrange Jewish Christians from their own people by calling them "proselytes." In this case a thorough-going change in policy and practice is necessary . . . That the ideal of an autonomous Jewish Christian church is closely

> connected with these aspirations regarding the right attitude of Hebrew Christians to their people is self-evident.[30]

We can't help but appreciate this gentleman's sensitivity to the profoundly difficult situation Jewish believers in Yeshua faced in his era; I look forward to meeting him one day. The fact that some of the Jewish believers used biblical passages to bludgeon others of their countrymen speaks to one of the sad social realities sometimes evident in marginalized communities. Reverend Lindhagen suggests that forming "Messianic Jewish" communities will help undo the negative effects of their outsider status.

As we continue to survey the MA motivational mix for starting Jewish-oriented congregations—later called "Messianic" or "Messianic Jewish" —we discern a strong tendency toward the pragmatic. Such congregations are helpful to Jewish believers, are a cost effective means of outreach for Jewish missions,[31] and are a more effective means of outreach to Jews than Evangelical churches.

Some voices moved beyond the pragmatic to what I will call the "quasi covenantal," a sense that Jewish life was important in God's plan for these Jewish believers. Lichtenstein and Rabinowitz are two examples. Some early practitioners actually lived quite "kosher" lifestyles, perhaps more so than some who identify with a bilateral approach to modern Messianic Judaism. But the underlying theology speaks to the differing orientations we see even today. Joseph Cohn, son of the famed Leopold Cohn, founder of the American Board of Missions to the Jews, wrote about his father's Jewish practice and its motivation:

> He followed the method introduced by Paul, "To the Jew I become as a Jew." Pork he would not touch and it was not allowed in our home at any time . . . The Mosaic law was adhered to . . . For all of this he was continually attacked, even by certain Jews who already had accepted Christ. The reason for my father's dietetic asceticism was not that he felt himself to be under the [L]aw of Moses, but by this method he was able to win Jews to Christ who could not have been won otherwise.[32]

One wonders if Rabbi Cohn's motivations were truly quite so utilitarian. His passion and consistency seems to suggest a deep reservoir of love for Jewish life. But, the social and theological climate of the day likely would mute one's ability to express, to speak, or even to think too much about other possibilities.

The pragmatic, helpful, fair-minded, aesthetic, utilitarian, and musicological seem to inform the deeper ethos of MA, the Missions Approach to Messianic congregational development. Arnold Fruchtenbaum seems "to say it all" in his defense of the idea of Messianic Jewish congregations:

> If the question is asked, "Are Messianic congregations a biblical necessity or requirement?" then the answer has to be no. The Bible does not require uniquely Jewish congregations for Messianic Jews any more than it requires other ethnic churches, such as black churches, Latino churches, Chinese churches or others.

If the question is asked differently, "Is it biblically permissible to have Messianic congregations?" then the answer is yes. Jewish believers have the right to set up uniquely Jewish congregations that reflect the Jewish culture and style of music, worship, teaching, and so on just as black, Latino, and Chinese churches would reflect their particular style of worship and culture.[33]

Arnold Fruchtenbaum is being characteristically generous-spirited in his remarks, "Let people live. Let them be themselves." His theological outlook is typical of modern missiologists who lament the sad cultural imperialism of an earlier time that demanded white shirts and ties of sub tropical converts to Christianity during Sunday morning services.[34] But notice: Messianic life is simply a Jewish expression of ethnicity, no more a mandated covenant than any other expression.[35]

A fair characterization of Fruchtenbum's theology recognizes that at one point he does go beyond the pragmatic to the covenantal. As a classic Dispensationalist, he has a strong commitment to the ongoing importance of the Jewish people, especially as our existence impacts the eschatological plan of God for planet Earth. Though very resistant to the idea that the Torah of Moses contains the blueprint for Israel's national life for Yeshua-believing Jews, he does retain one explicit command—circumcision. He states:

> "It is my conviction that Hebrew Christians should have their sons circumcised on the eight day." However, he explains that this command remains in force because it had been given to Abraham long before Moses. A second value issuing from the Abrahamic covenant is his commitment to the Land of Israel as the God-given homeland of the Jewish people.[36]

In *Everything You Need to Know to Grow a Messianic Yeshiva,* pioneer thinker Phil Goble finds a similar theological orientation with its pragmatic focus:

> In 1974 I began to see that many churches were not willing to change the routine of their style of ministry in order to reach the Jewish neighborhoods where God had placed them. I saw that new congregations needed to be planted, messianic synagogues, in those areas. I have never advocated putting Jews under the law, but if a Jewish community like Williamsburg, Brooklyn, is on its way to eternal death (under the law) and a church in that area insists on worshipping in the style of White Anglo-Saxon Protestants, something must be done. A new congregation—one that will identify its hymnology, liturgy, architecture and worshipping style—must become as if it were under the law to win those who are under the law. (I Cor. 9:20)[37]

Summarizing the above, we can see that the Missions Approach to Messianic congregational formation stresses: (1) a concern for the well being of Jewish believers or, in the case of Goble's comments, deep concern for the eternal souls of Jewish non-believers. (2) a pragmatic, needs-based approach to the enterprise when limited resources are considered. (3) a view of Jewish life, which unlike the bilateral view, sees Jewish law, custom, and tradition in terms similar to its view of the culture of any other people group.

One Body in Messiah

One further aspect of the overall character of MA needs to be considered before we move directly into the subject of Gentile involvement in Messianic Judaism. Characteristic of MA is its aversion to making distinctions between Jewish and Gentile believers. This reticence, which is deeply rooted in the Christian psyche generally, finds expression over and over again in the literature about Jewish believing identity and practice, both from Christian and Jewish believers. A few examples will suffice:

William Varner, former dean of the Institute of Biblical Studies with Friends of Israel Gospel Ministry writes:

> It has sometimes been charged that Messianic Judaism is rebuilding the dividing wall of hostility. Actually, no one can rebuild the wall. It is done away with forever. My concern, however, is that Messianic Judaism by its concern with laws that have no continuing spiritual relevance for either Jews or Gentiles, is creating an appearance that the wall still separates us.[38]

Eliezer Maass, in his practical Survival Guide for the New Jewish Believer, speaks to the issue very directly:

> With the advent of Israel's Messiah, the law of Moses was put to an end . . . No longer are we (believers generally) burdened by the weight of dietary laws and endless regulations of every kind . . . We believe that the Law of Moses as a rule of life has been fulfilled in the Messiah and therefore, believers, whether Jewish or non-Jewish are no longer under its obligation or condemnation. However, both Jewish and non-Jewish believers have the freedom in Messiah to maintain those aspects of the Law of Moses and Jewish cultural identity that do not violate Scripture.[39]

This widespread conviction will have titanic implications for the role of Gentiles in Messianic Jewish congregations. It arises out of the matrix of this traditional Christian understanding of Jewish particularity, the role of Torah, and the very nature of the relationship of Jews and non-Jews in Messiah. However, we note that unlike the prevailing view in the Church for many centuries, Fruchtenbaum, Varner, Maass, and other practitioners do allow and often encourage Jewish practices, not for covenantal reasons, but for evangelistic purposes or as sincere accommodations to the needs of Jewish people who may desire to live in familiar cultural territory.

To reinforce the point, even a cursory Google search of the phrase "Messianic congregations, Jews, and Gentiles" reveals the extent to which the idea that Messianic congregations are by nature and purpose, a home where believers, Jewish or not, come to fellowship and learn the Bible from a Jewish perspective. As noted at the beginning of this paper, the categories we have chosen to tease out the two basic approaches to Gentile participation are the Bilateral and Missions approaches. Undoubtedly, many congregations surveyed on the web will most often not see themselves as sprouting from either of these in any direct sense and would likely find aspects of either or both orientations with which to agree. However, the theologically attuned observer can discern genuine patterns of thought and practice which translate very definitely into differing mentalities, approaches, and desired outcomes for both Jews and non-Jews in their midst.

An interesting example of the leveling of the playing field among Jewish and non-Jewish believers in congregations, which gravitate to the MA outlook, can be found in the wording of the website of Baruch Ha Shem, a large assembly in Dallas, Texas. Its leader is my very good friend Marty Waldman. In the section entitled "Welcome Mat" we read:

> *Baruch HaShem* (BHS) is a growing Messianic community that meets in North Dallas. As a congregation, BHS is dedicated to the Great Commission of *Yeshua* (Jesus) as expressed in the Good News of *Mattityahu* 28:18-20, as well as Romans 1:16, which states: "For I am not ashamed of the Good News, since it is God's powerful means of bringing salvation to everyone who keeps on trusting, to the Jew especially, but equally to the Gentile." Consequently, BHS membership includes many Jewish believers and also people from a wide range of other cultural and religious backgrounds. Nevertheless, the Congregation is *echad* (one) in the L-RD, and remains united by the power of the *Ruach HaKodesh* (Holy Spirit) and by the simple belief that *Yeshua* is the Messiah of Israel and thus King over all the nations. He is the center and focal point of our faith.

With such an all-embracing, universal message and its warm and gifted leader, it is no wonder that Baruch haShem is a very large and well-funded congregation with a sizable majority of non-Jewish participants.

We are now ready to consider in some detail the roles of Gentiles in Messianic congregations as seen through the grid established thus far. We will find great areas of commonality and an equally great number of significant differences.

PART 2- GENTILES IN OUR MESSIANIC JEWISH MIDST: HOW SHALT THEY LIVE?

In light of the previous discussion, let us consider practical means whereby Gentiles may attain the place we believe they are destined to in our congregations. However, we must not gloss over the areas of theological distinction covered above if our discussion of practical strategies is to have more than mere surface resonance or dissonance among us. The fact is that leaders of both kinds of congregations worry about the viability of the other:

- BA leaders wonder about the integrity of using Jewish symbols, holy day observance, etc. if Jews have no covenantal obligation to live as Jews.
- MA leaders wonder if the strong identification with Jewish norms, particularly liturgy will dull passion for the Risen One, will be beneficial in the long run.
- BA leaders wonder about the legitimacy of Messianic Jewish congregations that have a strong majority of Gentiles.
- MA leaders wonder about the drift of those who lean towards traditional Judaism and the demonstrable loss of passion for Yeshua among new Jewish believers.
- BA leaders wonder about the ability of MA congregations to speak meaningfully to the Jewish world.
- MA leaders wonder about BA leaders' tendency to elevate Jewish texts aside from the Bible.

We must also keep in mind the great areas of commonality among leaders who represent these orientations:

- Both see non-Jewish believers as "co-heirs with the saints," people who are loved by the God of Abraham, Isaac, and Jacob with intensity revealed most clearly at Messiah's incarnation, death, and resurrection.
- Both agree MJ congregations will have at least some non-Jewish presence and that these people need to be treated with the love and respect they deserve.
- Though for different reasons, both agree that MJ congregations are important: There are thousands of churches, but only a few places where we Jews can be ourselves.
- Both would like to see more Jewish people in the pews of their congregations.
- Both see intermarried people as an important constituency.
- Messianic congregations, because of their organic connection with the larger family of Yeshua, should embrace some of its universally held faith commitments. These include the full deity and full humanity of Yeshua, the canon of Scripture, including the New Testament and participation in the Tevilah (immersion) and Ha Zikkaron (The Lord's Supper, Communion). Such practices are more easily embraced in the synagogue when some non-Jews are present because they are more comfortable and familiar with such concepts.
- Both desire to see the entire Jewish world embrace Yeshua our Messiah.

A Shared Concern: Why So Many Gentiles?

Another commonality between differing kinds of Messianic Jewish congregations is the fact that, although most leaders would like to see significantly more Jews than non-Jews in the pews, historical, cultural, and demographic factors make this difficult. Some of these are:

- The total number of Jews in the world today is dwarfed by the number of non-Jews. Currently, the worldwide Jewish population is 13.3 million with 46 % of these living in North America. In 2011 the world population was estimated at 7 billion. Thus, the worldwide Jewish population is a mere .2 % of that total. Thus, any aggregation of people that appeals to both Jews and Gentiles, especially those that open its doors equally to both, will tend to have more non-Jewish participants. Of course, local demographic realities may alter this result. This is a powerful reason for planting Messianic Jewish congregations in Jewish population centers.

- Evangelical Christians, among Christian groupings, are the most interested in Messianic Jewish things.[40] Evangelicals in the United States numbered, according the Website of Political Research Associates, 102 million souls in 2007. The number of Jewish believers in Messianic assemblies could be placed very generously at 25,000 (50 people in 500 congregations). Thus, congregations with no firewall seeking to sustain a Jewish majority will have a very difficult time indeed.
- Christians go to church much more regularly than Jews go to synagogue. This translates into more regular attendance in our congregations by Gentiles who are used to the idea of attending services regularly.
- Non-Jewish members are often in a better financial position to help build a local congregation than Jewish members. Though this is clearly not the case generally in America when comparing income levels of Jews and non-Jews, the particular subset of Jews attracted to our congregations often do not come from the stable home environments conducive to financial success. Gravitation to marginal religious movements often begins with other areas of marginalization. We may chafe at this observation—who doesn't want to be viewed as living among "the winners?" But we must remember Messiah's agenda. He has a very special place in his heart for the outsiders, so much so that he became one himself. One subtle but ultimately powerful result of this economic reality is that Messianic leaders are understandably reluctant to disenfranchise well-heeled and generous Christian members of the congregation by allowing the place to become "too Jewish" and thereby losing the support of these good folks. This can be especially true when a congregation has a large mortgage or responsibilities to multiple paid staff.[41]

Rabbi Tony Eaton, the spiritual leader of Congregation Simchat Yisrael in West Haven, CT, expresses the demographic problem in these terms: "The problem is not too many Gentiles, but too few

Jews." In other words, the emphasis of the Messianic leader in solving the problem of an ever-diminishing proportion of Jewish people in Messianic Jewish congregations should be outreach (*keruv*) among our people. I appreciate and agree with Rabbi Tony's desire for more outreach. However, I sense that the solution will also require serious rethinking of our approach to Gentile participation.

So much for theological abstraction, historical reflection, and collective psychological analysis. It's time to get practical. Because I know it best, let me tell you about the synagogue I've been privileged to serve for the past three decades. Congregation Ruach Israel, located in Needham, MA, a near-western suburb of Boston, has been in existence since 1978. I have spent much energy seeking to build a bilaterally oriented synagogue, starting long before Mark Kinzer's introduction of the term (though I am profoundly grateful to Mark for clarifying and articulating the theological underpinnings of things I could only intuit in earlier years).

Case Study: Congregation Ruach Israel

Congregation Ruach Israel had its humble beginnings in 1979 in Boston, Massachusetts. For the past 21 years, the synagogue's home has been in Needham, Massachusetts, with a population of 29,000. The growing Jewish community represents roughly one third of that total. Ruach Israel's formal membership is 44 family units. In four of these families, neither husband nor wife is Jewish.[42] The congregation is led by a nine member Board of Directors at the center of which is an Executive Committee composed of Senior Rabbi, President, and Vice President. All Board members, as well as our Rabbinical Team (Senior Rabbi plus two others who have UMJC Smichah) and our three member Cantorial Team, are all Jewish.[43] The four key agendas of the congregation are:

- Outreach (keruv) to other Jews so they may make teshuvah and put their trust in Yeshua
- Liturgical integrity
- Healing prayer, so that Israel may experience the powerful, supernatural intrusion of Olam Ha Baah among us through the Risen One
- Children's education— a full one third of the congregations are children and teens

Over the years we have sought to work out our bilateral approach to non-Jewish participation in our synagogue. Here are some of the values and strategies that have guided us:

Gently guide Gentile visitors. I as the Senior Rabbi try to discourage non-Jewish visitors from viewing Ruach Israel as a likely next spiritual home. A typical conversation best had after the first or second visit can go something like this:

> Visitor: Rabbi I just loved your service. I sense that you are the true church. I've been looking for a place with the kind of spiritual purity I see here. How can I become part?
>
> Rabbi Rich: Well, I'm so glad you enjoyed the service, and I hope you'll feel free to visit again sometime, but I must tell you that Ruach is a synagogue and not a church.
>
> Visitor: Oh.
>
> Rabbi Rich: We really are a home mostly for Jewish people and intermarried families. There are so many churches in Boston, but very, very few places Jewish people can be ourselves as we follow the Messiah. I'm sure you can understand our thinking here.
>
> Visitor: Oh yes. I understand.
>
> Rabbi Rich: Now here's a thought. When you come visit us again sometime, think about bringing a Jewish friend with you.
>
> Visitor: Yes, I have a friend I think might like to come.
>
> Rabbi Rich: Great! Meanwhile, can you join us for lunch in the Function Hall?

Produce a pamphlet. Here is a reality I have seen over and over again: Jews come late to services, but church visitors show up early or on time. We have a pamphlet describing our service and which defines the major symbols and defining moments in the liturgy. It also lets visitors know about our unique calling.

Congregation Ruach Israel especially welcomes Jewish people and interfaith couples and their families to join our community. Ours is a synagogue and not a church. This can seem a bit confusing at first because we share with the Christian community a belief in Yeshua. But, as an expression of Jewish life, we are a synagogue. (A church, by definition, is a multi-ethnic community of believers and is therefore, different from a synagogue). Our synagogue has a deep appreciation for the Church in its many denominations. We share a sense of spiritual brotherhood in Yeshua. In fact, we see the unity of church and synagogue as central to God's plan for our world. But, we are a synagogue, not a church.

If you are not Jewish, we want you to know we are pleased you chose to visit our Shabbat or other service today. If you are a member of a local church, we hope your visit will enhance your appreciation of the Jewish roots of your Christian faith. If you are not Jewish and are unaffiliated, we encourage you to find a church that can become your spiritual home. Just as all Jews need a synagogue in which to learn and grow, so all Gentile believers need a local home with familiar heritage and culture in which to grow.

As visitors sit, waiting for the service to start, they can get just a subtle taste for how we view our visitors, the majority of whom come from local churches. To soften the message about our unique calling and to make the service easier to follow, the pamphlet continues with brief explanations of the morning's flow.

Manage visitor cards. Simply stated, Jewish visitors and intermarried families get my best pastoral attention. I am less likely to follow up with people visiting from local churches. However, we will put visitors from local churches on our general e-mail list if they so desire.

Cultivate Hebrew-rich services. Our Shabbat and holy day services are roughly half in Hebrew, half in English. Of course our principle reason for using so much of the mother tongue is that the Hebrew language binds the Jewish people together perhaps more deeply than any other single cultural dynamic. Hebrew ties us to our people, creating a cohesion that reaches through the many centuries of our shared experience. But, a useful bi-product of having Hebrew-rich services is that they are not so easily accessible to the Evangelical Christian visitor who is used to total accessibility. The meta communication here is that "this synagogue is deep Jewish space—a place where Jews gather."[44]

Make keruv (outreach) intentional. Our strategies for keruv always are geared for Jewish seekers and intermarried folks whom we hope to interest in creating Messianic Jewish homes. For example, our Outreach Committee is geared almost entirely to the many intermarried families in the Boston area. It is these people we have in mind to interest in our congregation. A constant refrain in the synagogue should be, "We are here for Jewish and intermarried families." This core value must gradually seep into the collective consciousness of the assembly.

Develop Jewish leadership. A value which seems quite obvious in a bilaterally oriented congregation is that the leaders of a synagogue must be Jewish. Rabbis, cantors, and synagogue presidents should be Jewish.[45] Here, theology plays a big role in creating this reality on the ground. As mentioned in Part I of this paper, the bilateral outlook demands that our congregations are little pieces of Israel—expressions first and foremost of Jewish peoplehood, though rooted in Messiah Yeshua. Thus, the energy and sacrifice necessary to guide a congregation to seek Jewish majorities, to install Jewish leaders, etc. comes from the deep reservoirs of spiritual conviction, not primarily from pragmatic considerations. Though subtle, it is hard to overstate the importance of this dynamic as we leaders seek to shape the future of Messianic Judaism. This point deserves further exploration.

Any Messianic Jewish leader who has reflected on the things which "make people tick" knows that one of the most powerful forces in the human experience is the acceptance/rejection dynamic. People yearn for acceptance by those they look up to, the people they love and admire. When they feel accepted, they are responsive to others, just as God's love in Messiah, when felt deeply, moves us all to love him back and to respond to his demands on our lives. Conversely, feelings of rejection are very difficult to accommodate. Ask any congregational leader and he or she will tell you that much of the pain in his or her ministry has come from people who have acted poorly toward them because of their irrational feelings of being rejected (misunderstood, not valued, unappreciated) by their pastor or rabbi. Surely this is not the only source of pain suffered by ministers and pulpit rabbis, but it is a major one. And sometimes, the congregant is right. She has been rejected unfairly by God's representative.

The challenge we face as Messianic Jewish leaders is that Jewish particularity—the uniqueness of the Jewish people and our obligation as leaders among Am Yisrael to uphold that uniqueness—demands that we cannot accept everyone into our synagogues equally. This can and will produce resentment among some people towards us. How could it not? They at times will feel rejected and unappreciated. How could it be otherwise, even despite our very best efforts to honor and love them? Further, as sensitive spiritual souls yearning to please our heavenly Abba, we leaders feel an opposite impulse—to uphold the universality of the Gospel and its call to all the men, women, boys, and girls so they may become enfolded in the welcoming embrace of Messiah Yeshua.

So, lying within our hearts and minds are two opposite impulses, both worthy, both essential. The particularity of the call of the Jewish people to live as God's *segullah*, his precious possession from among the people groups of the world, stretches one of our arms to the right, and the universality of Yeshua's message stretches in cruciform fashion to the opposite pole. We are thus, crucified with Messiah as the bearers of a conundrum which proves almost beyond our ability to bear. Yet, we can make progress by embracing our co-crucifixion with Messiah and then thinking dialectically about a possible resolution.

Clearly, dialectical approaches to life's questions can be misapplied. We think of the false dichotomy between Peter and Paul imagined by some 19th century biblical scholars as a good example. Paul and his gospel of grace allegedly conflicted with Peter's Jewish, Torah-friendly message. Along comes John, with his gospel of love and the tension of thesis and antithesis was resolved in the new synthesis: the gospel of love—the true gospel. Actually, there really was no true dialectic between Peter and Paul as the best modern scholarship demonstrates but the appeal to love as a starting place for resolving the kind of true dialectic we Messianic Jewish leaders face is most worthy. More on the ways of love a bit later in our discussion.

We can legitimately think about the resolution of truly opposite impulses (universalism and particularism) if we allow ourselves to "be stretched between the polarities" as Messiah was stretched out on the cross, allowing ourselves to die while embracing the complexity of our calling. We imagine the tension on his attenuated limbs to be roughly equal. So, too we must feel the pulling in both directions. I suggest that the pragmatism of many Messianic Jewish congregations tends to pull too much to the side of the universal and not enough to the demands of the particular call of the Jewish people. I would criticize some Messianic Jewish synagogues as having an overdeveloped sense of particularism, which functionally removes them from all life in the larger community of Yeshua.[46]

I suggest the best resolution to date is the bilateral model of Messianic Jewish congregational development along with a clear understanding of exactly what it means to truly love the non-Jewish people in our midst.

Loving Gentiles in Our Midst

We begin with the clear awareness that Gentile believers are not the pagans of antiquity, but brothers and sisters in Messiah who deserve our deepest respect and love. With this clearly in mind we are in a position to ask the question, "How shall we love these people who come among us?"

We mentioned earlier that at Ruach Israel we resist seeking members from among Gentile visitors. Can we appeal to a love motivation for such "exclusion?" We surely can. Let's talk about children. When (the hypothetical) Bob and Sally O'Hara show up to services with their three children in tow and enthusiastically proclaim they loved what they find in our service, that they have finally found the true faith and they may want to become part of our community, we are less enthusiastic. We have found that often these parents are not thinking about the long-term effects of the identity confusion they bequeath to the children when they rip them out of Awana Club and Boys Brigade, Sunday school, and church so they can become part of "the Jewish church." The negative spiritual effects of this move may not be very pronounced among 3-10 year olds, but, eventually little Cindy O'Hara will become a teenager and as we all know, issues related to fitting in, feeling normal, and not being an outsider, become important at that age. So we ask, "Is it really loving for the Messianic Jewish leader to put out the welcome mat to the O'Hara family?" I would suggest that in most cases the answer is an emphatic "no." Are there exceptions to the above? Of course there may be. Such is the nature of the infinite variations we find in the human relational mix. We will consider some "exceptions" below. But, the general principle stands. It is usually not loving to bring children into an already identity-challenged community, thereby compounding their own confusion, potentially leaving them in a spiritual no-man's land instead of celebrating and reinforcing their God given identity as people who should attend church.[47]

But how shall we love the non-Jews already in our midst? I know of no worthy congregation that does not have at least a small number of non-Jews in attendance. This is true of mainstream synagogues as well as Messianic congregations. Below are some principles and examples that may prove helpful:

Discern the Difference. Our experience as leaders as well as the testimony of history from Ruth the Moabitess to the present demonstrates that some non-Jews should and must be among us. We know who these folks are:

- They don't demand to wear a *tallit* or make a Torah *aliyah* but are just happy to serve in the community and feel profoundly grateful to do so.[48]
- They appreciate the Church. Their presence in the Messianic Jewish congregation is not primarily a reaction formation to the bad pastor or bad Sunday school teacher of their childhood. Rather, they appreciate the historic community of Yeshua, understand that churches are the God-ordained home for most believers, but have felt the strong undertow of the Ruach, drawing them into Jewish space. They spend no time trying to get their friends in the churches to "quit those paganized, apostate assemblies and join the messianics, the true believers!" Encouraging such people has a very positive effect on our relationship with local churches. Pastors are very understandably wary of believers in their churches who begin speaking to others about the deficiencies of the Church and the "better way of the Messianic Jews who get it right," vis-à-vis Christmas, Easter, Torah, etc. We Messianic Jewish leaders in no way want to dignify or endorse such trite nonsense. Healthy non-Jewish believers who attach themselves to our congregations should ideally love and appreciate their Christian upbringing.
- They have high regard for the Jewish people, not as an idealized mass of eschatological mini Abrahams and Sarahs, but as the real people they know from real history, work, and the JCC.
- They are the good-hearted Catholic or Evangelical spouses of Jewish believers who, though initially don't understand the meaning of all the Jewish emphasis, are willing to follow their husbands (yes, usually these are Gentile wives) to the Messianic

Jewish congregation. At first they do it for the children or for the sake of family unity. In time, some desire to identify with the Jewish people and the Jewish Messiah for even deeper reasons.

Caution: The "rules" don't cover every situation. Sometimes, the only reason for justifying a particular Gentile's participation among us is simple love flowing from our mandate to love people who may not "get it" concerning the specifics of Messianic Jewish theology or practice. These souls should be welcome to sojourn among us for no other reason than the fact that they may have attended for a long time or because the community senses a goodness and holiness which ennobles the community or simply because they have nowhere else to go.

Make clear the rules. I'll have to admit, I was nervous. The Messianic Jewish Rabbinical Council (MJRC) had formulated and would soon jointly affirm a set of standards to be commended as norms for the non-Jews in our member congregations. I had determined to clearly articulate these at one of our brunches geared for intermarried people—one where I knew the vast majority of those present would be members of our synagogue and not visitors. After the meal, I gathered the twenty or so participants in our host's living room, passed out copies of the standards, and began to teach. To my delight, there were no objections to the fact that non-Jews would not be invited to the Torah scroll to read, would not be permitted to wear a tallit at services, etc. The key issue was expressed by Paul, a non-Jewish spouse of one of our Jewish members. "Rabbi Rich, we don't mind the rules at all. What we need is to be clear as to exactly what they are." Right, Paul!

All too often the Messianic Jewish enterprise appears trivial because the "rules of the game" vary so widely among our congregations. The question, most often unarticulated but felt, is this: Why should Jewish people take seriously a religious movement that is so ambiguous in its values and teachings? The Messianic Jewish Rabbinical Council (MJRC) was formed to give weight to Messianic Jewish understandings, particularly in the areas of congregational life and practice. Four intersecting questions have guided our deliberations over the past decade as we have wrestled with the issues of normative practice for our synagogues:

- What does Scripture say explicitly on a given subject?

- What does Jewish tradition reveal on the subject?
- What do the explicit teachings and example of Yeshua reveal on the subject?
- How do the realities of modern life inform our determinations?

Full members of the Messianic Jewish Rabbinical Council with voice and vote must be ordained rabbis. Associate members need not be ordained but serve the movement as recognized lay leaders with the intellectual and spiritual gifts necessary to contribute to the dialogue.

The discussion will likely continue on for years to come as new situations present themselves. Our contention is that loving the non-Jews in our midst demands the kind of clarity that a group process of like-minded rabbis working together over many years can generate. The pay-off comes in the form of a plan for clear identity formation for our synagogue members, resulting in a relaxed congregational atmosphere, the result of clarity where before there had been none. The payoff also comes from the joy we sense among those who have demonstrated they really have a "Jewish *neshuma* (soul)" whose need for full participation among Am Yisrael can finally be met in a communally-sanctioned fashion through the auspices of the MJRC. See below for more on this.

Rely on the power of symbolic gesture. At Ruach Israel, as in most spiritual communities, we look for ways to express love to our members, including our non-Jewish members, via small acts which demonstrate how much we appreciate them—a special poem or a song just for them, a "member of the month" announcement, etc. When we invite all the children up to the *bema* for a blessing before Shabbat school, I make it a point to connect with as many kids as I can reach. I pull the little girls ponytails and rub the *keppies* of the little guys. This is a moment for love for all in the midst of a Torah service, which in most every other respect reserves special space for Am Yisrael in our re-enactment of the Sinai experience.

Consider The Conversion Option. Though controversial in Messianic Jewish circles, we have found that having a mechanism whereby a very limited number of non-Jews among us can formally join the Jewish people is helpful. It can be a tremendous act of love to formally eliminate the huge psychic burden felt by some uniquely called non-Jews among us who feel caught in the "no man's land" of a confused personal identity and who yearn to be counted among the Jewish people. Others in our congregations can be helped as well. Here are some examples. Though hypothetical, they represent the kinds of concerns casting a mist of confusion and anxiety on many among the people we serve:

- "I wasn't born Jewish, but at the Messianic Jewish synagogue I attend all the guys wear tallises, which makes me feel Jewish. I suppose I am, but I'm not sure. No one really talks about it much. "

- "My name is Tommy O'Hara and I'm 10 years old. Mom and dad like to take me to a Messianic Jewish church and I like to go. I think I may be Jewish now, but I'm not sure."

- "My name is Rachel Sandler and I'm Jewish. I like going to temple but I end up confused when I go. My bat mitzvah is coming up in May, but my Jewish friends at school say our congregation is all wrong and their parents won't let them come. They say our rabbi shouldn't have bar mitzvahs for kids who aren't Jewish, but they know that we do. I kind of agree, because bat mitzvah is really a Jewish ceremony. But, there are more kids at our Messianic temple who aren't Jewish than kids who are. And we have bar mitzvahs for everyone. I don't want to act like I'm prejudiced, but it all feels weird. I'm confused about a lot of things. And I'm really sad my best friends from school won't be coming to my bat mitzvah."

- "I grew up in Messianic Judaism but frankly, on reflection, I think it is such a hodgepodge of confusion that I can't possibly stay in such an environment. It was nice when I was a kid, but as a young adult it really makes no sense to me at all. How can I possibly stay? I don't expect any religion to be perfect. I'm surely not perfect. But, I just cannot continue to support a faith that seems so utterly ambiguous about its very nature. Is it really Judaism? Is it Christianity? No one seems to offer clear answers to even such obvious questions."[49]

Under the right conditions offering conversion can help solve some of the challenges facing our constituencies and enhance the staying power of our movement.

Cultivate a gentle touch. The apostles remind us that, "love is kind" (I Cor. 13:4). True kindness will express itself as an approach to people that is relaxed, gentle, and good-natured whenever possible. Even in areas of great doctrinal import—or in areas of ecclesiology, which are meaningful and important as our subject—kindness must rule. After all, as Messianic Jewish leaders, we hold the hearts of other human beings in our hands. They deserve to be treated well and if we don't, God promises to hold us accountable. Here are some specifics:

- Wait until after the service to explain to the non-Jewish visitor donning a tallit that doing so is not the *minhag* (custom) of the synagogue.[50] If appropriate, gently touch his shoulder as you explain that the fringes of the tallit are key reminders of the Jewish people's obligation to the Torah and thus, are best not worn in our services by non-Jewish people. I have unnecessarily hurt some people's feelings by not being conscious of the timing factor.
- Be willing to meet with Gentile visitors to explain the congregation's views either during Oneg Shabbat or at some other time if you sense that such conversation will bring peace to their souls. Given the current climate among Messianic congregations, it is really not their fault if they begin with confusion in these matters.

Learn the value of grandfathering. For leaders who come to understand that the very nature of Messianic Judaism demands distinctions between Jews and Gentiles even within the four walls of our congregations, the transition can be difficult. As a general rule, it is best not to take privileges away that have already been offered but to allow a transition time sometimes lasting a few years. Of the five non-Jewish men accustomed to wearing a tallit at our synagogue at the time we made the transition to viewing the donning of a tallit as the province of Jews, we made no demands of these good men. They knew about our transition but were free to do as they chose. One kept wearing the tallit. One saw the transition as the next step in our maturation as a synagogue and though he had a prominent role among us, willingly gave up wearing his prayer shawl. Another, a man with some Jewish lineage, stopped wearing his tallit and later chose to enter the conversion process. The remaining two did leave the congregation for reasons tangential to this specific change in our policy but related to the overall development of our congregation's bilateral outlook. The point here is that though transitions are never easy, a light touch clearly helped minimize damage to the community and was appreciated by a majority of those who were affected.

Take away, but give back. Robert Frost's poem is the source of the familiar phrase, "Good fences make good neighbors." An application in our context is this: once clarity comes to Messianic Jewish leadership regarding the rules guiding Gentile participation, great liberty and largesse can be expressed within those boundaries. Non-Jews can have important roles among us. Why should a qualified Gentile not teach a Scripture study? Why not preach on occasion? Why not serve on a standing committee or lead an ad-hoc committee? Or, lead a musical group? *It is the ambiguity of their status that creates the up-tightness in the community and prevents the relaxed, good-natured feeling conducive to creativity and joy. Identity confusion is the curse. Clear boundaries with love embody the blessing.*

Explain, explain, explain. The other day I made my very first stock purchase on TDAmeritrade. It was a huge step because, though I enjoy fund-raising, I have always viewed involvement in the market with the trepidation one might feel approaching the entrance of an interesting cave while hearing a low animal growl from within. But there was assurance and help from the lady in the customer service department. She explained what an "option" was. Other terms, which undoubtedly were as clear as water in a mountain stream to her and her colleagues, went from completely murky to almost clear for me as she patiently answered my many questions.

We Messianic Jewish leaders sport a rich theological vocabulary and a glossary of in-house terminology. It is an act of love to explain transitions in the congregation's outlook clearly, simply, and with great patience. Had the very wealthy proprietors of TDAmeritrade expected me to penetrate their world without that lady's patient help, I would likely have opted for the piggy bank. It just smiles and says "klink" with each investment. But there can be much gain with oxen (I mean TDAmeritrade) so, explain, explain, explain and the good people of your congregation will, for the most part, respond positively.

Appreciate and Validate. Looking back over thirty-plus years, I am filled with gratitude for many of the non-Jewish believers who have come among us. Ruach Israel has been enriched by such people. In fact, I would argue that without the presence of these selfless servants of the King, ours, and many other Messianic Jewish synagogues, might not have come into existence at all. These folks deserve our highest esteem and love. Once clear boundaries have been established, it is fairly easy to show appreciation at every turn of the synagogue's life. Of course, such expressions of praise and appreciation should be "equal opportunity." Good-hearted Jewish members contribute to the whole and these need to know that the rabbi thinks they are terrific, too.

Guard their futures. I am not referring to stock futures here, but the possible futures of Gentile members of our synagogues. We must help them cultivate love for the church while they sojourn with us. We don't want these folks to burn their bridges with their own religious roots because in time, many will feel the tug of their early childhood experiences and desire to move back into familiar territory. This can be a very healthy thing for all. Help them celebrate their re-entry to church so they can look back at their experience in the Messianic Jewish congregation as a time of growth—a wonderful God ordained step along the way. Help them return with a mandate to help their church love the Jewish people and especially the remnant of Israel.

Find a sympathetic church or two. Particularly in the BA, but possible in the MA, it becomes very clear that most Gentiles should belong to healthy churches. As noted, there are exceptions. Would it not be a good thing for the rabbi to locate a couple of churches in the area which support the Messianic Jewish idea, have a regard for Israel and the Jewish people, and could make a comfortable home for the non-Jew who, having spent some time in the Messianic Jewish congregation, is ready to move on?[51] All these strategies intended to grow a healthy Messianic Jewish congregation, where a strong majority of Jewish members creates space with real love for others, takes courage and determination. Where do these come from?

CONCLUSION

Not long ago, I spontaneously declared to our Board, "The one thing I dislike about my job (as Senior Rabbi) is having to protect our boundaries." I was referring to my role as Center on the offensive line of our team, so often called upon to protect the community's Messianic Jewish identity from patterns that will likely assure that we will lose our essence in the years to come. Some of these patterns that are clearly observable among our larger Messianic Jewish world have to do with the role of Gentiles in our midst.

Being the gatekeeper is a role many of us would like to delegate (or theologize) away. But, at what cost?

We leaders need a deeply rooted set of convictions that arise from God's revelation so that we may be able to do the necessary "heavy lifting." Without such convictions, the social pressure to conform to the usual patterns will be too great to bear in the long term. Additionally, in a culture that values egalitarianism ("we are all winners here" says the kid's soccer coach), it is hard to escape the nagging feeling that we as leaders are acting from unworthy motivations like prejudice or ungodly exclusivity when in fact, such sinful attitudes may not be the true story at all. We need sources of strength that take us to the very substructure of our callings.

It is for this reason that I find the missions approach to Messianic Jewish communal formation to be less helpful than the bilateral approach. The inherent pragmatism and primary self-identification as a culturally Jewish expression of Evangelical Christian faith of the MA can make it vulnerable to a seemingly inevitable future, endlessly bested by the identity confusion, non-Jewish over-participation and perpetual outsider status among Am Yisrael. This is not to say that there are no blind spots and great areas of weakness attendant to the BA enterprise. MA congregations have much to teach as well, particularly in the areas of effective outreach, passion to persuade our people to consider Yeshua, and the ways and means of funding our work. And again as Mitch Glaser has reminded us, the missions movement produced the first self-consciously Jewish Yeshua-affirming communities. However, in the area of the roles of Gentiles in our midst, I contend that only bilateral ecclesiology creates "Messianic Jews with chests." I will explain this allusion.

The phase comes from the great C.S. Lewis and is the title of his short but penetrating analysis of the trajectory of modern Western culture generally and the ways of modern education in particular. *The Abolition of Man* expresses the fear that since the end of the Medieval outlook and the rise of modernity (c. 1800) thinkers have abandoned the Tao—the time-honored moral code agreed upon—by the purveyors of all the world's great religious traditions. In doing so, they have robbed men of necessary motivations to sustain life-affirming societies. They have created men without chests. They have heads representing thoughts about a desired future. They have stomach areas representing the appetites we all share for food, sex, etc. But, they lack chests—the place where animal instincts and desired ends meet, rooted in truths that are passed on *dor l'dor* (generation to generation) "the way old birds teach young birds to fly." It is these rock-solid truths passed down the line with real passion that enables a healthy society to resist seductive answers such as totalitarianism. The Tao is above and beyond the promises made by despots on the Left or the Right. Embracing the Tao with strong chests is the western man's only hope in an age when the tools of psychological conditioning have a power as never before to seduce us en masse.

"Messianic Jews with chests"—the women and men with the strength to make the tough choices in our congregations regarding non-Jewish participation—must be equipped with transcendent reasons for paying the inevitable price for the long-term gain. By analogy, God's revelation of both the unity and diversity of the human race—Jew and Gentile, one, *echad*, yet uniquely called—is the Tao. If we, some of the older birds, don't teach the young ones to fly, then what will become of Messianic Judaism in twenty-five years?

To summarize: If Israel, God's segullah, is first and foremost an enfleshed reality—an aggregate of people born to Jewish parents, then Messianic Jewish leaders should, as a matter of theological conviction, seek to protect the Jewish community from even self-inflicted dissolution.

If we are to protect Israel in this way, then our leaders should work hard to find ways to graciously, but effectively, grow and sustain Jewish majorities in our congregations, which, by our actions, suggest to the watching world that ours is Jewish space.

If, while sustaining strong Jewish majorities, we nevertheless leave room for some non-Jews in our midst (e.g. intermarried spouses, some uniquely called Gentiles), then we must develop clear boundary markers circumscribing the appropriate roles for these members of our communities. Health and joy spring from such clarity. Confusion and pain result when the game seems to have endlessly obscure or changing rules.

If clear boundary markers are important, than we need a body of leaders who are willing to do the "heavy lifting" of deciding which these should be based on a solid foundation of principles which factor in all the necessary criteria.

If we have a body of leaders to which we belong that derives through prayer, reflection, and argumentation of the specific standards for non-Jews in our midst, then we need winning ways to convince our members that these are holy, life-giving, and good.

If we have all the above in place, with large measures of passion for Yeshua, *ahavat Yisrael* (love for Israel), love for the Church, effective outreach, and the other elements of successful congregational development, then we can go to sleep at night with confidence that Messianic Judaism will flourish in the decades ahead. How our congregations relate to non-Jewish participants is one vital element in the equation, one which requires clear thinking admixed with the heart of Messiah Yeshua, whose love and commitment extend to the "Jew first," through our people, to all humanity.

ENDNOTES

1. "Summary of Opportunities and Boundaries Report," JRF Task Force on the Role of Non-Jews in JRF Congregations, Oct. 2007.
2. The Jewish community is talking about outreach and this necessarily relates to non-Jewish participation. In the Spring 2006 edition of the CCAR Journal, Reform leader Eric Yoffie argues strongly for open-armed acceptance of non-Jewish spouses within a framework of strong Jewish particularity. He notes, "If we have learned anything at all over the past twenty-five years, it is this: you do not draw people in by erasing boundaries and eliminating distinctions. If there are no clearly defined distinctions between our Jewish values and the values of the world around us, then what reason would serious people—Jews or non-Jews—have to cast their fate with ours? We have learned that intermarried couples are not attracted by minimalism or watered down Judaism." Might there be lessons here for Messianic Jewish leaders?
3. I have long since changed my position in this matter, and in 1994, produced a booklet entitled, "The Case for Conversion; Welcoming Non-Jews Into Messianic Jewish Space."
4. Two examples: A childhood friend, Harry, and I became followers of Yeshua in 1971. Harry resisted wearing a tallit in his worship, not because he lacked respect for his Jewish upbringing or life, but because, as he explained to me, he had such great respect for a tradition he felt he could no longer honestly claim as his own. A newer Messianic Jewish friend and colleague in Boston clearly aligns with a more missions orientation professionally. But, he clearly has deep Jewish sensibilities as reflected in sermons he has brought in our synagogue and with the high regard he expresses regarding Jewish religious life.
5. Early on, I published my experience of turning to Jesus in the Ithaca College newspaper. The following issue, a traditional Jewish student published his outrage at my claims that Jesus was for Jews. I wrote again appealing to Jesus' Jewishness as adequate justification for my own. Now, some forty years later I can see the limits of my argument.
6. Alan M. Dershowitz, *The Vanishing American Jew* (Boston: Little, Brown and Company, 1997), 169.
7. Mark S. Kinzer, *Post Missionary Messianic Judaism* (Grand Rapids, Brazo Press, 2005), 39.
8. Kinzer, Post Missionary, 98.
9. In his audio taped series, "Gen Eden and Gehena" Dr. Kinzer discusses the strands of biblical teaching on heaven, hell ,and implications for us today. Clearly, he is no universalist.
10. Kinzer, *Post Missionary*, 50.
11. Ibid., 53.
12. Ibid., 107.
13. Michael Wyschogrod, *Body of Faith* (Minneapolis: Winston Press, 1983), xv.

14. In truth, this verse is not diminishing the central importance of transgenerational physical family membership in the Jewish people. Paul knows well that his people are the physical seed of Abraham, Isaac, and Jacob. Rather his rhetoric is similar to that of John the Immerser who emphasized that without "walking the walk" of covenant faithfulness to God, an individual's Jewish pedigree will not count for much. Quoting Kinzer, "physical descent from the patriarchs, and matriarchs, (Romans 9:8), the covenantal sign of circumcision (Romans 2: 25-29), and the possession and knowledge of the Torah (Romans 2: 17-24) are all privileges of enormous value, but they cannot guarantee the inheritance of the life of the world to come" (Kinzer, Israel's Messiah 39).
15. R. Kendall Soulen *The God of Israel and Christian Theology* (Minneapolis: Fortress Press, 1996), 154-155.
16. Kinzer, *Post Missionary*, 21.
17. I like to refer to "Israel and the nations" as "the irreducible dyad of human existence." This seems to me to be the basic biblical paradigm.
18. Are Messianic Jews Christians by this definition? In the strictest sense, if the word "Christian" is used in its barest, most literal meaning of "messianist," then we Messianic Jews could own the term. But we must consider the fact that in historical, contemporary, and common usage, the term misleading because it leaves little room for the bilateral nature of our faith. Every community must decide when it is worth it to reclaim a commonly misused term and when energies can be better spent creating new ones. The emotional baggage attendant to the use of "Christian" for Jewish believers is simply too great to overcome.
19. No doubt there is an invisible body of the truly redeemed. But, our ability to know exactly who belongs in this category is very limited.
20. The concept was insisted upon during the Protestant reformation as a way of distinguishing between the "visible" Roman Catholic Church, which according to the Reformers was corrupt, and those within it who truly believe as well as true believers within their own denominations. John Calvin described the church invisible as "that which is actually in God's presence, into which no persons are received but those who are children of God by grace of adoption and true members of Christ by sanctification of the Holy Spirit . . . [it] includes not only the saints presently living on earth, but all the elect from the beginning of the world" (*Institutes* 4.1.7).
21. Mark Kinzer, *Israel's Messiah and the People of God* (Eugene: Cascade Books, 2011), xiv.
22. Congregation Ruach Israel expresses this unity by having jointly built a building in Needham, MA, with a Mennonite Church. The arrangement has been rich in mutual blessings these twenty years. Our synagogue also sponsors a yearly Pastors' Day—an Oneg Shabbat dedicated to the honor of our guests from among Boston's clergy who have become friends of our synagogue over the years.
23. Kinzer notes: "The abolition of the dietary laws is in effect an abolition of the Jewish people itself."
24. Michael 116-117.

25. Dr. Stuart Dauermann has written a very helpful little book called *Keeping the Faith in Interfaith Relationships* (Wiph and Stock Publishers, Eugene, Oregon). It reflects an actual discussion between a Christian young woman, her Jewish fiancée and Stuart, sitting at a restaurant and discussing the practical out-workings of some of the issues raised to this paper. I highly recommend it for its subtle theological sophistication as well as its value as a tool for outreach among Intermarrieds.
26. Actually the distinction between the Christian assembly and the Jewish is not quite as dramatic as suggested here. Churches make internal distinctions rooted in revelation, too. For example many would not allow a woman pastor to serve the assembly. Conversely, every Messianic Jewish congregation I know of has meaningful roles for non-Jewish members, even those congregations that strongly identify with the bilateral approach.
27. The price Jews have paid for seeking to remain a unique people has been steep. Jewish particularity has occasioned unspeakable violence against the Jewish people for centuries: "Those Jews . . . they don't mix with others . . . Who do they think they are?"
28. Some may argue that there is a third way: "We are neither a church, nor a synagogue, but a Messianic congregation." On the surface this may seem plausible insofar that our congregations are something of a new and different thing on the religious scene. However, at root level, the actual contours of our assemblies fit the dyadic model of "little piece of Israel" or "little piece of the world wide community of Messiah with a Jewish ethos." Neither in Scripture nor in past history can we discern such a third form of communal identity.
29. Dan Cohn-Sherbok, *Voices of Messianic Judaism* (Baltimore: Lederer Books, 2001), 172.
30. Dan Cohn-Sherbok, *Messianic Judaism* (London: Cassel, 2000), 25.
31. "In the 1930s a new development came about. Presbyterian missionaries initiated the establishment of a number of Hebrew Christian congregations under their auspices. The director . . . considered it more economical to create independent Jewish congregations that served as centers for evangelism and raised funds on their own" (Ariel 221).
32. Cohn-Sherbok, *Messianic Judaism*, 40-41.
33. Louis Goldberg and Stanly Gundry, ed. *How Jewish is Christianity?* (Grand Rapids: Zondervan, 2003), 111-112.
34. For a fuller discussion of the modern openness to the cultures of the world among modern missiologists see *Understanding Church Growth* by Donald A McGavran.
35. Of course, this is a very incomplete picture of my friend Arnold's theology. His classical Dispensationalism sees much more in the Jewish experience than one's preference for blintzes over baklava, but the fact remains, congregations that bear his theological stamp would have a very different self-understanding than bilaterally oriented ones.
36. Arnold Fruchtenbaum, *Hebrew Christianity—Its Theology, History, and Philosophy* (Washington D.C.: Canon Press, 1974), 29.
37. Philip E. Globe, *Everything You Need to Grow a Messiainic Yeshiva* (Pasadena: William Carrey Library, 1981), xi.

38. Goldberg and Grundy, 20.
39. Eliezer Maass, *Stand Firm* (Lansing: American Messianic Fellowship, 1990), 89,173.
40. Why are these Evangelicals so interested in us? First, there is a mystique about the Jews because we are the people of the Book. Second, many Evangelicals yearn for a sense of the transcendence of God which often is absent from their churches, which tend to place a great deal of emphasis on God's immanence. Third, and related to point one, Evangelicals often see involvement in our congregations as a way to "get back to the primitive church. Though largely a naïve belief, this has a powerful appeal for many, especially those who have seen the seedier side of their own communities. They imagine that we are the "pure" followers of Christ whom they long to emulate. Fourth, a kind of "covenant envy" has lurked in the collective psyche of the Church generally for centuries. Often this has resulted in the kind of reaction formation resulting in hostile action. For evangelicals, this can translate into a desire to get close to Jewish believers. Finally, it is much easier for Christians to cross the great religious divide and to attend a Messianic Jewish assembly than for a Jewish person to do so. Yeshua remains a difficult pill for our people to swallow in light of the realities of history.
41. This insight is the product of personal observation and discussion only. It is not statistically verifiable and certainly does not reflect the inner motivations of any particular leader.
42. The Messianic Jewish Rabbinical Council's definition of "Who is a Jew" forms the basis for this statistic.
43. Aside from the rabbinical staff, the Bylaws of the congregation do not demand that all the governmental roles are filled by Jewish people, but that "the composition of the Board shall be predominantly Jewish."
44. A complication, of course, is that a Hebrew-rich service can be off-putting to some Jews, not just to Gentile visitors.
45. At Ruach Israel, we would be sure to have Jewish Senior and Associate Rabbis and cantors, both lay and professional. . Currently our Board also is entirely Jewish. However, there may at times be the need to place a non-Jewish person on the Synagogue Board since our by-laws do not prohibit such.
46. Two spiritual pathologies converge in some of these groups: an over-idealization of the Jewish experience characterized by stereotypic Chasidic dress (and often, a Gentile leader) and an irrational disdain for the Christian church.
47. It can be argued that the same reasoning would keep Messianic Jews from inviting their own children into our "marginalized space." The key difference here is that God's covenantal calling to all Jewish people is that "dor l'dor" – from generation to generation – we are obligated to bring our children into the fullness of the covenant.
48. In our synagogue two wonderful examples come to mind. Dave N. had been with us for twenty five or so years and served as our cantor. It was a time of less theological maturity when we failed to see the incongruity of a Gentile cantor. He willingly gave up donning a tallit when it became clear to us and to him that this was inappropriate. His comment about the congregation made without any sense of

bitterness or regret was, "The baby has grown up," meaning that Ruach Israel was at the point of moving into her calling as a true synagogue. The second example is that of John and Carol M., an older couple of strong Italian background. They came to me many years ago and announced they felt it was time for them to relinquish their formal membership in the synagogue because this was a home for Jews. However, they wanted to continue giving generously financially and to serve the synagogue. They are among our most faithful couples, serving in multiple capacities.

49. Richard Nichol, *The Case for Conversion* (Needham: Congregation Ruach Israel, 2004), 6-7.
50. Or, wait until the next time the visitor comes. This gives the leader opportunity to ascertain if in fact the person is Jewish or not.
51. It seems to me that every Messianic Jewish rabbi should cultivate friendships among Christian pastors and if possible, among mainstream rabbis.

HOW JEWISH WILL THE MESSIANIC JEWISH COMMUNITY OF THE FUTURE BE?

Steven Charles Ger
B.A. in psychology and interpersonal communication from Trenton State College,
Th.M. from Dallas Theological Seminary,
Founder and director of Sojourner Ministries

Brief presentations such as this one, by their very nature, demand generalizations. It extends beyond this project's scope to drill down into the gathering of hard evidence and measured evaluation. Therefore, it necessitates exchanging the academic for the anecdotal, as these generalizations are based upon subjective observation. It is also true that when dealing with generalizations, the audience may immediately call to mind their own observations that lead them to an opposite conclusion. This is why the participation of a three-member panel is so indispensable and allows for a clearer, three-dimensional view of the issue at hand.

The author is neither a prognosticator nor the son of a prognosticator, and this exercise has moved him into a subjective realm far from his native comfort level of objective biblical exegesis. He has never been one to gaze into a crystal ball nor does he even enjoy reading books that attempt to forecast future predictions through interpreting current trends. (And there is nothing as doleful as the fellow attempting to sell his used copy of *Megatrends 2000* after the year 2000.)

Nonetheless, in the spirit of the men of Issachar ("who understood the times," 1 Chron. 12:32), this paper will attempt to identify specific challenges and opportunities facing the messianic community in the future, specifically regarding levels of "Jewishness." However, prior to addressing the question, it is a Jewish (messianic or not) prerogative to take umbrage with the parameters of the initial question as lacking sufficient specificity. (And as a late substitution presenter, the author claims the privilege regardless.)

Within the topic itself, “How Jewish will the Messianic Jewish community of the future be?” are significant levels of ambiguity. Just what is meant by “Jewish?” Does the concern regard ethnicity, culture, adherence to Torah observance, identification with Judaism (rabbinic or otherwise), dissociation with mainstream Christianity, congregational percentage of Jews vis-à-vis Gentiles? Specifically which Messianic Jewish community is being referenced? The non-congregational participating community or the congregational community? If congregational, which theological or observational flavor? If non-congregational, is it the actively involved or the self-identified Messianics who, nonetheless, remain on the fringe? North American messianic community or global? Finally, how far into the future is the author being asked to forecast? It is particularly problematic that this presentation addresses a group that collectively holds diversely modified definitions for every word in the topic question with the exception of "the," "of" and "be." Nevertheless, the author has done the best he can with the material he was given, inherent ambiguity notwithstanding.

THE VIEWS OF THE YOUNGER GENERATION REGARDING JEWISH IDENTITY AS COMPARED AND CONTRASTED WITH VIEWS OF THE OLDER GENERATION.

Defining and then differentiating the views regarding Jewish identity between older and younger generations is no small task. The answers are dependent upon how much older and how much younger the generations are that we choose to place under the microscope. The author believes that the messianic movement as it stands today is composed of three distinct generations possessing various degrees of overlapping characteristics and perspectives: older, younger, and somewhat in-between the two poles. The author’s place is among the “in-betweeners.”

There are actually two subsets that comprise the older generation: those who are veterans of the messianic movement, who came of age prior to the Jesus movement in the 1970s, from the generational cohort known as the Silent Generation (Arnold Fruchtenbaum would be an example), and those who arrived to the movement with accompanying long hair, beards, faded blue jeans and guitars (Mitch Glaser, Sam Nadler, and many others present at this conference would fit this category). These are the Baby Boomer generation.

The younger generation would roughly be defined as those who are members of what is called Generation Y, the Millennials, or the Echo Boomers, born during the two decades that span the Reagan and Clinton administrations. These are largely the teens and twenty-somethings within the messianic movement who will provide the movement's leadership in future years. A large portion of these are second or third generation messianic believers and were born and raised within the messianic movement.

The middle group is aptly called Generation X, those born between 1965 and 1981. There is a small percentage of this generation that was part of the Hebrew Christian stage of the messianic movement, that is, that stage which preceded the 1970s Jesus movement. The author, a fourth generation Jewish believer, would be a member of that select group and writes from this perspective. The remainder of this group is composed of a mix of those born into the messianic movement and first generation believers who found the Lord as they traversed their spiritual journey/quest.

As opposed to older generations of messianics who possess a clearer sense of identity, younger messianics of both Jewish and Gentile persuasions, are literally facing an existential crisis. They are asking themselves, in a paraphrase of a reference they are too young to remember from those noted pop philosophers Donny and Marie (who famously sang that one was "a little bit country" and the other was "a little bit rock and roll"), just how to reconcile their dual identities as "a little bit Jewish" and "a little bit Christian." More specifically, they wonder how to reconcile the concepts of belonging to a movement that claims affinity with both Judaism and Christianity. The old classic questions of "Who am I," "How do I fit in?" and "Where do I belong" are very present (and for some, paralyzing) for this generation of messianics.

While certainly every Jewish believer, from generation to generation, undergoes some manner of identity crisis, the younger generation appears to be stumbling over this issue more intensely, especially those raised from childhood within the movement. Many older messianics, both from the Hebrew Christian stage and Jesus movement stage, came to faith as teens or young adults and by virtue of having had to explain, confront, and (in some cases) separate from their families over the issue of Messiah and their adherence to an exciting burgeoning movement, were able to transition more rapidly to an identity acceptance.

However, the 21st century Messianic movement is in a very different place and condition from its 20th century fits and starts. The innovation, creativity, and energetic experimentation of previous decades have given way to both a maturing consolidation and at the same time, a disconcerting fragmentation. Traced over the course of the past eight decades, the movement has transitioned over time from a fairly homogenous and unified Hebrew Christian missionary model, where communities of exclusively Jewish believers gathered together for worship, fellowship, teaching, and evangelism, to today's broad, modern movement composed of Jews and Gentiles gathering in a diversity of charismatic, dispensational, Torah-centric, or post-missionary congregations. In other words, while some attend Bene Assemblies of God, others are attending Bene First Baptist. Within one century, the messianic movement has become the Baskin Robbins of denominations, with available congregational flavors to suit every taste and preference. And for the majority of Jewish believers in the movement who fail to choose congregational affiliation, there are many welcoming churches eager to have genuine Jewish residents within their local bodies.

This diversity of messianic perspectives has necessarily engendered a diversity of answers to basic messianic questions. The obviousness of this point is recognized by this symposium itself. It is the very diversity of heart-felt answers to these basic questions, relating, for example, to which self-designation is *de rigeur* and which is now *declassee*. Are we still called "Messianic Jews"? Is "Completed Jew" now politically incorrect? Will the designation "Hebrew Christian" ever come back in style? Are we even comfortable using the term "Christian" at all? Is our faith system properly designated as a qualified or unqualified "Christianity" or is a qualified "Judaism" more accurate? What does it mean to be Jewish? Can a Messianic Gentile ever be considered to be Messianic Jewish, and if not, is he truly a member of Messianic Judaism? Should Gentile teens become bar mitzvah? The questions go on and on.

It is no wonder that the younger messianic generation is confused—the movement itself remains confused and fractured in theology, mission, praxis, purpose, and approach. It sometimes may appear as if our small movement is as splintered as mainstream Judaism and as differentiated from one another as Chabad, Orthodox, Conservative, and Reform. In point of fact, the same words (such as Judaism, Jewish, missionary, grace, justification, New Covenant, etc.), are given different shades of nuance or even different meanings altogether depending upon which subset of our movement is using them at the time. This is the legacy and the challenge that older messianic generations have left for those that follow in their footsteps.

Young messianics are attempting to figure out what the Jewish component of their lives means and practically, how it fits with who they are, what they believe, and with whom they associate. Are they, for example, abandoning the Jewish people by rejecting Judaism as a religious system and choosing Messiah? Does choosing Messiah itself necessitate rejection of rabbinic Judaism? What does "being Jewish" mean if not adherence to rabbinic practice? Is it possible that rabbinic tradition itself could somehow be antithetical to authentic Jewish expression? Is there any way, any contortion, short of abandoning Jesus that would cause the unbelieving Jewish community to accept them? Should the purpose of Torah observance be based upon a licensed, situational, or cultural expression or the result of timeless theological mandate? What do you do with the internal emptiness of what feels like abandoning and being abandoned by your own people?

Some young messianic Gentiles have existential questions of their own. Often, they are part of a congregation through parental circumstance and didn't get much of a say in the matter. The major issue here is a sense of inferiority, of second-class citizenship. The accommodation and acculturation of the Gentile family members of Jewish believers (spouses, step-children, etc.) is often an issue as well.

Finally, while the author somewhat enjoys his Jewish Christian status within the church at large as a novelty guest speaker (it's a living, after all) and mature Jewish believers have learned to endure and capitalize on their distinctness, the younger generation, if given the choice, would choose rather to "fit in" and prefer not to stand out with such novel distinction.

THE ROLE OF TORAH AND TRADITION, MARRIAGE WITHIN THE JEWISH COMMUNITY, AND THE IMPORTANCE OF ISRAEL IN THE YEARS AHEAD

Many within the 20th century's larger evangelical movement emphasized an approach to our faith with the overt and specific accent on Christianity not being a religion, per se, but rather, a relationship. Religious rules and behavioral boundaries were purposely deemphasized, and the personal relationship between believers and God was placed at the forefront. We can, however, observe a general shift in 21st century culture toward, and not away from, certain religions and religious systems, specifically those that emphasize the liturgical, possess demonstrable historic roots, provide exceptionally clear behavioral boundaries, and unambiguously express requirements. This trend can travel some length toward explaining Islam's inroads into American culture; the emerging church movement; the move of evangelicals toward the Anglican, Episcopal, and Eastern Orthodox (and the like) churches; the uptick in conversions of evangelicals to Judaism; and the attraction of many Jews and Gentiles to a Torah observant lifestyle. Yet this is only a recognizable trend and obviously does not characterize the generation as a whole.

Indeed, the inability of the messianic movement to come to theological agreement regarding the continued relation of Torah to the believer (Jewish or Gentile), and the role, if any, that Jewish tradition plays in the messianic community will continue to divide the movement, symposia notwithstanding. Riding current trends, there are those young messianics who will gravitate toward Torah observance, whether through theological conviction, anthropological preference or missiological passion. Many others will choose to express their faith apart from overt Torah observance and will retain more of a grace/Christian liberty perspective. All, however, will remain confused by the continued and ever-expanding diversity of opinion among respected messianic leaders as regards this issue and each side's seeming inability to sensitively persuade the other.

On marriage and dating, the author presumes that the present trends of intermarriage within the larger nonbelieving Jewish community as well as among messianic believers will continue. Practically, not necessarily preferentially, speaking, it is far more challenging for two Jewish believers of the opposite sex within a particular geographic region to make a love connection than it is to connect with a Gentile believer (and far more important to marry a believer than to marry a Jewish unbeliever for ethnicity's sake). It is simply a matter of percentages. While the ideal of "marrying Jewish" will continue to have appeal, that appeal will be muted by a lack of parental pressure, the wide number of intermarriages among respected messianic leadership, the presence of large numbers of Gentiles within messianic congregations, non-messianic church affiliation, and above all, circumstance and opportunity. As increasing numbers of intermarried, mixed, and blended families affiliate with the messianic movement, questions of accommodation and integration will be ever more central to messianic life.

The importance of Israel will continue to increase. Many young Jewish believers will solve (or at least, salve) their identity crises through Jewish nationalism. Many of the younger generation, through visiting Israel, have observed the demonstrable fact that Israeli believers rarely suffer the same levels of identity crisis experienced by American Jewish believers. Jewish Nationalism, while never absent from the contemporary messianic movement, will undoubtedly move further to the forefront of messianic consciousness.

TOWARDS A MESSIANIC CONGREGATIONAL FUTURE: FACING THE CONGREGATIONAL CHALLENGES IN FORMING JEWISH IDENTITY FOR A NEW GENERATION

The congregational challenges in forming Jewish identity for a new generation largely stem from the movement's continued fragmentation. What some would charitably label as "lively diversity" regarding such basics as defining what an observable, authentic messianic faith looks like in action (not to mention the issues of charismatic/non-charismatic, Torah observant, non-Torah observant, subset of Judaism or Christianity, role of Gentiles, etc.), may provoke the reticence of younger messianics regarding their continued participation in messianic congregational life. Many may tire or grow weary of uncertainty and confusion and may find a greater ability to express authenticity of faith within a non-messianic church setting.

There are some among the younger messianics in the movement who yearn for a place to belong, where they can fit in and dig in among other believers. Again, the idea here is of a culture where the expression of faith feels authentic, or more authentic than within a messianic setting. To that end, it must be freely admitted that messianic congregations have a history of attracting what seems to be a larger percentage of eccentric personalities than do many other faith venues. For a Jewish believer to look down the row and see a Gentile believer, beard grown, tallis-wearing and, in some cases, looking like an escapee from a road company of *Fiddler on the Roof*, can be disconcerting. For the Jewish believer, it may seem as if some participants are playing "dress-up," finding identity not in Messiah but in Jewish trappings. It will be interesting to see whether the long-standing trend of "Jewish wannabe-ism" continues to gain traction. On a personal note, this author, on the basis of personal conscience and conviction, turned down a lucrative opportunity to spend a weeklong Tabernacles conference with a campground full of messianic Gentiles in holiday costume. (Looking at their website, it looked more like Halloween than Sukkot, so the author politely begged off.)

To feel a sense of genuine belonging is a powerful motivator, not just for the gang at *Cheers* (where everybody knows your name). Couple a genuine sense of belonging with a legitimate sense of purpose, calling, and mission, and the local church may have a powerful appeal over and above membership within the messianic congregation. The rise of the missional movement bears watching and perhaps the incorporation or adaptation of some core concepts may prove fruitful when applied to the messianic congregational context. At any rate, to compete with the attraction of the local church, the congregation must provide the younger generation with clear answers not only pertaining to messianic Jewish identity, but messianic Jewish mission as well.

The danger ahead is for those who know us best, those who have been raised from infancy in the movement, to ponder questions such as, "Just what are they playing at? Whom are they trying to please? What is the point?" Young people will not stick around or truly commit themselves to anything less than an authentic expression of faith and an articulated, intentional mission. The moment the movement is perceived by any generation as mile wide but inch deep, that generation will bolt from the movement.

Furthermore, the messianic movement should be prepared with a measured, considered response regarding the next generation's congregational participation. Is it more optimal for every Jewish believer to be involved in a messianic congregation? If someone chooses to be a member of First Baptist, is that choice somehow inferior, a betrayal of his heritage, a betrayal of his responsibility, or a betrayal of his people? And if that is our conviction, what is our strategy going forward other than to "guilt" the next generation into staying within the movement? Does detachment from congregational life necessitate estrangement from other Jews? Can it be effectively argued that a Jewish believer is de facto less in touch with Jewish identity by fellowshipping within a church but more in touch with Jewish identity within a congregational context?

The greatest example of God's historic and ongoing faithfulness is to be found in the preservation of a believing remnant. From the times of the patriarchs through the coming future tribulation, the principal evidence provided for all believers, Jew and Gentile, to confidently place their trust in Him to keep His promises and bring His program to completion is His sovereign and gracious preservation of the remnant (Rom. 9-11). It is the enduring, organic, and growing remnant of Israel, the very Israel of God, which is the luminous beacon of God's faithfulness throughout history, past, present, and future.

Younger messianics want to explore whether the testimony of God's Jewish remnant is most potent while sequestered away from the church in a messianic "ghetto," or smack dab in the midst of a church full of inquisitive Gentiles. They may wish to revel in our distinctions, because then our unity is that much more captivating to an observing world. A monochromatic tapestry possesses limited visual interest but a tapestry of two colors, skillfully and brilliantly woven together, shows far greater artistry. After all, one of the mysteries of the church is that believing Gentiles are co-heirs and co-participants with believing Israel (Eph. 2:11-19; 3:6). The absence of a localized, tangible Jewish presence within the church arguably robs the church of blessing.

In addition, the younger generation has somewhat different musical tastes and preferences regarding congregational worship (as appalling as the concept may be for many of us). They do not respond in the same fashion or with the same intensity as previous generations of American Jewish believers do to the strains of Eastern-Europe-minor-key-Fiddler-on-the-Roof-Liberated-Wailing-Wallish messianic-style music. They may enjoy singing Hebrew worship songs, but often in major keys, not just minor. They especially rebel against being segregated into a messianic musical ghetto, demanding both familiarity and solidarity with the contemporary worship strains and styles being enjoyed by their friends in the church at large. There is a great deal of room for our definition of what constitutes messianic Jewish worship music to be reexamined and perhaps extended.

Finally, size still matters. Most of us are familiar with many of our congregation's families at a certain point either departing from congregational life or "double-dipping" (the split loyalty caused through attending a church in addition to the congregation, as the church provides a needed element, for example, a large and vibrant youth group, that the messianic congregation may presently lack). It is the rare messianic congregation that grows large enough to provide that which is provided by many a substantial local church. Divided loyalties and erratic attendance are likely continuing trends.

NEXT GENERATION SPIRITUAL DYNAMICS OF CONCERN

One area of concern as the messianic movement presses forward is the divergent and sometimes unclear philosophy regarding the mixture of Jews and gentiles within our congregations.

Contextualization principles: It is possible to construe the participation of Gentiles within messianic congregations as a mixed blessing. Specifically, the general purpose of any intentionally, ethnically, and contextualized church is to provide a more authentic and culturally comfortable setting in which homogeneous groups of believers could worship. Thus, Chinese church services are conducted in the Chinese language, utilizing cultural cues for predominantly Chinese people; Hispanic churches are conducted for Hispanics; African-American churches, those of the Greek Orthodox, etc., follow the same principle.

Among intentionally ethnic contextualized churches, it is only in messianic Jewish congregations where it might be normative for eighty percent of the worshippers to be Gentile. If on a normative Sunday morning in an African-American church, even fifty percent of the people were Caucasian, that church would cease to have the character of a black church. It is more equally unthinkable for that church to continue on as a black church with a white majority or to install a

Caucasian pastor. While it might be a spectacular church, its change of demographics makes it implausible to posit its continued success as a specifically black church. Yet it is extremely common to find messianic Jewish congregations led by Gentile "rabbis" and for messianic Jewish congregations to have so few Jews, even on their highest attended day, that it would still be incapable of assembling a *minyan*. In no other setting would this be viewed as a viable or sustainable model of contextualization. The resolution of this issue is the first area of concern regarding next generation spiritual dynamics.

A second major area of concern as the messianic movement goes forward is the disagreement among us as to our relationship with rabbinic Judaism, indeed, even the movement's own inability to agree on a definition of Judaism. This should not be surprising, however, as the Jewish community itself cannot agree on a definition of Judaism. A recent issue of *Moment* magazine provides a few examples of the diversity of opinion among well-known Jewish authors:

> "Being Jewish is not about beliefs, but about connections with other people, sharing values and a collective destiny" —Robert Putnam
>
> "For nearly seven decades, (Soviet) Jews maintained a separate identity without religion . . . common experience . . . forged a common destiny" —Masha Gessen
>
> "Many of us make a distinction between Judaism as religion and Judaism as a cultural and ethical outlook" —Rebecca Goldstein
>
> "When one speaks about Judaism as an idea or a culture, it becomes quite ridiculous; it is like an attempt to write literature by using only three or four letters of the alphabet" —Adin Steinsaltz
>
> "It depends on what you mean by Judaism" —David Klinghoffer[1]

Considering this diversity of Jewish opinion, the question should be asked as to why there is an insistence in some quarters that the messianic community accept traditional rabbinic orthodoxy's model. Will our ortho-praxis ever make our allegiance to Yeshua more acceptable to them? If only we could innovate a formula that provides the correct ratio of Torah observance and theological reframing while maintaining consistent fidelity to Yeshua! This continued messianic quest for a genuine acceptance as Jews within the larger Jewish world transforms us into Don Quixote-steins, forever tilting at imaginary windmills. The pipedream of an envisioned era when messianic faith is finally recognized and validated as part of Judaism by the corporate Jewish community is the impossible dream.

It must be recognized that some within our movement are perceived as being focused more on the rabbis than our Messiah. The Messianic Jewish movement is not the *Moshianic* Jewish movement. It requires an indomitable and unshakeable focus on the Messiah. The key to the movement's future is to press on toward Him. The movement should never exchange a full and robust messianism for what can only be, at best, a status of qualified tolerance within Judaism.

It is instructive to be reminded of the identity of the most stringently observant group of messianic Jewish believers of any generation or century: the first generation church in the book of Acts. No group of Jewish believers has adhered to Torah more affectionately or rigorously. Nonetheless, the non-believing Jewish community turned virulently on them, in an ever-increasing expression of vitriolic rejection. Alternatively, consider the messianic Jewish community addressed in Hebrews. The whole argument of the entire letter is designed to strengthen the believers to endure the rejection they had and continued to experience from the surrounding Jewish community. The apostles themselves, if they suddenly beamed down, would not be accepted today as Jews by the Jewish community.

The palpable Jewishness of the future messianic movement can be ensured by the community's unyielding and untiring emphasis on living authentic lives that reinforce Jewishness through reflecting the New Testament's apostolic teaching as well as that of our Lord. The Jewish lifestyle values that we are commanded to stress are specifically found there. Coupled to unwavering fidelity to New Covenant instruction is a focus that remains solidly fixed on Yeshua, our Messiah, steadfastly refusing to turn to the left or right.

This leads to a final area of concern vis-à-vis next generation spiritual dynamics, that of our movement's stark disagreement as regards foundational philosophic emphases on either the Mosaic Covenant or the Abrahamic Covenant. In other words, while our movement is indivisibly centered on Yeshua, the open question is whether our Messiah stands on the shoulders of Moses or Abraham.

The author of Hebrews makes a passionate case that the Mosaic Covenant is inferior to the New Covenant (7:22; 8:6-7), that God's guarantee of the Mosaic Covenant is inferior to that of the New Covenant (7:22-24), and the Mosaic Covenant's promises are inferior to those of the New Covenant (8:6-7). Two thousand years later, the argument of Hebrews' stunning indictment of first century Judaism's inadequacy in light of Jesus' superiority still possesses the power to astonish. Implicit in God's promise of a new covenant is His recognition of the previous covenant's inadequacy. It is not as if God's plan to establish a new covenant was a midcourse adjustment in His divine master plan for Israel, a celestial "plan B" of sorts. He had always intended to replace the Mosaic Covenant with the New Covenant. If the nation of Israel's spiritual maturity could be perfected through the Mosaic Covenant, another covenant would prove redundant. The New Covenant's very existence demonstrates the deficiency and provisional nature of the Mosaic covenant, which could produce neither the justification of humanity nor the internal righteousness that God requires.[2]

No matter the contextual or grammatical evidence, many believers, particularly within the messianic community, hold fast tenaciously to their misunderstanding that the New Covenant inscribes onto our inner being a copy of the "the one and only Torah," albeit an abridged version that excludes the priestly legislation and which is interpreted through our Jesus-centric perspective. This position views Torah as eternal (in an absolute sense) and rejects that God would ever contemplate a replacement.

To hold a conflicting position means opening oneself up to accusations of disloyalty to one's Jewish heritage for abandoning Torah, as if adherence to the Torah was ever the premium hallmark of Jewish identity. According to Stephen's presentation in Acts, Jewish identity might more accurately be indicated not through adherence to Torah but by rebellion against God.[3] That is precisely the reason that the Mosaic legislation, as a package, was found by God to be deficient and in need of replacement with the superior New Covenant. In reality, for Jewish believers in Jesus, it is their participation within this better covenant along with that of the Abrahamic Covenant that defines genuine Jewish identity according to the New Testament.[4]

The author proposes that the pendulum has swung too far, regarding the movement's focus on Moses and that it must swing back and refocus on Abrahamic Covenant. Many in the younger generation are discovering that Moses is nice, but Messiah is everything, our all in all. To the extent that the younger generation perceives our loyalty is divided between Messiah and Moses, they will reject the movement actively by leaving or passively by disengagement.

Yet the Abraham Covenant's provisions address the movement's foundational theological issues and practical concerns. Within the Abrahamic Covenant is found a four-fold emphasis on land, seed, blessing, and divine relationship. This provides a solid theological basis for the messianic movement's focus on strong, continued Jewish identity, the centrality of the land of Israel, the inclusion of Gentiles, and the Jewish people's irrevocable, unconditional, and covenantal relationship with God. Although Jewish and Gentile believers alike are partaking of the spiritual blessings of the covenant as Abraham's spiritual seed, Jewish believers are Abraham's physical seed as well, and additional elements of the covenant apply specifically to them. Elements that still apply to Jewish believers would be the divine right of possession of the land of Israel, the reciprocal blessing and cursing on those who bless and curse Israel, and the sign of circumcision, which, finding its foundation within the Abrahamic Covenant, is still incumbent upon all Jews, including those within the believing remnant.[5]

THE SOURCE OF THE MESSIANIC COMMUNITY'S FUTURE LEADERSHIP

The movement's need for quality, i.e. qualified, trained future leaders is no secret. Right now, there is no shortage of self-proclaimed and self-commended leaders. Today when any Jew comes to faith, he seems to think that he is qualified by virtue of having had a bar mitzvah twenty years ago to hang out a shingle and call himself a "rabbi." More of those leaders are not needed.

We face unprecedented challenges today, of both sophisticated and unsophisticated varieties. The arguments of Jews for Judaism, while not getting any better, seem to be becoming more persuasive among young people. The anti-missionaries appear to be on the ascent in their influence, and if not completely successful, seem to be productively sowing doubts that our young people cannot readily answer. Ignorance, i.e. biblical illiteracy, is the enemy. We must examine why the latest generation of messianics are struggling with the defense of our faith. It is possible that some of us have become distracted by the sexy exotic nature of rabbinic contexts and Torah praxis and require a return to the old basics like messianic prophecy and apologetics, arming the next generation with much needed answers and biblical reassurances. Intentional programming like the Isaiah 53 campaign is a wonderful, restorative step in the right direction. But we must be alert and ready to recognize, foster, and nurture the next Michael Brown or the next Arnold Fruchtenbaum.

It is possible that the movement's leaders have pushed a quest for unity and identification with the Jewish people to the detriment of laying a solid theological foundation for our young people. Yet, therein lies a central component of the messianic movement's problem, as we do not agree theologically with one another regarding some very basic theological issues. In the quest for unity, there remains a danger of inadvertently placing theological doctrine in the role of enemy. Young people, especially, want to get along. Yet, whether young or old, we must remain true to our core theological convictions. If we fail to persuade one another of the rightness of our positions, so be it. However, let us nonetheless never abandon our quest for unity even in the absence of theological agreement,

As to formal training programs of study for developing future leaders, there are many positive developments on that front. Christian seminaries, like Dallas Theological Seminary, are still preparing capable expositors of the word. Now available in every geographic region of the country are other seminaries, graduate schools, and institutions of higher learning with Jewish studies emphases like Pasche Institute of Jewish Studies, Feinberg Center for Jewish Studies, Denver Seminary, Kings University, Western Seminary, to name just a few. Regarding less formal training, Ariel Ministries' Camp Shoshanah has been training the messianic community for over three decades and still provides a rigorous, multi-summer program of biblical, messianic instruction that has had an inordinate impact on multiple messianic generations of leaders.

Within our own congregations and churches, the older generations of messianic believers must make a commitment to safeguard the instruction of the up and coming generation. One way to systematize and formalize that commitment is through an intensive and rigorous bar and bat mitzvah training program.

CONCLUSION AND NOSTALGIC MUSING

When considering the future of the messianic community, the challenge remains for contemporary congregations to make up their minds as to what they are about and what exactly it is that necessitates their continued existence. So many ideas, so little consensus. From the author's perspective, as one of the few still around who personally experienced the old ABMJ Hebrew Christian missionary model, it may be instructive to reexamine elements of what made that ministry paradigm so effective for so many decades.

In those days, a local Jewish mission existed for two main purposes: to introduce unsaved Jewish people to their Messiah and to provide an emotionally and culturally comfortable place where those Jews could worship and receive biblical instruction and fellowship together. The movement was phenomenally successful at achieving those two goals. The author's first eleven years were spent within the nurturing matrix of the Coney Island mission, led by his great-aunt, Hilda Koser. In a good month, there were approximately 200 members attending every Sunday morning, perhaps 40-50 kids/teens and 150 adults. The "40-50 kids/teens" is not a typo. The NY missions ministered to many future messianic leaders like Michael Rydelnik and Arnold Fruchtenbaum, just to name a few.

At that time, there was no Gentile integration problem. All attendees were Jewish (although an occasional Gentile may have flown under the radar now and then, and there were occasional Gentile guest speakers). There were no crises of Jewish identity amidst a group so demonstrably Jewish. (There was arguably a level of *yiddishkeit* we enjoyed, absorbed through our collective pores, merely by virtue of having breathed Brooklyn air.) We sang from the Baptist hymnal, not from Liberated Wailing Wall overheads (and we never danced or, God forbid, clapped). We read responsively from the KJV (King James Version of the Bible), "thee's," thou's," and all. The only Hebrew we ever saw was a plaque affixed to the podium that said, "Shalom," and we said Jesus Christ without stuttering. (Aunt Hilda considered it "truth in advertising," so that there would never be a question concerning Whom she was proclaiming and in Whom her people believed. The first time the author heard the name Yeshua was when he was 18, reading Moishe Rosen's little paperback. Coney Island (and the other missions as well), saw thousands of Jewish people saved throughout their tenure. (Bit of trivia: Q -What was the single most successful Jewish evangelistic event of the year? A – the annual Christmas pageant.))

The following is the author's take on what happened, more or less, to this *goldene medine*. While there was still life left in this missiological paradigm, a longer-haired generation arose that knew not traditional Jewish missions (or rather, thought they knew better). The Jesus movement brought fresh enthusiasm to the messianic movement, but it also brought immaturity. And so, the pieces of the old paradigm, along with accompanying experience and maturity were dramatically swept off the table by those convinced they knew better than their predecessors. The new paradigm brought big, bold ideas—Hebrew language, folk music, dancing, clapping, the replacement of certain words that had been comfortably in use but were now labeled as being universally offensive, and most importantly, the modern messianic congregation. The rest is history.

Four decades later, innumerable blessings have accrued through the modern messianic movement. Yet it is unavoidable to note the fragmentation and confusion it has sown. Over time, for example, somehow it became acceptable (and later, expected) practice for the movement to attract and welcome groups of Gentiles bored with common Christianity, looking for novel ideas and experiences. In addition, we have been unfortunate witnesses to the birth and rise of very creative fringe and heterodox groups like the Two House Movement and those who reject the deity of Messiah.

Could the messianic movement ever return to former days and previous methods? Not completely and only then in highly concentrated geographic pockets of Jewish population. Would doing so help ensure the Jewish future of the Messianic Jewish movement? It couldn't hurt. Perhaps the answer to the challenge of just how Jewish the messianic movement will be methodologically lies in going back to the future and cherry picking a few of the older generation's approaches, distilling a few timeless principles ripe for rediscovery and reapplication. Amid the popular quest for Jewish roots, perhaps a re-visitation to our own "Jewish roots" is in order.

ENDNOTES

1. *A Moment Symposium*, Moment magazine, Sept/Oct, 2011, 34-39.
2. Heb. 8:6-13.
3. Acts 7:51-53.
4. Rom. 9:6-8.
5. Jn. 7:22; Acts 16:3; 21:21-24; Rom. 3:1.

HOW JEWISH WILL THE MESSIANIC JEWISH COMMUNITY OF THE FUTURE BE?

Mara Frisch
National Ministries Director for the Young Messianic Jewish Alliance

The Messianic Jewish community is approaching an exciting time. We are living out one of the most cherished phrases in Judaism, "L'Dor V'Dor, from generation to generation." The pioneers of our movement are in the process of symbolically passing the torch to the younger generation. During this process, many questions come to mind including, "How Jewish will the Messianic Jewish community of the future be?" In order to attempt to answer this important question, we need to understand who the Messianic Jewish younger generation is, where they are headed, and how we can help foster their growth, while paying special attention to cultivating and encouraging future leaders. In the following paper, I will share my experiences as Ministries Director of the Young Messianic Jewish Alliance and offer my insight into these important questions.

WHO IS THE MESSIANIC JEWISH YOUNGER GENERATION?

A generation encompasses many individuals, and while it is not my desire to make generalizations about the Messianic Jewish individuals within our movement, there are certain struggles and spiritual dynamics that appear consistently in the Messianic Jewish younger generation. Further, I believe that these struggles and spiritual dynamics have a direct impact on young people's sense of Jewish identity. One cannot determine how to foster growth in the younger generation without first understanding the spiritual struggles and dynamics pervading young people.

Through my interactions with teens and young adults from different regions of the country, I have come to believe that identity formation is one of the most important and challenging struggles that young people face. While battling physical and emotional changes, young people are simultaneously trying to find their place in the world and understand who they are. Even the most well adjusted young adults seem to struggle through this process.

There is a youth ministry video ("I Am," Bluefish TV) that illustrates this concept well. The video opens with a young girl walking around, appearing confused and timid. The silence in the video emphasizes her loneliness. She finds a closet and begins trying on different outfits, essentially changing her identity with each new outfit. At this point, the music begins, demonstrating the positive impact the new outfits, or new identities, have upon her. For each new outfit, the girl wears a different nametag. The labels read, "I am athletic," "I am punk," "I am preppy," "I am a druggie," and finally, "I am confused." I showed this video to young people all over the country during our 2009-2010 youth retreat season. It was sobering to hear how many young people strongly resonated with the video. Young people are starving for approval and acceptance, and yet they cannot genuinely gain either without developing a strong sense of identity.

In the Messianic Jewish community, the common teenage identity struggle is even more trying. Many young people do not know how to define their Messianic Jewish identity. They compare themselves to labels, which are already understood and accepted within society. I've heard the following statements: "I'm sort of Christian and sort of Jewish." "My friends at school think it's weird that I go to synagogue and believe in Christianity." "I try to explain it [Messianic Judaism], but nobody gets it." Ascribing to a faith that is difficult to explain and not readily understood by one's peers makes identity formation all the more difficult.

A need that is closely related to identity is a sense of belonging. Almost every young person is ultrasensitive to any small way that he or she differs from his or her peers. Some cope with this by attempting to stand out and embrace the concept of being different, while others do their best to conform. For example, many young people today do not try drugs or alcohol for the first time because they are curious about how it will affect their bodies but because their peer group is using drugs or alcohol. I have heard teens explain that they just wanted to "fit in" when explaining why they first experimented with drugs.

In addition, just as with identity, a Messianic Jewish young person may struggle to belong even more than a typical young person, isolating them even further in their school settings. Their Christian friends may not understand why they are practicing their faith in a Jewish context, especially if they are not Jewish. Similarly, their Jewish friends may mock them for practicing what they see as a counterfeit form of Judaism. All this is in addition to the pressure teens may feel to conform to their secular friends.

If these issues of identity and belonging are not addressed, they can act as barriers to young people's spiritual growth and development. In Abraham Maslow's (1954) hierarchy of needs, which is often referenced in the psychological community, Maslow identifies levels of needs that must be satisfied before other needs come into focus and can be realized. A sense of belonging is identified as being just above (or after) safety and physiological needs such as needing food, water, shelter, security, and stability. Higher up on the pyramid are the "personal growth" needs. Spiritual growth and faith formation can be categorized in the higher "growth" category, and according to Maslow and the psychological community at large, this cannot be achieved without first satisfying a sense of belonging.

Another important spiritual dynamic of Messianic Jewish young people is building one's *Messianic Jewish faith identity*. Many times, children take on, or essentially inherit, the faith of their parents and believe because their parents believe. Though this provides a wonderful foundation, it needs to progress into taking ownership of one's faith. Further, young people need to make the transition to solidifying their own faith identities by asking Yeshua to be their personal Lord and Savior and by actively maturing in their faith. Unfortunately, this is not always an easy, linear process and it can be challenging for young people to make this transition. "*Therefore, my dear friends, as you have always obeyed—not only my presence, but now much more in my absence—continue to work out your salvation with fear and trembling*" (Philippians 2:12, New International Version).

In a Messianic Jewish setting, there is the similar dynamic of Messianic vision. Often teens attend a Messianic synagogue because their parents feel called to the Messianic movement and have chosen to raise their children in a Messianic Jewish context. Again, this provides a foundation for young people, but the process is not always seamless for teens as they develop their own vision for Messianic Judaism and hearts for the Jewish people. I personally think this is a large reason that young people leave the movement. If a teen's personal Messianic Jewish vision has never had the opportunity to flourish on its own, then it is difficult to withstand the challenges of Messianic Judaism, and young people often fully assimilate into a church or may abandon their faith altogether.

I would also like to address three other issues that pervade our youth: depression, fear of the future, and broken relationships. Depression is rampant in young people. According to an article published in Clinical Psychology Review, where Twenge (2009) looked at the increases in psychopathy in high school and college students over seventy years, there has been a significant rise in depression and anxiety in young people today. In fact, they are five times as likely to suffer from major depression and/or anxiety disorders as young people in the 1940s. It seriously concerns me how many Messianic Jewish young people I meet who are depressed and do not know healthy coping strategies. Further, they are often told to "just pray about it" and "let the Lord heal them." Hearing these oversimplified responses to their pain can leave them confused and feeling that their pain is being minimized. When Messianic Jewish young people attempt to pray and do not receive instant, supernatural healing, they may either feel that G-d has abandoned them or that they were not worthy of being healed. The consequences can be devastating for their mental health, theology, and relationship with G-d.

Another difficulty teens and young adults face is a fear of the future. Two years ago, the YMJA retreat season's theme focused on fear. Young people were encouraged to recognize the fears that were operating in their lives through detailed teaching during the first half of the retreat, and then during the second half, they were taught how to overcome those fears through practical Biblical strategies. There was also a specific time scheduled for prayer. Though there were many different types of fear discussed, an overwhelming number of young people privately confided that "fear of the future" is what they struggled with the most. This encompasses worries about where to attend college, what to do after school, whom to marry, etc. In addition, there is another layer related to faith that affects Messianic Jewish young people. Many voiced fears about discerning G-d's will incorrectly, fearing His call on their lives, fearing disappointing the Lord, and experiencing confusion about whether to pursue a secular career or one in ministry. In fact, many young people hold the incorrect belief that if they really love G-d and desire to serve Him, then that should translate into pursuing a career in full-time Messianic ministry. The potential for this type of fear to drastically influence Messianic Jewish young people's futures is serious and needs to be addressed.

Lastly, young people are deeply hurting from broken relationships in their lives, specifically in their families. Young people crave unconditional love, stability, and acceptance. When parents divorce, these basic needs are tested and injured even when parents attempt to continue to provide loving, stable homes. I cannot begin to tell you how many hurting Messianic Jewish teens and young adults I have encountered, who are children of divorced parents. Of course, there are plenty of other reasons that young people experience broken relationships in their lives, but in my experiences, I believe that divorce is one of the most common and most damaging. I will never forget one young teen at our Northeast retreat who came up to me for prayer with tear-filled eyes. She was having such a difficult time dealing with her parents' divorce, and I sensed that her hurt was also making it difficult for her to relate to G-d as loving and unconditional. Now, we know that the Lord can renew broken spirits and that children of divorce or other sources of broken relationships can absolutely become healthy, stable individuals. However, we must recognize that many Messianic Jewish young people experience broken relationships in their lives, and this can have a large effect upon their spiritual identity and understanding. Often times, these young people wear the label or identity, "I am hurting."

JEWISH IDENTITY

I believe that many of the struggles and spiritual dynamics noted above have a direct impact on young people's sense of Jewish identity. In order to understand their identity, I think that we need to start by looking at our framework. It has always been tempting to view Messianic Jewish identity in light of a Venn diagram, or overlapping circles of Judaism and Christianity. However, I do not believe that Messianic Judaism is the intersection of two circles; it is not a Christian faith with Jewish practices nor is it traditional Judaism with Christian theology. Rather, I believe that Messianic Judaism is its own circle encompassing its own expression and unique identity. In that case, I prefer to utilize the term, "Messianic Jewish identity," rather than "Jewish identity." I believe that it is more beneficial when one is not viewed as separate from the other; Messianic Jewish identity encompasses Jewish identity woven together with an identity in Yeshua the Messiah.

As I stated earlier, it is not easy for young people to define their identity, and I believe the same is true when it comes to defining their Messianic Jewish identity. However, I have witnessed some common values, which relate to the spiritual struggles and dynamics previously stated.

Young people desire very much to be authentic; it is a buzzword in youth culture and relates to their desire for belonging. One complaint that I regularly hear is that we are trying too hard to be like other people. When pressed further, young people explain what can be translated into an identity crisis. Either, they feel we are trying too much to be like the church or are trying too hard to appear Torah observant. Trying to be like another faith is perceived to them as being inauthentic, and that does not line up with their value system. This is one reason that I push the "non-Venn diagram"' approach to Messianic Jewish identity. If Messianic young people can accept that we are unique and are *not* trying to measure up against Christianity or traditional Judaism, then they will be able to define their identity as being authentic. Further, if they can perceive our style of worship, practices, and traditions as distinctly Messianic, rather than a potpourri of traditional Judaism and Christianity, then these facets will be incorporated into their Messianic Jewish identities.

While I suggest defining Messianic Jewish identity as unique, I am not advocating isolation from either the Christian or traditional Jewish communities. In fact, I believe that Messianic Jews benefit greatly from participating in both of these communities. When Messianic Jewish young people participate in the larger Christian community, they gain a sense of how we fit into the greater body of believers and can foster connections with other believers.

In terms of the traditional Jewish community, I have witnessed that many young people either have a strained or non-existent relationship with the traditional Jewish community. I believe that this relates to the high value placed on authenticity. Several years ago, I brought our local Messianic Jewish youth group to a Holocaust remembrance ceremony at our local Jewish Community Center. Prior to attending the event, I felt that it would be a great opportunity to allow our youth group to be involved in the Jewish community, giving them a chance to participate in observing an event that was already familiar to them. However, when I brought them to the event, I noticed that they were very uncomfortable. The young people did their best to adapt and were very respectful, but they seemed to have a difficult time engaging in the ceremony. After the event, I asked them about their experience. Some of them felt that we were trying to "fit in" when we really did not. Others were uncomfortable because they did not know some of the prayers and felt out of place. Lastly, some were afraid that they would be ridiculed if others found out that they were Messianic Jews. These feelings point to the desire to belong and also relate to authenticity. The young people felt that they were inauthentic members at this traditional Jewish event, and thus, their desire to belong was not satisfied. In their minds, only authentic members of a community could belong to the community. My challenge was to encourage them that they were, in fact, authentic—as Messianic Jews—and that they did not have to "fit in" in order to belong.

Though it can be difficult, I believe that we need to encourage our young people to engage with the traditional Jewish community. Yeshua explains to His disciples that though they are in the world, "they are not of the world" (John 15:19). Rather than isolate ourselves from the traditional Jewish community, I am advocating that we prepare our young people for encounters with the traditional Jewish community. We need to explain to our young people that they should not expect to "fit in" seamlessly, and also, that we should not be ashamed of our differences. At the same time, we need to teach them to be respectful when participating with the Jewish community. There is a delicate balance between affirming one's uniqueness and respecting the norms of the community. In this case, I believe that our young people's Messianic Jewish identity needs strengthening. When they are comfortable as Messianic Jews and feel that they are authentically practicing *their* faith, then they will be able to participate in events in the traditional Jewish community without feeling inauthentic. Just as we are encouraged to be "in the world, but not of the world," we can encourage our young people to participate in the Jewish community, while authentically embracing their Messianic Jewish identity.

In contrast to my experiences with Messianic Jewish youth relating to the American Jewish community, I have observed that identifying with Israel is a natural and integral part of young people's Messianic Jewish identity. I believe that a large reason that this is the case is because identifying with Israel does not conflict with young people's need to belong or make them feel inauthentic. Messianic young people can actively support Israel in school through social media and anywhere else outside of their Messianic Jewish synagogues without being told that they are inauthentic. In other words, they feel that they belong to Israel.

I witnessed a beautiful example of this in Israel this past summer. Rabbi Kevin Solomon and I took nearly thirty Messianic young adults on a month-long ministry trip to Israel, where our young people served in the Land, participated in outreach, and visited biblical and historical sites. One of the most profound experiences of the trip was when Ofer Amitai, a Messianic leader in Israel, led our group out on a night hike in the Negev desert. Eventually, we stopped walking, and Ofer Amitai asked us to sit in silence, looking up at the stars. After some time, he read to us from Genesis, where G-d asks Abraham to attempt to "number the stars," promising that Abraham's descendants would be as numerous (Genesis 15:5, 26:4). Then, Ofer Amitai turned to us and spoke softly, "You are the stars that G-d spoke of. You belong to this land; you are part of that promise." That moment was so powerful and months after the trip, I still hear the youth referencing that time in the desert. I believe that it will continue impacting them for a lifetime. It was a moment of pure belonging to a land and cause greater than themselves.

In addition, there is a clear directive in Scripture to "pray for the peace of Jerusalem," and Messianic young people may feel as though they are living out an important aspect of their spiritual calling by standing prayerfully and practically for Eretz Yisrael (Psalm 122:6). Consequently, identifying with Israel, politically, practically, and prayerfully, is a critical aspect of young people's Messianic Jewish identity.

From my experiences, Messianic Jewish young people approach Torah and tradition differently than the senior generation. First, many people in the Messianic senior generation grew up in traditional Judaism and became Messianic Jewish believers later in life. Torah and liturgy have a special role in connecting them to their Jewish heritage and people, and it triggers a sense of familiarity and perhaps even sentimentality. I relate to this as someone who grew up in Reform Judaism. For me, chanting the familiar liturgy the first time I stepped into a Messianic synagogue was transformative; it brought together my Jewish heritage and my faith in Yeshua and allowed me to worship Yeshua while living out my Jewish identity. I also felt the same liturgy that I grew up chanting come alive as I proclaimed it knowing Yeshua fulfilled the Messianic prophecies and Scriptures. However, most Messianic Jewish young people in our movement grew up in Messianic Judaism. I believe that liturgy is still meaningful to them, connecting them to their Jewish heritage, but it does not carry the same link that it does for many in the senior generation who grew up in traditional Judaism.

I have seen Messianic Jewish young people engage the most with liturgy when it is integrated into worship. For example, many times there is a specific liturgical section of a Messianic Jewish service. The praise and worship team usually leads worship before or after the liturgy. When liturgy and the Torah service are included as separate components of a service, I have seen youth disengage during the liturgy and engage during the worship. Often, they will still verbalize the importance of liturgy and the Torah service, but it is not a vibrant aspect of their Messianic Jewish identity. Further, the liturgy and worship seem to be understood as two distinct concepts. At a conference several years ago, a young rabbi led the liturgy at our youth Torah service. This was the first time that I had witnessed liturgy and worship being woven together, and the result was astounding. I witnessed our youth worshiping through liturgy and flowing from the traditional Jewish prayers to contemporary Messianic Jewish songs in one continuous stream of worship. I have also witnessed a similar experience when a young songwriter in our movement led worship at our national Messiah conference this past summer. She had written a beautiful worship song that incorporated the *Aleinu* along with modern lyrics. In addition, I have heard of vibrant Torah services incorporating worship, liturgy, and musical instruments. I believe that Torah and tradition are important aspects of young people's Messianic Jewish identity, but young people desire to bring fresh expression and meaning. When they are able to worship through liturgy, it brings life to our traditional prayers, along with a reminder of Yeshua's fulfillment of the Scriptures.

I think it is important to acknowledge that Messianic Jewish youth worship has had several major influences. First, I have noticed that Messianic Israeli youth worship songs have become a thriving part of worship repertoire. The sound is different from Messianic Jewish American artists, and Messianic young people seem quite excited about worshiping as Messianic Israelis worship. Secondly, IHOP (International House of Prayer) has had a large musical influence on the Messianic Jewish movement, and Messianic Jewish young people have gravitated toward the prophetic styles of worship. Messianic Jewish worship leaders will often introduce IHOP worship songs with Messianic modifications at conferences and retreats. Overall, worship is an integral part of young people's Messianic Jewish identity.

Lastly, I believe that community plays a large role in Messianic Jewish culture, for both the younger and senior generations. As stated earlier, a sense of belonging and acceptance, along with experiencing stable and loving relationships, are extremely important, and community plays an important role in a Messianic Jewish young person's identity. I have heard a great deal of talk about the need for stronger community and discussions on the difficulties of achieving community within our movement, especially among the post-college-age Messianic young adults. I believe that this is one reason that AMF, Asheville Music Festival, was so overwhelmingly successful. Nearly one thousand Messianic young people (including some from the Messianic Jewish senior generation) gathered together for three days of Messianic Jewish music, communal experience, and intimate fellowship. It was incredible to see young people flock from all over the country and beyond to this event, demonstrating the desire for a strong community.

Though young people's Messianic Jewish identity is constantly evolving, one can note that a commitment to authenticity, community, relationships, solidarity with Israel, and a fresh expression of liturgy and Messianic worship are all vital components.

WHERE IS THE MESSIANIC JEWISH YOUNGER GENERATION HEADED?

It is essential to take a look at where the Messianic Jewish youth is headed. Realistically, there are three major paths that they may take: living a Messianic Jewish lifestyle, assimilating into the church, or walking away from the Lord. However, we also must recognize that young people often do not follow linear paths in life, and their choices and decisions may not solely belong to one of the three possibilities stated above.

It is our hope that the younger generation will commit themselves to the Messianic Jewish movement, marry Messianic Jewish believers, and birth the next generation of Messianic Jews. We must be careful, though, to acknowledge that a "Messianic Jewish lifestyle" in the next generation may look quite different than it has in the current generation. In addition, it may vary greatly within a single generation. Rather than surmise what characteristics the Messianic Jewish *lifestyles* of the future generation will comprise of, I would like to focus on asking ourselves how we can help foster their growth as individuals and help strengthen their identities. In supporting Messianic Jewish young people, we can help prepare them to carry on the movement of the future.

First, I believe that we need to nurture our youth spiritually by offering them spiritual mentorship and discipleship. Young people need strong role models of Messianic Jewish men and women who are firm in their identities and live out authentic Messianic Jewish lifestyles. This involves explaining why one is practicing certain Jewish traditions such as keeping Biblical Kosher or keeping Shabbat. It is not enough to simply say to young people, "We do this because we are Jews." Young people must learn of the Messianic Jewish significance, incorporate it into their identities, and see examples of people they trust who live out genuine Messianic Jewish lifestyles. It also involves offering young people solid discipleship, walking them through the process of maturing spiritually and feeding them spiritual meat. Yeshua mentored the twelve disciples and demonstrated the importance of investing in another person, and I absolutely believe that we must do the same.

Secondly, I strongly believe in providing Messianic youth ministry, both in local congregations and nationally, where young people can build their Messianic Jewish identity and fellowship with their peers in a setting relevant to their experiences, age, and needs. A strong Messianic youth ministry program will encourage identity, help students to take ownership of their faith, offer students a sense of belonging, and give them opportunities to grow in their relationship with Yeshua and personal Messianic Jewish vision. I believe that on the local level, young people must be able to attend regular youth meetings, and on the national level, young people must have the opportunity to engage with the larger Messianic Jewish youth community.

It is important to note the distinction between offering a Messianic youth ministry and isolating young people from their Messianic Jewish community at large. A solid Messianic youth ministry program will provide a foundation for young people to be vital members of their congregation. Judaism is community oriented, and Messianic youth ministry should reflect that. In order to flourish and grow, young people need the wisdom and guidance of their elders and they need to be part of a congregational community. Further, they need to be held accountable not just by their youth leader, but also by their rabbi and those who have walked with the Lord longer than they have. Young people need the freedom to build their own identities, but their faith also needs to be cultivated by the Messianic Jewish community. This can be achieved in a practical way by ensuring that the local youth group meetings are held during a time that is separate from the congregational service, allowing young people to engage in both the Messianic youth ministry and the congregational community.

Next, I believe that it is critical for young people to engage in first-hand experiences with Israel and Holocaust remembrance opportunities. It is not enough to hear about the importance of standing with Israel from the senior generation; young people must set foot in the land of Israel for themselves, walking the land of their ancestors, interacting with Israelis, and visiting important Biblical and historical sites. Further, Messianic Jewish young people need to learn of the prophetic and Biblical significance of Israel. As previously explained, they also need to develop their own hearts for unsaved Jewish people and take on the spiritual burden of praying for Israel.

Similarly, the younger generation of Messianic Jews is much more removed from the Holocaust than the senior generation, who likely had family members who escaped. But the young generation must not become apathetic to the devastation of the Holocaust, and we must give them regular resources and opportunities to commemorate the Holocaust. Identifying with both Israel and the Holocaust are important aspects of Messianic Jewish identity, and it is our responsibility to ensure that the younger generation of Messianic Jews will continue to carry these burdens.

Lastly, acknowledging the rise of mental illness among young people, we must be aware of the resources available to those who are struggling and equip people in our congregations to reach out. I strongly advocate recommending and/or offering faith-based counseling when necessary and removing the stigma attached to those who struggle with depression. A strong Messianic Jewish faith and depression are not mutually exclusive, and our young people need to gain that understanding.

FUTURE LEADERS OF THE MESSIANIC JEWISH COMMUNITY

Finally, in discussing our future Messianic Jewish generation, we must highlight the need to raise up future Messianic Jewish leaders. I believe that this need is already strongly recognized across the Messianic Jewish movement, and it is encouraging to note that different ministries and organizations have been creating various opportunities for Messianic Jewish leadership development.

In continuing the conversation, I will share what I believe are critical components of this important task of training up young Messianic Jewish leaders. First, we need to be serious about identification and recruitment. It is necessary to constantly look for potential in the areas of spiritual maturity, Messianic Jewish vision, and a high level or morality and character. If these qualities are identified in young people, current leaders should begin the process of directly and indirectly training them up. This should not be confused with locking them into positions of ministry or placing too much responsibility on their shoulders prematurely. Rather, I believe that long-term mentoring and opportunities for character building should precede formal ministry training.

Once someone has been identified as having potential and has demonstrated strong character and spiritual maturity, we need to offer them formal training and equipping opportunities. I am pleased that formal leadership training, both through short-term and long-term opportunities, are already being offered throughout the movement, and I hope to see this initiative continue and grow. Additionally, it is important to train leaders for all different kinds of ministry; we need future Messianic Jewish worship leaders, rabbis, elders, youth leaders, intercessors, evangelists, children's ministry workers, sisterhood coordinators, administrators, humanitarian coordinators, etc. Consequently, we should be aware of the array of possibilities for future volunteer, part-time, and full-time ministry when training up future Messianic Jewish leaders.

Lastly, I want to encourage every congregation to the opportunity to begin serving immediately. Experience, paired with mentoring, is one of the most fertile grounds for learning to occur. Perhaps there are needs in your congregation that young people could fill as they are paired with a mentor who will give them feedback and guide them through the process of leadership development. The opportunities for growth are endless.

In conclusion, I would like to return to our original question, "How Jewish will the Messianic Jewish community of the future be?" I propose asking this question slightly differently. I prefer to ask, "How strong will the future generation's Messianic Jewish identity be?" I believe that shifting our focus to identity will offer a greater lens into the future of our Messianic Jewish movement. I hope that this paper has offered insight into the struggles and dynamics of this vibrant generation and has brought attention to the need for strengthening Messianic Jewish identity. I believe that the Lord has great plans for the future of our movement. We all have an important role to play in helping cultivate the younger generation's Messianic Jewish identities, giving them opportunities to flourish and grow, and training up future Messianic Jewish leaders. Let us continue to cry out, "L'Dor V'Dor, from generation to generation."

Printed in the United States
by Baker & Taylor Publisher Services